# 中国会计服务市场开放与监管

财政部会计司
普华永道中天会计师事务所（特殊普通合伙） 著

中国财政经济出版社

**图书在版编目（CIP）数据**

中国会计服务市场开放与监管/财政部会计司，普华永道中天会计师事务所（特殊普通合伙）著．—北京：中国财政经济出版社，2015.8

ISBN 978－7－5095－6290－1

Ⅰ.①中… Ⅱ.①财…②普… Ⅲ.①会计－市场－对外开放－研究－中国 ②会计－市场监管－研究－中国 Ⅳ.①F233.2

中国版本图书馆 CIP 数据核字（2015）第 155102 号

责任编辑：宋学军　　　　责任校对：张　凡

封面设计：耕　者　　　　版式设计：康普宝蓝

中国财政经济出版社 出版

**URL**：http：//ckfz.cfeph.cn

E－mail：ckfz@cfeph.cn



社址：北京市海淀区阜成路甲 28 号　邮政编码：100142

营销中心电话：010－88190406　北京财经书店电话：010－64033436、84041336

河北省零五印刷厂印刷　各地新华书店经销

787×1092 毫米　16 开　13 印张　206 000 字

2015 年 8 月第 1 版　2015 年 8 月河北第 1 次印刷

定价：38.00 元

ISBN 978－7－5095－6290－1/F·5068

（图书出现印装问题，本社负责调换）

质量投诉电话：010－88190744

**打击盗版举报热线：010－88190492，QQ：634579818**

# “中国会计服务市场开放与监管”项目组


**财政部会计司联合研究组**

**组　长**　高一斌、刘光忠

**成　员**　王　宏、韩　冰、王　晶、冯翠平、邱　颖

**普华永道中天联合研究组**

**组　长**　李　丹、吴卫军

**成　员**　Addison L. Everett、Paul F. Winkelmann、Jan McCahey、Kenneth R. Chatelain、吴　蔚、陈　波、黄洁莉、沈　洁、丁　松、于　玮、董　洁

# 为全面深化中国会计服务市场开放与监管提供科学理论指导

（代序）

会计依托经济、反映经济、服务经济，“经济越发展、会计越重要”。近年来，中国经济改革和对外开放取得了举世瞩目的成绩，“四个全面”的战略布局、“一带一路”的发展规划，以及中国倡导成立的亚洲基础设施投资银行等多边开发金融机制，更为新常态下中国经济持续发展和全球经济复苏注入新的活力。

党的十八届三中全会提出放开会计审计等领域外资准入限制，为推动中国会计服务市场开放定下基调、指明方向。伴随着中国经济的持续健康发展和中国企业“走出去”参与国际竞争，为企业提供传统审计鉴证服务和新型高端增值服务的注册会计师行业得以蓬勃发展并逐步走向国际。作为中国注册会计师行业的主管部门，财政部积极参与世贸组织等多种机制下会计服务市场的开放磋商，大力推动在上海、广东、天津、福建等自贸区试点扩大会计服务市场开放，并建立与之相适应的行业监管体系。总体来看，通过世贸组织（WTO）、自贸区（FTA）以及双边经贸安排等多种机制，中国会计服务市场已基本形成全方位、多层次、有深度、高质量的开放格局，会计服务业已经成为中国国际化程度很高的专业行业之一。

在推动中国会计服务市场开放的进程中，我们深感使命光荣、责任重大，既要顺应我国改革开放的新形势、促进会计服务市场对外开放和国际化发展，又要维护国家主权、强化监管、保障我国注册会计师行业的合法正当权益。特别是2015年2月，国务院发布《关于加快培育外贸竞争新优势的若干意见》（国发〔2015〕9号，强调要“重点培育和扩大通信、金融、会计等新兴服务贸易，提升服务业国际化水平，提高服务贸易在对外贸易中的比重。”面对日益繁重和紧迫的开放任务，深入研究国内外会计服务市场开放与监管模式，为宏观政策制定提供指导和借鉴，成为一项重要而迫切的任务。有鉴于此，财政部向亚洲开发银行申报了“会计服务市场开放与监管”技术援助项目（TA8192_Comp3）。普华永道中天会计师事务所（特殊普通合伙）受托担任该项目的合作研究机构，在财政部的指导和亚行的监督下承担具体研究任务。

项目研究历时一年多。项目组克服了研究议题多、涉及地域广、资料搜集难度大等种种困难，通过文献翻译、档案查证、实地考察、现场访谈、问卷调查、统计分析等多种方式，对世界主要经济体的会计服务市场开放和监管现状进行了归纳、总结和分析，并结合中国国情提出相关政策建议，最终形成《中国会计服务市场开放与监管》研究报告。报告分为两部分：第一部分为项目概要，第二部分将主项目分解为十个子项目，结合国内外相关热点问题逐项研究国际经验和中国实践，并提出政策建议。十个子项目分别是境外人士成为注册会计师管理、境外会计师事务所开展法定审计业务、负面清单管理模式、注册会计师行业监管法规、会计师事务所强制轮换、政府购买会计师事务所专业服务、金融机构审计、职业责任保险、联合审计和跨境监管合作。

该报告旨在对国际通行的会计服务市场开放原则、国际监管惯例和世界主要经济体现行做法进行全面梳理和深入研究，并将其与中国的制度背景和实践做法进行对比分析，不仅为国内政府部门制定相关政策提供了有益参考，更为国际社会认知中国注册会计师行业的制度选择打开了一扇“窗口”。我相信，该报告的原创性、前沿性和建设性能为全面深化中外会计服务市场开放与监管合作提供理论指导，必将进一步增强中国注册会计师行业国际化发展的理论自信、道路自信和制度自信。

是为序，并与国内外会计同仁共勉。

财政部副部长 

2015 年 7 月

# 前　言

FOREWORD

2014 年 7 月 11 日，普华永道中天会计师事务所（特殊普通合伙）与亚洲开发银行就推动财政管理与会计服务监管技术援助项目（TA8912）第三部分（“会计服务市场开放与监管”）签署了协议。本项目旨在通过提高财务报表透明度和会计信息质量，加强会计服务业在国内和国际的市场竞争力，并增强国际会计服务监管机构间的合作，进一步支持中国政府在推动会计服务市场开放及培养专业人员方面所付出的不懈努力。项目组将本项目的研究成果汇编为本书。

本书总结了项目组对项目课题的调研分析，全面阐述了项目组的研究发现及有关建议。在调研过程中，项目组主要通过访谈及对相关文献的解读，对各个课题在其他国家的事实范例和背景渊源进行研究，探访特定国家/地区的政府及非政府监管机构的洞见，并通过收集报道和采访，了解国际知名非政府组织的观点，当然本书也参考了来自财务报表编报者、使用者及审计师[①]的不同视角的意见。

① 如无特别说明，本报告中的审计师与会计师事务所系同义语。

中国财政部会计司设计了一套分析框架，供项目组以此为基础，构建项目的研究发现和建议。此框架非常明确有效，反映了财政部和项目组在选定最切题论据的深入讨论。此框架的基本逻辑如下，具体内容体现在本书的第二部分：

（一）中国会计服务的开放（第一章—第三章）；

（二）中国会计服务的竞争力（第四章—第九章）；

（三）跨境会计监管与合作（第十章）。

财政部框架不仅帮助项目组选取了明确且客观的事实进行分析，还考虑到了事实范例的相关背景及各种因素之间的互相依赖性，这些都保证了项目组的研究结论及建议具有充分的相关性，能够确保本书中的监管政策建议实现预期目标。

# 目　录

CONTENTS


PART 1　第一部分

项目概要 / 3

Executive Summary / 27

PART 2　第二部分

第一章　境外人士成为执业注册会计师 / 63

第二章　境外会计师事务所开展法定审计业务 / 77

第三章　会计服务市场开放负面清单管理模式 / 88

第四章　注册会计师行业监管法规 / 93

第五章　会计师事务所强制轮换 / 107

第六章　政府购买会计师事务所专业服务 / 120

第七章　金融机构审计 / 138

第八章　会计师事务所职业责任保险 / 151

第九章　会计师事务所联合审计 / 163

第十章　跨境会计监管与合作 / 174

参考文献 / 187
附录　国际监管合作的全球实践 / 193
后记 / 195

# 第一部分

# THE FIRST PART

# 项目概要

商业的全球化和跨国企业的扩张从不同的角度推动着会计职业成为最为国际化的职业之一。与此同时，鉴于会计服务，特别是法定审计服务在一个国家整体经济中的重要性，注册会计师行业在大多数国家/地区已经成为了一个受到广泛而严格监管的行业。同样，中国在提升注册会计师行业的监督和管理上也付出了持续不断的努力。

本书对比了注册会计师行业的国际基本法律法规和实践，分析了每种范例的优势和面临的挑战。本书的分析依据上述财政部框架而展开，研究的重点领域包括：中国会计服务的开放、提升会计服务的竞争力、跨境会计监管与合作。



## 一、中国会计服务的开放

从很多角度来看，会计行业可以说是最国际化的行业之一。商业的全球化带动了对会计服务开展全球合作的需求。随着跨国企业在全球拓展业务，大型的会计师事务所也需要放眼全球，为这些企业提供全面服务。商业交易（包括跨国并购）的复杂性、编制在国际证券交易所上市所需财务报表以及准备公司纳税申报材料等都增加了对高质量并满足多重监管要求的会计审计专业服务的需求，以确保商业交易能够平稳高效地推进。

中国作为世界大型经济体和大型市场之一，在每年吸引着数十亿外资投入的同时，也在国际市场上积极地参与了大量的重大交易。在此背景下，中国会计服务的开放就成为了一个必然且必要的趋势，也是时下的热点话题。对此，项目组研究分析了美国、英国、澳大利亚等具有代表性的国家在提供跨境会计服务方面的监管规定和实务操作。项目组的研究分析集中在以下三方面：对境外人士成为境内执业注册会计师的监管规定和实务操作、对境外会计师事务所在境内开展法定审计业务的管理规定和实务操作、会计服务市场开放负面清单管理模式。

### （一）境外人士成为执业注册会计师

注册会计师可以提供多种服务，比如审计、代理记账、代理报税、咨询服务以及承担财务人员的职责。在这些服务之中，法定审计是注册会计师提供的最常见的服务，也是在各个国家都受到广泛监管的服务。在这里我们有必要将提供审计和鉴证服务与其他未受监管的会计服务加以区分，同样地，我们也有必要将那些想加入会计职业组织成为其会员的人，与那些希望通过执业申请程序在会计师事务所提供审计服务的人员加以区分。

在大多数国家，加入会计职业组织首先要成为其会员，之后要持续对专业技术方面的知识进行更新，以满足会员资格要求。在很多国家/地区，这样的专业团体会员都活跃在专业会计岗位（公司财务职位）、税务咨询岗位以及提供代理记账、公司秘书或者其他与财务相关的服务岗位上。会计职业组织会员的资格已经可以满足以上服务需求，同时会计职业组织通过对其会员的后续教育以及通过会计、职业道德及独立性等准则约束以保证其会员的专业技术能力。因此，对这些专业从业人员通常不需要进一步的监管。



然而，对于那些希望加入会计师事务所或由其个人提供法定审计服务的人员来说，他们往往需要在经济法及税法等方面进行额外的深造，同时必须通过审计专业考试。执业注册会计师的这一服务领域一般都受到独立监管部门的监管。在阅读本书时需要时刻注意以上区别。

项目组选取了美国（主要为四个具有代表性的州——纽约、伊利诺伊、加利福尼亚和德克萨斯）、英国、澳大利亚、新西兰、新加坡和中国香港这几个国家/地区作为代表进行研究分析。项目组发现，在这些国家/地区，成为注册会计师会员的要求和流程都是大致相同的。具体来说，其对成为注册会计师都有一些共性的要求，如完成特定的专业课程、通过行业准则及会计服务相关其他专业知识（尤其是境内法律和税务知识）的考试、完成职业道德测试且具备相关工作经验。同样在中国，注册会计师也需要满足相似的要求才能获得中国注册会计师协会会员资格。

然而，在取得法定审计报告签字权（“执业资格”）的要求方面则存在一定的差异，进一步解释如下：

1. 会计职业组织会员资格（非法定审计师）

（1）公民与居民身份要求。很少有国家/地区要求会计职业组织会员必须是当地公民或者居民。通常情况下，在一个地区求学的学生可以加入当地的会计职业组织，通过考试并获得相关工作经验而成为其会员。成为会员后，他们可以去境外工作并继续保留会员资格。很多在境外工作的会员也会再次取得他们工作所在地的会计职业组织会员资格。

（2）工作经验。大多数会计职业组织要求申请成为其会员的申请者在申请时已具备一定的工作经验。通常要求这些工作经验需要从会计师事务所或者是在该会计职业组织会员监督下的商业机构中获得，无论其是在境内还是境外的会计师事务所或商业机构取得。

2. 提供法定审计服务的会计师

通常这样的会计师被称为“执业注册会计师”或者“注册会计师”，他们或者是会计师事务所的合伙人（合伙制事务所），或者是公司制会计师事务所中的董事，或者由个人挂牌签署法定审计报告。不同国家/地区对这类执业会计师的监管要求存在很大区别。在大多数国家/地区，成为会计职业组织会员并不意味着该会员可以签署法定审计报告，“签字会计师”需要满足额外的登记注册要求，并且每年都要符合这些资格要求。在另外一些国家，例如美国和中国，成为注册会计师即可以签署法定审计报告。下文将进一步介绍对各国执业注册会计师的要求：

（1）公民与居民身份要求。大多数国家/地区不要求执业注册会计师申请人是本地公民，但通常都要求申请人拥有本地居民身份。这是为了保证申请人熟悉当地经常变换的环境，并且方便本地监管者执行监管及在必要的情况下执行纪律处罚。各地对居民身份的要求有所不同，但通常都要求是“常住居民”，即在当地居住达到一定的时间。另外，大多数地区要求在本地注册成立的会计师事务所的多数所有权为本地居民持有，或者主管（首席）合伙人/董事为本地居民。

（2）工作经验。大多数国家/地区要求执业注册会计师必须具备从境内会计师事务所获得的相关工作经验。这样就要求境外人士必须在境内会计师事务所工作而取得充足的本地经验后才能够成为执业注册会计师并签署法定审计报告。

（3）执业资格要求。在某些国家如美国，只要事务所授权的注册会计师都可以代表事务所签署法定审计报告。然而，在其他一些国家/地区，如英国、澳大利亚、新加坡和中国香港，注册会计师须取得额外的执业资格，才可以拥有当地法定审计报告的签字权。获取此种执业资格须满足额外的要求。例如在英国，注册会计师取得执业资格需要满足一定的当地相关工作经验及工作年限的要求，并购买达到一定额度的职业责任保险。此外，拥有执业资格的注册会计师与普通的注册会计师相比须缴付更高的会员费，并接受监管机构的严密监管。因此在实务操作中，注册会计师个人只有在成为事务所合伙人以后才会申请该执业资格，并代表事务所签署法定审计报告。通过对执业资格的额外要求，及对执业资格人员的严密监管，监管机构可以提高审计质量并规范审计市场。

3. 互认协议

许多国家/地区的会计职业组织（如行业协会或公会）和其他国家/地区一些相对应的会计职业组织签订有一个或多个互认协议（Mutual Recognition Agreement，MRAs）。这些互认协议有多种形式，互认的程度和范围也各有不同。在互认协议安排下，考生有时需要接受额外教育并进行考试，但通常都会取得一定的豁免以避免重复性考试。在签署互认协议前，双方须评估对方的注册会计师资格认证系统，根据评估结果确定互认的程度和范围。通常，如果评估认为对应会计职业组织的注册会计师资格认证系统和境内等效，即可安排注册会计师会员资格互认。互认评估一般由有资质的第三方专业机构进行。虽然互认协议为境外注册会计师获取境内注册会计师会员资格建立了一条“快速通道”，但互认协议不会授予注册会计师签署境内法定审计报告的签字权，在大多数国家/地区，如英国、澳大利亚、新加坡和中国香港，注册会计师须取得上述额外的执业资格才能签署法定审计报告。此外，若代表会计师事务所签署法定审计报告，注册会计师须取得该事务所的授权，而通常能获得该授权的须是该事务所的合伙人。但是，一些欧盟成员国之间的互认协议存在一些特殊安排，这些安排包括法定审计签字权的互认。举例来说，英国和德国允许欧洲经济区（European Economic Area，EEA）内各国的执业注册会计师和事务所在境内提供法定审计服务，当然德国额外要求签字会计师通过一项能力测试，该测试包括笔试和面试，内容主要涵盖法定审计相关法律规定、经济法、税法以及德国注册会计师（Wirtschaftspr ü fer）行业的监管规定。

4. 有关建议

(1) 中国可考虑与境外知名会计职业组织，如美国注册会计师协会(AICPA)、英国特许公认会计师公会（ACCA)、澳大利亚及新西兰特许会计师协会（CAANZ)、澳洲会计师公会（CPA Australia）等建立会员互认制度。中国也可以考虑进一步扩展目前与香港会计师公会（HKICPA）以及英格兰及威尔士特许会计师协会（ICAEW）的部分考试科目互免安排。这样会帮助中国注册会计师更容易成为境外会计职业组织会员，并在境外工作。此举也会吸引更多的海外优秀人才成为中国注册会计师，并在全球范围增强中国注册会计师协会的影响力。通过互认协议授予的会员资格并不等同于授予其在境内签署法定审计报告的资格，这也是互认协议的常规做法。监管机构可以考虑设立额外的执业资格要求或类似手段来管理执业许可，这样就可以更好地对有签字权的注册会计师进行监督管理。

(2) 随着越来越多的中国公司在境外设立分支机构或开展兼并收购，越来越多的国际公司来中国设立公司，中国应与境外会计职业组织或会计监管机构安排更多的交换项目，来增加境内注册会计师的国际经验，此举能够帮助中国注册会计师接触海外实务、获得海外经验，从而拥有了更开阔的视角和良好的国际关系网络，为中国公司吸引外资和海外投资活动提供更好的服务。另一方面，此举也会帮助经验丰富的中国注册会计师走出去，将中国的专业经验和知识带到国外，以便其他国家更好地了解中国的实务。

(3) 中国可以考虑将注册会计师资质与法定审计报告签字权分离，建立签字注册会计师管理制度。取得注册会计师资质的会员需要满足额外的要求方能取得法定审计报告签字权。这样有利于监管机构对具有法定审计报告签字权的会计师进行单独管理，提高监管有效性。此举将有效避免对所有注册会计师进行“一刀切”的管理，有利于针对非法定审计服务的注册会计师制定更加灵活的政策措施，吸引更多的注册会计师会员。法定审计报告签字权分离也有助于中国与国外会计师职业团体在互认协议中进行更加灵活的安排。

(4) 中国香港作为一个国际性金融贸易都市，吸引了大批国际性人才。中国可以考虑在香港设立中国会计师人才培养基地，培养拥有中国知识及实践经验的国际型会计及审计人才，为推动中国会计行业发展贡献力量。中国也可以考虑进一步完善注册会计师考试制度，吸引港澳台及海外考生参与中国注册会计师考试，根据这些考生的特点给予一定的灵活安排。例如外界有些观点提出中国注册会计师的机考制度使得部分港澳台及海外考生由于在电脑上输入中文不熟练而难以通过考试，给予这些特定考生手写考试的选择将会大大提高考生的积极性。

## （二）境外会计师事务所开展法定审计业务

项目组探讨会计师事务所能否直接到国外提供法定审计服务，或通过在国外设立分支机构的方式提供法定审计服务。项目组还考察了审计工作底稿跨境转移的问题。研究选取美国、英国、澳大利亚、新加坡、日本、德国和中国香港为代表，考察结果如下：

1. 境外会计师事务所在境内提供审计业务

法定审计是一个国家主权管理的体现，在各个国家都受到广泛监管。一般而言，各国的法律要求，法定审计必须由在境内注册/许可的会计师事务所来执行，这些事务所的所有权或控制权必须由境内居民持有（100%持有或者占多数比例持有）；还有一些国家要求会计师事务所的所有者必须是境内公民，例如美国的个别州就有此要求。因此，法定审计服务无法由境外会计师事务所提供。对于在本国证券交易所上市的外国公司，某些国家/地区允许境外会计师事务所在满足特定要求并在本国监管机构登记的前提下，出具符合本国上市要求规定的审计报告。比如在美国，发行人的审计可由任何一个注册于美国公众公司会计监督委员会（PCAOB）并接受其监管的事务所执行，无论该事务所来自美国还是其他国家/地区。在实践中，提供法定审计服务的会计师事务所一般来自于美国发行人的主营业务所在国，原因是该会计师事务所具备与被审计客户相关的本地知识及技能以胜任该审计业务，相对于境外事务所而言，其审计更有效率。在欧盟的规定下，境外会计师事务所在满足某些监管要求的前提下，或境外会计师事务所所在的监管环境等效于欧盟的监管环境（“欧盟等效国家或地区”），可以对在欧洲证券交易所上市的外国公司出具审计报告。在中国，法定审计报告必须由具有中国注册会计师资格的人员签署。由于中国尚未允许外国公司在本国证券交易所上市，目前尚无有关境外事务所为在本国上市的外国公司提供审计服务的相关规定。

2. 境外会计师事务所在境内设立分支机构

世界上大多数会计师事务所的法律形式为合伙制（有限责任合伙或普通合伙）。由于合伙人为自然人，这就使得合伙制会计师事务所无法拥有子公司。此外，上文分析了各国对在境内提供法定审计服务的事务所提出的一系列要求，境外事务所的分所很难满足这些要求，因此也就无法提供法定审计服务。另外，法律责任的归属问题也使会计师事务所很难在境外开设分所。因此，合伙制会计师事务所就很难通过设立海外分/子公司的形式来拓展其在海外市场的业务。在那些允许有限责任公司制会计师事务所的国家中，大多数国家要求有限责任会计师事务所的股东为拥有境内注册会计师执业资格的自然人，这样会计师事务所也不可能通过设立境外分/子公司而在国外提供审计服务。项目组还注意到，大型会计师事务所在境外市场的业务拓展都是通过建立由“本地所”组成的国际网络而实现的，“网络所”为独立的法律实体，他们彼此间不存在隶属关系，这些网络所通过遵守网络中统一的质量标准、共享同一品牌而结合在一起。它们遵守同样的内部控制政策，互相之间还开展内部质量检查以维护品牌声誉。

3. 审计工作底稿的管理

审计工作底稿是会计师事务所的资产。虽然各国法律没有明文禁止或限制，但审计工作底稿都是由会计师事务所在境内保存，在大多数情况下，不会被转移出境。审计师在他们的业务约定书中通常都会包含这样的条款，约定审计工作底稿是会计师事务所的财产，不得对外提供或转移，除非法律或者审计准则要求。根据审计准则的要求，在集团审计中，当海外分支机构对集团来讲相对重要时，集团审计师须对分支机构的审计工作取得信心，因此可能需要审阅分支机构审计师的工作底稿。在这种情况下，监管措施需要保障集团审计师能够有渠道在分支机构所在国，或在集团审计师所在国，对这些审计工作底稿进行审阅，在通常情况下，不应存在障碍。

4. 有关建议

由于法定审计在世界范围内所有国家均受到监管，中国会计师事务所很难直接或通过设立海外分支机构的方式在境外市场拓展其法定审计业务。项目组建议中国会计师事务所遵循国际注册会计师行业惯例，按照国外监管要求，在境外市场设立具有中国品牌的“网络所”，以便拓展境外业务。如何设立并扩张具有中国品牌的国际“网络所”并维护良好的品牌质量及声誉将成为中国会计师事务所的研究重点。像“四大”这样的大型会计师事务所通过在中国按照中国法律要求成立本地会计师事务所的形式已经将其网络扩展至中国。这些“本地”会计师事务所共享网络品牌、信息系统以及内部控制系统等来确保全球统一的服务质量。

### （三）会计服务市场开放负面清单管理模式

本章主要讨论负面清单能否被有效地使用在注册会计师行业国际服务贸易协定当中以及这种服务贸易协定中常见的负面清单条款。负面清单是指一系列不被允许的活动的清单，列明了企业不能投资的领域和产业。那些没有被包含在负面清单里的活动就是“允许的活动”或外资享有国民待遇的事项。以负面清单为基础的管理模型遵循“法无禁止即可为”的原则。负面清单概念首先被用在北美自由贸易谈判中，以美国为首的北美各国同意除个别单独讨论的领域以外，在各自国家全面放开自由贸易，取消贸易壁垒。在以负面清单模式为基础的自由贸易谈判中，市场开放和市场准入是谈判各方的核心目的。现在，越来越多的国家开始将负面清单概念用在双边贸易协定和控制外商投资当中。包括会计审计专业服务在内的服务业中，例如法定审计服务，也开始使用负面清单方法进行双边服务协定谈判。



根据调查，世界上在会计审计服务领域较有代表性的负面清单应当为中国香港与欧盟部分国家在自由贸易协定中使用的负面清单。项目组总结了中国香港与冰岛、瑞士及挪威在自由贸易协定中对会计审计服务领域的保留性限制措施。在美国与韩国的自由贸易协定中，双方同意成立一个由双方代表组成的“专业服务工作小组”，协助进行包括审计服务在内的专业服务相关事项。各国的世贸组织承诺表也提供了部分限制性措施信息。对此进行分析，有助于各国在市场开放磋商谈判中找到彼此的利益关切点，制定更高水平的负面清单。

中国政府近年来开始通过在特定区域使用负面清单的方法进行双边服务贸易管理。对负面清单模式的运用体现在对内和对外两个方面，对内主要是运用在国内自由贸易试验区的政策措施管理中，对外主要体现在与港澳的双边服务贸易自由化协定中。此外中国监管机构也在考虑进一步加强负面清单在其他双边投资协定中的使用，如中美双边投资协定。

有关建议如下：

(1) 负面清单方法可以通过加强自由贸易及对境外人士实行“国民待遇”来增进双边服务协议谈判的有效性。这对会计审计服务行业是尤其重要的。随着越来越多的公司向国外发展业务，会计审计专业服务也需要在全世界范围内放开。中国政府应该鼓励在与其他国家/地区的服务贸易协定中使用负面清单的方法实现更高水平的开放，从而增强在注册会计师专业服务领域的全球合作。

（2）会计审计专业服务在中国是一个新兴产业，而这种专业服务，尤其是审计服务是一个需要高度监管的领域，如果监管者没有能够及时发现需要被限制的新兴商业行为或没有能够及时更新负面清单，可能会导致负面清单被商业滥用的现象。中国的监管者需要密切关注在会计审计专业服务领域的新兴商业行为及其他国家/地区监管者的管控措施，以在必要的情况下，及时对新兴商业活动制定相关管控政策并且更新负面清单，以满足对会计专业服务领域的治理需要。

（3）对境外人士及境外会计师事务所在本国执业的管理措施都应该反映在双边协定的负面清单当中。由于法定审计是一个国家主权管理的体现，对于一个国家的经济来说具有至关重要的影响，各国政府也都在这一领域制定了严格的管控措施。因此针对会计审计专业服务领域的负面清单应该明确反映以上管控措施，以确保相关政策的一致性。

（4）对比研究分析可以发现，中国会计审计领域的负面清单是极少的，开放程度在全球首屈一指，这与当初中国加入 WTO 的承诺密切相关。认真总结正反两方面的经验，对于中国既扩大开放又有效维护国家利益是十分必要的。



## 二、中国会计服务的竞争力

以上针对会计服务开放的相关法规和实践的观察分析显示，项目组调研的国家/地区全部采取了各种措施来应对会计服务开放可能带来的风险和挑战。因此，境内注册会计师行业需要持续不断地发展壮大，提升竞争能力，为这一行业向国际发展奠定坚实的基础。从这个角度出发，项目组选取了六项重点议题，涵盖了与提升境内注册会计师水平有关的当今市场关注重点及政策讨论热点。项目组对六项议题分别进行了详尽的研究和分析，找出关键性问题并提出了相应的建议。这六项重点议题为：

- 注册会计师行业监管法规
- 会计师事务所强制轮换
- 政府购买会计师事务所专业服务
- 金融机构审计
- 会计师事务所职业责任保险

- 会计师事务所联合审计

### （一）注册会计师行业监管法规[①]

本章探讨的是在注册会计师行业提供审计服务方面现行的监管法规和规定，以确保对该行业实施有效的监督。项目组选取了美国（主要为四个代表州——纽约、伊利诺伊、加利福尼亚和德克萨斯）、英国、澳大利亚、加拿大、新加坡这些国家和中国香港地区作为代表进行研究。鉴于注册会计师行业提供的审计服务对一个国家资本市场和整体经济的重要性，研究范围内的所有国家/地区，注册会计师行业都存在广泛的监管。项目组的研究重点集中在四项监管要素上：对注册会计师个人和会计师事务所的资格认证/注册要求、会计师事务所的法律形式、注册会计师服务的质量控制/检查以及对注册会计师个人和会计师事务所的纪律处罚。



1. 资格认证/注册要求

在所有国家/地区，注册会计师及事务所开展审计服务，都需要进行资格认证或注册，以确保从事审计服务的个人和事务所具有恰当的执业资格。对事务所的管理，各国或地区的做法不一，具体来说，在美国、英国、新西兰和新加坡，会计师事务所须在公认的政府机构登记注册，获得提供法定审计服务的资格。类似地，会计师事务所若在中国开展法定审计服务，必须取得审计执照。这些负责会计师事务所注册的监管机构会评估事务所是否满足提供审计服务的条件，包括专业知识、能力及其他与执行法定审计服务相关的资质。各监管机构的具体要求也许不同，但通常要求绝大多数事务所主管人员（一般为合伙人和总监）具备专业资格。会计师事务所经过注册或认证后就会接受注册政府机构的持续监督。

与对事务所的管理有所不同，对注册会计师个人的管理通常通过授予执业资格（例如英国和中国香港），或是要求在公认的监管机构注册（例如澳大利亚和新西兰）这两种形式来实现，当然这些要求都只针对代表事务所签署审计意见的审计项目负责人。拥有执业资格或注册成为法定审计师的注册会计师个人须接受监管机构的监督。此外，所有的注册会计师都要取得足够的后续职业教育（Continuous Professional Education，CPE）以保证其专业资格的有效性。

---

① 主要针对注册会计师提供审计服务方面的法规。

2. 法律形式

大部分国家/地区允许会计师事务所采取不同的法律形式，事务所可以是合伙、独资或公司制。美国、英国、德国和新加坡还允许有限合伙制的会计师事务所。在中国，根据有关规定，财政部鼓励会计师事务所从有限责任公司形式转制为特殊普通合伙制形式，中国所有的证券资格会计师事务所已经完成了转制。

3. 质量控制/检查

每个国家/地区都设立了独立的审计监管机构，对审计活动进行持续的质量控制。这些机构的设立和监管活动的安排大多依据独立审计监管机构国际论坛（International Forum of Independent Audit Regulators，IFIAR）制定的11项核心原则。这套原则在国际上被普遍认可，涵盖设置独立审计监管机构的三个方面，即组织结构、经营管理和检查活动，同时也针对注册会计师行业审计服务质量控制的常见问题，例如独立性和执业能力，提出了解决方案框架。IFIAR原则建议各国审计监管机构采用“风险导向”的方法实施对会计师事务所的检查。比如为“公众利益公司”提供审计业务的事务所及审计业务量较大的事务所通常应当受到更为频繁的检查。项目组还注意到，政府对确保不同监管机构间的合作与交流也作出了努力。通过建立有效的沟通渠道，各监管机构就可以协同彼此、互通信息，从而实现更好的资源配置，避免重复检查。相比而言，中国由财政部门（包括财政部和地方财政厅局）和中国注册会计师协会对事务所进行系统的定期检查，但除此之外，一些其他的监管机构也会对一些事务所进行延伸检查。具体来说，中国证监会对提供中国上市公司审计的事务所进行延伸检查，中国银监会对为银行提供审计服务的事务所进行延伸检查，中国保监会对为保险公司提供审计服务的事务所进行延伸检查，这样的安排就导致了重复检查的可能性。

4. 纪律处罚

各国对在检查中发现的注册会计师和事务所的违规行为均有一系列的纪律处罚措施，这些措施通常包括罚款、通报批评、限期整改及暂停或永久吊销执照。有时，监管机构也会要求事务所聘请独立的第三方对其某一个或几个审计项目进行检查并出具检查报告，或者请专人设计公司内部管理政策以确保其符合行业要求。

5. 有关建议

（1）针对审计师的检查，中国应该考虑将各部门和各级的监管机构的检查结合起来，形成一个统一的系统化的检查方案，以便有效地利用政府资源，避免重复检查。对各国审计监管机构的各项安排比照 IFIAR 原则逐一进行的分析可以帮助我们了解一系列可行的监管方案。中国应建立统一的检查方案，且该方案需要符合 IFIAR 原则的要求。

（2）中国可以考虑对事务所进行分类监管，由监管机构依据过往检查经验和监管实践，以事务所的规模、收入、质量控制考核结果、公共利益公司及其他被监管的客户的数量等为分类依据，对不同类别的事务所采取不同的监管措施。事务所的质量提高，对该所的监管力度与检查次数可以相应减少；反之，如果一家事务所质量下降，则降低其级别，加强对其监管的力度。

（3）纪律处罚的重心应从事务所转向注册会计师个人。此建议基于三点考虑：①对于小型事务所，如果纪律处罚主要针对事务所，那么事务所的合伙人就可以选择关闭该事务所，再重新设立一个新所继续从业（除处罚个人外，该项风险还可以通过建立适当的注册会计师个人及事务所从业资格认证/注册要求体系来进行控制，通过认证注册过程将曾有不良行为记录的会计师及事务所剔除在外）；②对于大型事务所，鉴于声誉对其事务所至关重要，如果纪律处罚是针对事务所而不是个人，事务所就会聘请律师竭尽全力来维护自身声誉，这就将导致一个冗长且昂贵的诉讼过程；③证明大型事务所的质量控制系统缺陷比证明单个审计项目的缺陷更为耗时费力。因此，处罚负责单个审计项目的会计师个人要更为有效和快捷。将监管和纪律处罚集中在对会计师个人的管理上不失为一种更好的手段，而且这种做法的有效性在某些国家已经得到了验证，比如澳大利亚和新西兰。

（4）中国审计监管机构有必要进一步提升胜任能力。对比国外监管机构，由其监管人员配置和能力、经验等可看出，只有监管机构处于更胜一筹的地位，才能推动监管工作取得实效。由于历史原因等多方面条件的制约，中国一些监管机构同会计师事务所相比仍存在本能欠缺，导致监管工作偏离执业质量这一核心而停留在其他次要层面；同时，也存在监管机构内部权责配置不当等问题，需要结合职能定位、胜任能力等加以调整完善。

## （二）会计师事务所强制轮换

项目组重点分析了对从事法定审计服务的会计师事务所实行强制轮换要求的相关国际惯例，以及强制轮换所带来的影响。考虑到这些国家/地区能够较好地代表国际惯例，研究围绕着美国、英国、欧盟、新加坡、日本、澳大利亚、巴西、印度、荷兰、土耳其和中国香港展开。项目组了解到，在美国，监管机构针对审计强制轮换要求开展了冗长的辩论，由于强制轮换事务所带来的明显弊端，美国国会于2013年7月经投票否决了PCAOB提出的对事务所实施强制轮换的要求。英国监管机构经历了漫长的辩论过程，最终，竞争委员会（而不是会计师行业监管机构）要求立法者不要对事务所实行强制轮换，而是实行强制招标。即鉴于强制轮换存在弊端，为了增加竞争（而不是提升审计质量），要求对那些连续服务年限达到10年的会计师事务所进行强制招标，现任审计师可以参加招标。考虑到强制轮换事务所给银行和审计师双方都带来严重的负面影响，新加坡金融管理局于2008年撤销了对国内银行审计的强制轮换要求。

目前虽然对强制轮换会计师事务所仍存在一定的争议，但在主要的金融中心，该争议已进入尾声。推行强制轮换会计师事务所的监管机构大多是希望避免审计师与客户由于长期合作而产生过度亲密的关系，从而损害审计师独立性。此外也有部分人士认为强制轮换会计师事务所会增加审计市场的竞争，以降低审计市场的集中度。反对强制轮换会计师事务所的人士认为，强制轮换会计师事务所，尤其是当轮换期限过短时，会给审计质量及公司治理带来相对的弊端，主要体现在以下几个方面：

- 增加时间、成本及管理层负担
- 损害现行公司治理制度
- 减少选择
- 降低审计质量
- 进一步提高行业集中度
- 全球环境导致强制轮换难以实施
- 对审计行业的不利影响
- 过度市场干预

有关建议如下：

（1）鉴于强制轮换会计师事务所带来的种种弊端，建议中国考虑加强对轮换审计师个人的要求，以代替对会计师事务所的轮换，这样既能避免审计师与客户之间长期合作引起独立性问题，又能避免轮换事务所带来的不利因素。目前，中国对上市公司已经采取了轮换签字审计师的要求，中国可以考虑进一步完善这种对签字审计师的轮换制度，加强对签字审计师强制轮换的监管力度。

（2）对于特定行业（例如国有企业和金融机构）现行轮换会计师事务所的要求，监管机构可以考虑在短期内适当延长轮换期限（例如延长轮换期限至10年），避免轮换期限较短带来的各种不利因素。同时监管机构可以结合中国整体经济改革，发挥市场在经济资源配置中的决定作用，鼓励企业建立起良好的公司治理环境。在良好的公司治理环境下，独立的非执行董事可以有效地发挥作用；会计师事务所也应该采取合理的内部控制措施保证其独立性。当公司的治理环境得以全面提升时，中国可以考虑取消对会计师事务所的强制轮换要求，而侧重于轮换签字审计师个人及其他对独立性的治理需求。



### （三）政府购买会计师事务所专业服务

项目组对各国政府从会计师事务所购买专业服务的实务操作进行了对比分析，通过研究各自的优势和挑战，探讨在中国公共部门从会计师事务所购买专业服务的可行性方案。本议题选取了美国、英国、澳大利亚、新加坡、新西兰这几个发达国家和中国香港地区作为代表进行研究，学习其成熟经验。研究结果显示，这些国家/地区均存在政府从会计师事务所购买专业服务的惯例，也有一整套适用于如政府机关和非营利性组织等公共部门的审计准则。

1. 政府从会计师事务所购买专业服务的优势

（1）可以增加政府的透明度和确保地方公众对公共机构实施监督的权利。

（2）将减轻国家审计机关的政府审计负担。

（3）会计师事务所可以将其在为企业提供专业服务时获得的宝贵经验用于为政府部门提供的服务上，该优势在提供管理咨询等非审计服务时更为显著，这对提升中国公共部门管理水平和透明度将十分有益。

2. 政府从会计师事务所购买专业服务的挑战

（1）由于市场竞争机制的存在，不同政府机构在公开的市场上采购类似的专业服务所支付的费用可能有所不同，这就可能增加政府预算管理的困难。然而，项目组也注意到，英国的社区和地方政府部门（Department for Communities and Local Government，DCLG）认为，从长期来看，政府审计项目外包给外部审计师将会为纳税人节约相当可观的资金。

（2）政府的业务常常涉及高度机密的信息。会计师事务所为政府部门提供专业服务将有机会接触到这些机密信息，因此对这些机密信息需要进行额外的保护。

（3）鉴于公共部门和企业的审计目标不同，会计师事务所在处理公共部门的审计时可能缺乏足够的背景和专业知识。因此，会计师事务所开展政府机构审计，相比企业审计，需要更高水平的监管。

3. 中国特有的挑战

（1）目前在中国，会计师事务所参与公共部门审计的情况较为有限，公共部门的审计主要由国家审计机关负责执行。对比会计师事务所审计和国家审计机关审计，双方在独立性要求、职业道德要求等方面具有相似之处。但由于企业审计和公共部门审计的关注点不同（企业审计关注财务报表的真实性公允性，公共部门审计除关注财务报表的真实性公允性外，还关注财政资金使用等的合规性执行情况），会计师事务所审计主要针对财务信息发表意见，而国家审计机关审计主要对公共部门的合规性发表意见（如财政拨款使用的合规性），因此会计师事务所审计与国家审计机关审计在审计目标和策略、适用的审计准则、接受的监管等方面都存在差异。此外，国家审计机关审计还包含对单位主要负责人的经济责任审计以及对预算执行情况和特别项目的财政收支情况等的专项审计。这些差异就要求建立起一套针对会计师事务所进行或参与公共部门审计工作的准则，来明确会计师事务所参与公共部门审计的范围、方式和行为规范等等。

（2）中国在公共部门审计方面的准则规范还需要进一步明晰和完善。目前，与政府审计相关的法规准则更多的是一些基础规则，而不是审计师执行具体审计程序时应遵守的行为准则。因此，如果计划让会计师事务所大规模地参与到公共部门的审计工作中来，就必须制定及完善针对会计师事务所对政府机构进行审计的专业准则。目前，中注协已经开始组织专员着手该准则制定工作。

（3）中国的政府会计体系正在经历一系列的改革和完善。中国共产党的十八届三中全会要求，积极推进政府会计准则体系的建立和以权责发生制为基础的政府综合财务报告制度。根据现行的《行政单位会计制度》，中国目前各行政单位会计核算一般采用收付实现制，特殊经济业务和事项按照制度的规定采用权责发生制核算。因此，现行的政府会计准则和财务报告制度需要加快改革，财政部也在积极推进这一工作。

（4）需要推动和加快对政府部门会计审计人才的培养，尤其是要提升他们对政府会计、审计准则相关知识的掌握水平。一方面，政府财务报表的编制者，应当熟练掌握更新的政府会计准则和综合财务报告制度，同时相关领导阶层能对政府审计准则进行总体上的把握。另一方面，若计划让会计师事务所大规模地参与到公共部门的审计工作中来，也需要加强对会计师事务所和注册会计师与政府部门会计审计准则相关知识的培训。

（5）会计师事务所也许会因为缺少适当授权，在执行某些政府审计程序时遇到困难。

（6）虽然短期内在中国，针对政府机构的审计，会计师事务所的平均收费标准与国家审计机关内部审计师相比可能略高，但从长远看，政府购买审计服务能够大大节省公共部门的总审计成本。因此，从长远看，目前的政府预算管理需要进行修改，将这部分审计费用纳入财政预算的考虑范围内。

（7）在中国，政府从会计师事务所购买专业服务尚处在初步探索阶段，还需要进一步建立和完善一套透明且公平的政府专业服务招标体系，而选聘符合要求的会计师事务所的评估标准将是该体系的一项重要内容。

4. 有关建议

（1）会计师事务所向政府部门提供专业服务可以增加政府财务状况的透明度，增强政府公信力，确保公众对公共机构实施监督的权利，对加快推进廉洁政府、透明政府能够起到积极的作用。我们预期在中国，政府部门对会计师事务所的专业服务有着很大的需求，比如中国正在大力推进政府会计准则体系建设和以权责发生制为基础的政府综合财务报告制度，未来对政府及公共部门的注册会计师审计有较大需求。中国应当在实施必要监督的基础上，大力支持和鼓励政府从会计师事务所购买专业服务。

（2）政府部门应考虑建设一套标准的政府购买专业服务的体系，包括由哪些部门负责采购、采购方式（如公开招标还是直接指派）、公开招标文件、招标文件应涵盖的内容、要求事务所提供的信息、选聘事务所的评估标准以及对聘用的会计师事务所工作质量的监督等等。其他国家在这些方面的实施情况可作为参考。

(3) 政府在计划向会计师事务所采购专业服务的同时也要考虑其成本构成。这些成本需要被妥善地纳入政府预算控制体系。政府可自行决定这些成本应由政府直接支付还是由接受服务的部门自行承担。

(4) 应按照中国共产党的十八届三中全会要求，尽快建立政府会计准则体系和以权责发生制为基础的政府综合财务报告制度。同时，应进一步改革和完善政府部门审计准则，使其标准化、具体化，明确会计师事务所作为政府部门审计师的责任，是保证政府购买专业服务顺利进行的决定性前提和关键。作为中国注册会计师审计准则的一部分，这些准则和应用指南需要具体且清晰，可以最大限度地参考企业审计的一般公认准则，并加入政府部门审计的特殊领域（如合规性）的特殊审计要求。这些准则和应用指南也为政府审计各方提供了一个行为标准的框架。

(5) 全面推进对政府部门会计审计人才的培养。首先，应当加强对政府部门财务报表编制者，即政府财务人员的专业培训，使其具备充分的政府会计准则知识及编制以权责发生制为基础的政府综合财务报表的专业胜任能力，并对政府审计准则有一定的了解。同时，为政府部门提供专业服务的会计师事务所和注册会计师应当熟练掌握公共部门会计准则和制度、审计准则与实务，具备公共部门事务尤其是特殊行业（如社保基金）的充分了解并具有相关经验和资质。对此，中国可以考虑在注册会计师考试和后续教育要求中增加公共部门会计准则、审计准则相关的内容，同时，各会计师事务所内部也应增加相关的培训内容，注重对政府部门专业服务人才的培养。

(6) 与其他审计一样，财政部作为监管机构，应总体上对会计师事务所开展的政府部门审计业务实施监管。其他相关机构，如国家审计机关，也可以对其委托的审计业务参与监管。下一步，财政部、审计署应加强对推进公共部门注册会计师审计制度建设的沟通协调，促进政府审计与注册会计师审计相互补充、相互支持、相得益彰。

### （四）金融机构审计

项目组研究了法定审计在金融机构监管体系中扮演的角色，以及如何进一步提升金融机构法定审计的质量。项目组的调研主要围绕着美国、英国、新加坡和澳大利亚展开，因为这些国家都是世界上重要的金融中心。研究结果显示，金融机构大多数为公众利益实体，大多数国家对金融机构都采取严格的监管措施。每个国家的监管结构不同，但通常都涉及审慎监管、消费者保护和市场稳定。其监管目的是构建一个稳健与活跃并存的金融市场，预防金融危机的再次发生。在人民币国际化及利率市场化的进程中，中国的金融审计也面临着更多挑战。

1. 法定审计师在金融市场监管中扮演重要的角色

各国政府都试图通过直接监管金融部门来消除或减缓潜在的金融危机。监管的主要目标之一是提高透明度：通过要求金融机构定期提供并公开其按照相关会计准则编制的财务报表使公众了解金融机构的财务状况；监管的另一个目标是通过准备金、资本要求以及其他杠杆比率的限制确保金融机构有足够的资产以满足其契约义务。审计师在政府对金融机构的监管中发挥如下重要作用：

（1）提高透明度。审计师通过对金融机构的财务报表展开高质量的审计以提高其透明度。

（2）确保资本充足。通过对准备金、资本金及其他杠杆率进行合规审计[①]，确定金融机构的资本是否充足。

2. 从近年金融危机中取得的教训

近年的金融危机显示，金融机构的法定审计师需要关注以下领域并拓展其相关审计专业技能，以应对审计高风险环节：

- 计算机技能在审计中的运用
- 对金融资产的信用分析及减值评估
- 公允价值评估及利用评估专家的工作
- 财务报表合并及对特殊目的公司的会计处理
- 内部控制和欺诈风险
- 披露

金融审计的特殊性要求其审计师拥有充足的审计经验、专业审计队伍以及特殊行业专家，例如计算机专家、精算专家、评估专家等等。此外，鉴于大型金融机构的规模庞大，审计团队也需要具有相匹配的规模。这些特殊要求使得

① 金融机构的合规审计没有强制要求由法定审计师执行，金融机构可以聘请另一家有资格的会计师事务所提供该审计服务。然而，在实际操作中，法定审计师通常比其他事务所在执行合规审计方面更为高效，因此合规审计通常仍由法定审计师来执行。

世界主要国家/地区的大型金融机构一般倾向于选择大型会计师事务所为其提供专业服务。

3. 有关建议

（1）夯实教育。针对金融审计高风险领域，应对金融机构的管理层及金融机构审计师开展有效的教育及培训，以确保金融机构的财务报表“透明且充分”地反映金融机构的财务状况。对市场上的潜在投资人进行这些方面的教育也是必要的，这样可以保证这些投资人能够正确阅读并理解财务报表，进而根据经审计的财务信息及其他信息作出明智的投资决定。

（2）人才储备。中国会计师事务所应该注重在金融审计方面的人才储备，培养相关人才，扩大金融审计团队规模以应对大型金融机构审计项目的需求。中国财政部高度重视会计审计人才培养，目前开展了多项会计领军人才培养和特殊支持计划。中国会计师事务所可以结合财政部的人才培养计划来规划其自身人才培养及储备计划，进一步提高其金融审计能力。

（3）监管检查。监管检查可以保证法定审计服务的质量。鉴于金融机构对整个国家经济的重要性，监管机构可以考虑进一步提高对金融机构法定审计师的检查频率，扩大覆盖范围，以营造一个稳健有效的金融管理控制体系。监管机构的检查机制应对公众透明，向公众提供其采用的抽查方法及检查范围等信息，这将进一步提升公众信心并建立市场信任。监管检查应该集中考察审计师的经验、能力和审计工作的质量。此外，在一些特殊情况下，尤其是当被审计金融机构存在严重违规现象且不愿更正的时候，为了保护公共利益，审计师应该有渠道直接与相关监管机构沟通违规事项。

（4）惩戒措施。良好的质量控制环境离不开合理的惩戒措施，这些措施通常包括通告批评、经济处罚以及通过限制事务所的业务范围来进行惩戒，例如限期禁止有问题的事务所及其合伙人对金融机构提供审计服务。此外，在金融机构审计检查中发现的问题也可能反映了该被审计金融机构也许存在合规性问题，这些问题应该通过合理的渠道向金融机构的监管者进行反映，以便在必要情况下对相关金融机构采取惩戒措施，以确保市场的稳定性。在一些国家，监管机构可以要求与金融机构及其审计师召开三方会议来共同讨论与会计及控制有关的问题。

### （五）会计师事务所职业责任保险

项目组讨论了对提供法定审计服务的会计师事务所强制要求购买职业责任保险的国际范例，事务所在市场上购买适当的责任险所面临的阻碍以及如何克服这些阻碍。项目组的研究围绕世界上具有代表性的主要经济体，如英国、德国、澳大利亚、新加坡、美国和中国香港而展开。研究发现，大多数国家/地区都通过立法或通过会计职业组织的规定，要求会计师事务所或执业注册会计师个人购买最低限度的职业责任保险。在大多数国家/地区，如新加坡和中国香港，这种强制职业责任保险都仅限于法律实体为有限责任的会计师事务所，如有限责任合伙制或有限责任公司制会计师事务所。对于无限连带责任的普通合伙制会计师事务所则没有这种强制保险的要求。项目组同时注意到，由于“四大”会计师事务所通常无法完全从商业保险市场上购买到所需的全部职业责任保险，因此，“四大”在国际范围内都建立了各自“网络成员所”间的专业自我保险机制。



1. 各国对注册会计师职业责任保险的支持措施

为了保证执业注册会计师能以合理的价格购买到所需要的职业责任险，各个国家的政府或者会计职业组织都作出了很多努力。以美国和英国为例，会计职业组织与保险公司协商为会计师职业责任保险制定了双方认可的标准保单，所有的会计职业组织的会员都可以在市场上购买到这样的保险产品；澳大利亚通过立法规定了会计行业的最高赔付限额，保险公司据此可对风险进行更准确的估算，这就使保险公司能够在更广的范围内为会计师提供保险。劳合社是世界上一个比较特殊的保险市场，在这里来自不同国家的保险公司集中对某个行业提供保险以共同承担风险。这也为如何将注册会计师行业的责任风险进行分散提供了优秀范例。

2. 中国在此领域取得的成效

注册会计师责任保险在中国处于刚起步的阶段。在 2011 年年末，上海注册会计师协会在上海市为会计师事务所开展了集体公开招标。招标协商的结果是会计师事务所和保险公司之间实现了双赢。会计师事务所不仅扩大了保单中涵盖的责任险范围并且降低了保险成本，这样对于事务所来说在一定程度上就提供了可靠保障；另一方面，由于更多的会计师事务所愿意参与投保，中标的保险公司的相关保险业务得到了显著发展。此外，保险公司和事务所双方都能因风险分散而从中获益。2014 年年末，财政部发布征求意见稿，就会计师事务所购买职业责任保险相关规定征求公众意见，预计将于 2015 年正式发布。

3. 有关建议

（1）中国监管机构应鼓励全部会计师事务所采取风险保障措施，建立完善的风险控制体系。结合特殊普通合伙转制，对职业风险基金不足的会计师事务所实施强制职业责任保险，以便更好地保护投资者利益。

（2）上海市注册会计师协会引导全市会计师事务所进行集中投保的做法值得借鉴，事务所可以以合理的价格投保其所需的险种。这种集体招标安排可以在分散风险的同时降低保费。此举可以推广至中国其他省份，从而扩大投保的会计师事务所数量。此外，一些国际保险组织联合起来组成专业保险市场，为高额风险提供“辛迪加”式的保障服务，例如劳合社。中国监管机构可以考虑从这些国际保险组织获取国际上保险业及再保险商的操作经验，从而为向会计师事务所提供全球化的保险服务提供借鉴。



### （六）会计师事务所联合审计

项目组重点研究了欧洲市场上存在的联合审计的情况，并针对强制性联合审计制度的影响进行了分析。目前法国是实行强制性联合审计制度的主要国家，项目组的研究主要针对法国展开。联合审计与常见的集团审计相比，虽然都有超过一家会计师事务所参与审计，但两者的关键区别在于联合审计由参与审计的所有事务所对工作分工达成一致意见并联合发表审计意见，共同签署审计报告，而集团审计则是由担任集团审计师的事务所单独签署审计报告。项目组的研究显示，联合审计的支持者设想的联合审计的优点（降低市场集中度、提高审计质量）在实践中并未得到体现，相反，一些实证分析表明联合审计存在以下弊端：

- 增加审计成本
- 可能带来潜在风险，如审计分工不均问题或分工不明晰导致的重大审计程序遗漏的问题，因而不一定能提高审计质量，反而可能降低审计质量
- 可能增加市场集中度、减少审计师的可选择性
- 阻止审计委员会获得最佳的审计方案

有关建议如下：

（1）基于中国审计市场现状，引入联合审计是一个不经济的选择，联合审计

很可能增加资本市场的经济负担，并且可能很长一段时间内不会产生经济效益。

（2）鉴于中国会计师事务所在规模、资源、专业技能和审计方法等方面确实存在明显差距，以及联合审计在会计师事务所责任划分方面存在固有局限性，目前在中国引入联合审计弊大于利。

（3）联合审计在提高独立性和审计质量有关方面的理论优势可以通过其他替代途径来获得，如提高独立性及合规性的要求，并加强审计行业监管。

## 三、跨境会计监管与合作

上文研究分析表明，中国和其他国家有关注册会计师行业的监管规定和操作实务在许多方面存在差异，而这些差异会导致对跨境交易的监管冲突，比如对境外上市的本国公司的监管。然而，商业和会计服务的全球化要求建立有效的跨境监管合作机制来解决这些监管冲突，保护全球资本市场上投资者的利益。因此，项目组对现有的跨境监管合作方案和中国面对的主要挑战进行了研究，探讨能够解决中国跨境监管矛盾的可行性方案。

项目组选取欧盟、美国、澳大利亚和新西兰为代表进行研究，它们是当今世界主要的几大经济体，同时澳大利亚和新西兰在跨境监管方面也已实现区域合作。研究结果表明，在跨境检查方面，存在两种典型的国际合作方式，即欧盟模式和美国模式。

欧盟模式下，欧洲委员会（EC）通过“等效性决议”，已确认包括中国在内的十个非欧盟国家的审计监管体系与欧盟等效。在此模式下，欧盟成员国可以依赖认同等效的国家对事务所的检查，而无需额外进行现场审查。

美国模式下，PCAOB 对在 PCAOB 注册的对美国上市公司出具审计意见的境外事务所进行现场检查，此类检查可以由 PCAOB 独立进行，也可由 PCAOB 协同当地监管机构，比如澳大利亚证券和投资委员会（ASIC）联合进行。美国模式要求存在超越区域管辖权的立法才能保证美国具备实施跨境检查的能力，这一模式独树一帜但也存在很多弊端。

有关建议如下：

（1）解决跨境监管冲突、实现有效合作的根本是能够在保护投资者利益的同时，尊重各国国家主权，尊重各国对经济信息安全的关注，加强相互理解与协助，构建系统性的国际合作机制，既重视整体的协调又重视个体的差异，既重视标准的形成又重视执行中的落实，从整体效果最优的角度来考虑合作机制中各要素的相互关系。

（2）中国可以考虑与欧盟进行更多的交流与合作，在全球范围内推动相互信赖与相互协助这一合作理念，以解决目前的跨境监管冲突。在这一理念下，如果境外监管者发现中国的会计师事务所在为境外上市的中国公司提供审计服务时存在潜在的过失，境外监管者可将这些发现告知中国的独立审计监管机构，并要求其对该事务所实施检查或调查，并将检查或调查结果以及对该事务所的处罚决定与上市地的境外监管者进行充分沟通。适当的情况下，也可以考虑采用联合检查的形式实施检查。

（3）中美在跨境监管合作方面的冲突源于美国推行的跨境检查方案与地域管辖权的固有矛盾，中国也深知美国的跨境监管模式存在各种弊端，但若这些冲突不能尽快得到很好的解决，在美国上市的中国公司的形象将受到不必要的损害，中国会计服务开放的进程也会受到一定的阻碍。对此，中国可以考虑主动举办圆桌讨论或对话，促进双方在存在的冲突和困难上达成共识，呼吁通过共同努力来解决冲突。同时，中国应考虑加强对以间接上市的方式进入海外资本市场的中国企业的监管，向全世界展示中国解决跨境监管冲突的信心和决心，为进一步开展多层次的跨境监管合作奠定基础。2015 年 5 月，中国财政部发布《会计师事务所从事中国内地企业境外上市审计业务暂行规定》，朝着这一目标迈出了重要步伐。

（4）中国在跨境监管合作的国际活动中需要发挥更加积极的作用。作为世界上大的经济体之一，中国参与全球范围内的活动是必需的。中国可以考虑主动参与或举办定期的圆桌讨论，与其他国家共同讨论全球跨境合作中面临的冲突和挑战，探讨可行的解决办法。中国也可以考虑就跨境合作问题与其他国家协商和签订一些谅解备忘录或双边协议。此外，中国也可以对包括独立审计监管机构国际论坛（International Forum of Independent Audit Regulators, IFIAR）和国际证券事务监察委员会（International Organization of Securities Commissions, IOSCO）在内的大型国际组织的平台加以更好的利用。通过这些平台，中国可以学习到其他国家在审计监管方面的先进经验，也可以将中国的监管体系展示给其他国家，从而提高世界对中国监管体系的认可。同时通过参与各种国际性的讨论与经验分享，增强中国在国际监管规则制定方面的话语权。

（5）中国可以考虑加强对各国法律法规和实践的研究与分析，为中国法律法规的修订提供建议。同时，学习国际上的先进经验，领导解决其他国家或国际机构提出的中国市场目前的缺陷和问题，消除这些国际机构对中国市场的误解，改善中国在国际上的形象，增强全球资本市场上投资者对中国及中国上市公司的信心。

# Executive Summary

The globalization of businesses and expansion of multinational companies are promoting the accounting profession as the most international profession from various perspectives. Meanwhile, given the importance of accounting services, especially statutory audit services, to a nation's economy as a whole, the CPA profession has become an extensively regulated profession in most countries and territories. As such, continuous efforts have been made on improving the regulations and supervision over the CPA profession in China.



In order to contribute to the policy development, this report reviews the global practices for benchmarking rules and regulations relating to the CPA profession, and analyses the merits and challenges of each practice. Research and analysis were carried out according to a framework developed by the MOF as introduced above, with key focuses over the following three areas, which also form the structure of this report: opening-up of accounting services in China, competitiveness of accounting services in China, and cross-border accounting regulation and cooperation.

## A. Opening-up of accounting services in China

In several respects, accounting is one of the most international professions. Globalization of business has increased the demand for global co-ordination of accounting services. As multinational clients expand their operations worldwide, the large accounting firms have had to become more globally focused to provide comprehensive services. The complexity of commercial transactions (including international mergers and acquisitions), the preparation of financial statements for listings on international stock exchanges, and the preparation of company tax filings requires skilled and multi-disciplinary accounting and auditing services in order for companies to operate in a smooth, efficient and cost-effective manner.

China, as one of the strongest economies in the world, attracts billions of inbound investments every year and actively participates in large volumes of significant transactions in the global domain. Under such circumstances, the opening-up of accounting services in China is an inevitable and necessary trend. To support this trend, the project team performed research and analysis on the rules and practices regarding the performance of cross-border accounting services in representative territories including U. S., U. K., Australia, Singapore and Hong Kong, and the review and analysis focused on the following three topics: rules and practices regarding accepting a foreign individual as a local certified public accountant, administrative rules and practices for allowing overseas CPA firms to conduct statutory audit services in the local market, and the "Negative List" approach for accounting services.



(A) Rules and practices regarding the ability of a foreign individual to practice as a CPA

A CPA can provide various services such as audit, book-keeping, preparation of tax returns, consultancy services and occupying finance officer roles. Among these services, the statutory audit is the most common service provided by external CPAs and such service is normally extensively regulated in various countries. It is important to distinguish the provision of audit and assurance services from those of other accounting services which are generally not regulated. It is also important therefore to distinguish the wishes of an individual to be recognised as a member of an accounting professional body from a licensing mechanism over the provision of audit services by firms and the individuals in those firms who provide auditing services.

In almost all jurisdictions, individuals join their local accounting professional body, first as a qualified member as an accountant and thereafter to retain membership of that body to keep up-to-date with professional standards and be recognized as a member of that body. In many jurisdictions, such members are active as professional accountants in business (finance department) or perhaps as tax advisors or providers of services such as book-keeping, company secretarial and other such accounting related services. Being a member of the accounting professional body is sufficient for these purposes and the accounting professional body ensures quality through its membership requirements in areas of continuous professional development and the issuing of accounting standards, code of ethics including independence. Further regulation on these professionals is usually not undertaken.

For those individuals who wish to undertake statutory audits, either through a registered firm, or as individuals, additional qualifications are needed in areas such as local law and local taxation. In addition, these individuals must have undertaken auditing examinations. It is this part of the CPA profession that is generally regulated by an independent regulatory body. In reading the remainder of this topic it is important to keep this distinction in mind.



Research was conducted regarding the U. S. (four representative states – New York, Illinois, California and Texas), U. K., Australia, New Zealand, Singapore, and Hong Kong as representative territories. In all of these territories, the requirements and process for becoming a CPA are similar. Specifically, a CPA candidate must meet a number of broadly consistent requirements which include completing a specified education curriculum; passing an examination on professional standards and knowledge of areas relevant to providing accounting services, notably local law and taxation; completing an ethics test; and achieving experience thresholds. Similar requirements have been established in the PRC for candidates to obtain membership of CICPA.

However, when it comes to having rights to sign statutory opinions (practicing rights) there are notable differences between territories which are explained further below.

a. Membership of accounting professional bodies (NOT statutory auditors)

    - **Citizenship and residency** - Very few territories require a member of the local accounting professional body to be a local citizen or resident in their territory. Usually, students residing in a territory will join the local accounting professional body to pass the exams and obtain relevant work experience. Once this is completed and they have become a member, they can work overseas and retain their membership. In addition, once qualified many CPAs can travel and become members of the accounting professional body of the territory they have chosen to work in.

- **Work experience** - In order to become a member of an accounting professional body, candidates are required by most bodies to have obtained a certain level of practical experience. Many territories require this experience be obtained in a CPA firm or in a commercial organization under the supervision of a member of the accounting professional body. Such organization can be either a local CPA firm/commercial organization or an overseas CPA firm/commercial organization, as long as it meets the criteria set by the accounting professional body.



b. CPAs performing statutory audits

These are generally known as CPAs in practice, either as a partner of a partnership CPA firm or as a director of a corporate CPA firm, or as a sole practitioner signing statutory opinions. There is a fundamental difference between territories that needs explaining. In most territories, being a member of an accounting professional body of itself does not give that member the right to sign statutory audit opinions. Further registration and licensing requirements exist to qualify for this category of CPA and there are annual licensing requirements to adhere to. However, in some territories, such as U. S. and China, once an individual has become a CPA, it is sufficient to give the individual the right to sign statutory audit opinions. The importance of this distinction is elaborated below.

- **Citizenship and residency** - Most territories do not require a CPA candidate in this category to be a local citizen. However, most territories do require that this individual be resident in the local territory. This ensures that the individual is familiar with the local requirements which often change and can be located where disciplinary action is warranted. Residency is sometimes defined differently in territories and there are usually definitions to indicate "generally resident", i. e. those who meet the residential time threshold in a local territory. In addition, where a local CPA firm is registered, most territories require that they are owned by a majority of local residents or that the controlling partners or directors reside locally.

- Work experience - Most territories require the CPA candidates to have relevant working experience in a locally qualified CPA firm. This effectively requests that the candidates must work in the local territory and obtain sufficient local knowledge in order for him/her to sign the statutory audit report locally.

- Practicing certificate or registration requirement - In certain countries such as U. S., all CPAs can have signing rights for the statutory audit report if a registered accounting firm permits him/her to sign on the firm's behalf. However, in other territories, such as U. K., Australia, Singapore and Hong Kong, a CPA must obtain an additional practicing certificate or registration before he/she obtains the signing rights for the statutory audit report in the local market. To obtain such practicing certificate or registration, there are some additional requirements. E. g. in U. K., the candidate must have relevant local working experience with relevant nature and tenure, and purchase indemnity insurance up to a certain level as a precondition for obtaining the practicing certificate. Furthermore, a practicing certificate holder must pay higher amount of membership fee and be subject to close monitoring by the regulators. Thus in practice, a CPA individual will only apply for the practicing certificate once he/she becomes a partner of a CPA firm and will sign the statutory audit report on behalf of the CPA firm. Through the additional requirements for obtaining the practicing certificate or registration and the closer monitoring of CPA individuals with signing rights, the regulators improve audit quality and discipline in the market.

c. Mutual Recognition Agreements

The accounting professional bodies (e. g. , societies or institutes) in many territories have one or more mutual recognition agreements (MRAs) with selected counterparts in other territories. There are different types of MRAs providing different levels of "recognition" with the counterparties. Sometimes, additional education or exams are needed to achieve the mutual recognition, but credit is given for certain examination criteria to avoid duplication. Before an MRA can be entered into, both parties to the MRA need to evaluate the counterparties' CPA qualification system and the level of recognition provided is based on the evaluation results. Normally, if the counterparty's CPA qualification system is considered equivalent to that of the home territory, mutual recognition of the membership is agreed. The MRA evaluation is normally done by a qualified third country's accounting professional body. While MRA grants a "fast track" for the counterparty's CPAs to obtain local CPA membership title, it DOES NOT provide the candidates with the signing rights for local statutory audit reports. This is because in most of the territories, such as U. K. , Australia, Singapore and Hong Kong, a CPA needs to obtain a separate practicing certificate to sign the statutory audit report. Furthermore, as a CPA signs the statutory audit report on behalf of a qualified CPA firm, he/she must obtain the authorisation from the qualified CPA firm for the signing right, which normally requests the individual to be admitted as a partner of a CPA firm. European countries, such as U. K. and Germany, have some special treatment for the EU member states where mutual recognition is normally granted among EU countries, including the signing right for statutory audits. E. g. in U. K. and Germany, the CPAs and CPA firms from countries in European Economic Area (EEA), which includes the European Union member states, are allowed to practice statutory audit service in U. K. and Germany, while in Germany the signer of a statutory audit report needs to pass an aptitude test which comprises of a written and oral examination relating to legal provisions of statutory audits, commercial law, tax law and the regulations governing the profession of Wirtschaftsprüfer – Chartered Public Accountant.

Recommendations:

- China should consider establishing MRAs with overseas recognized accounting professional bodies, such as the AICPA, ACCA, CAANZ, CPA Australia and others. Consideration should also be given to extend the current arrangements with HKICPA and ICAEW relating to the exemption of certain tests. This would make it easier for Chinese CPAs to become a member of an overseas accounting professional body and, obtain employment overseas. This will also help attract more people to become CICPA members and thus enlarge the influential power of CICPA globally. The membership title through MRA SHOULD NOT give the candidate the signing right for the local statutory audit report. This is normal in such MRA arrangements. The regulators can implement additional licensing requirement through practicing certificate requirements or other similar measures, which can help the regulators better monitor and discipline the CPAs who have signing rights for statutory audit reports.

- More and more Chinese companies are setting up or acquiring businesses overseas, as well as more and more international companies are setting up business in China. Consequently, China should continue to train up local CPA professionals with rich experience by setting up more exchange work programs with overseas international bodies. This will help provide the Chinese accounting professionals with overseas exposure and experience so that when these Chinese accounting professionals come back to work in China, they can have a broader view in order to better provide services to Chinese companies in attracting global capital into China and helping Chinese companies conduct outbound investments. On the other hand, this will also help promote Chinese CPAs with special China practice and knowledge to go out and bring China related knowledge and practice to the foreign countries so that other countries will have a better understanding about Chinese practice.

- Chinese regulators may consider separating the statutory audit report signing rights from CICPA membership, which means that CICPA members should meet additional qualification requirements to obtain signing rights for statutory audit reports. Thus the regulators can control and monitor CPAs with signing rights separately from other members and improve the effectiveness of regulatory control. This approach can help mitigate the weakness of the single regulatory policy over all CICPA members. Under this approach, more flexible arrangements can be applied to members who do not provide statutory audit services and thus more people will be attracted to become CICPA members. Separating the statutory audit report signing rights can also help make China more flexible in setting up MRAs with overseas accounting professional bodies.

- As an international financial center, Hong Kong is attracting many international talents. China can consider establishing a CPA training center in Hong Kong to foster international accounting and auditing professionals with China related knowledge and experiences, which can help further develop the CPA profession in China. China may also consider further improving the CICPA examination administration to attract more candidates from Hong Kong, Macao and Taiwan, as well as candidates from overseas countries to participate in the CICPA exam by providing flexible examination arrangements based on the needs from these types of candidates. For example, there are views that the computerized CICPA examination requirement make it difficult for the overseas candidates to pass the exams given they are not good at typing Chinese. To provide a hand written exam option to such candidates can significantly motivate them to participate in CICPA exams.



（B） Administrative rule and practices for allowing foreign CPA firms to conduct statutory audit services in a local market

This topic discusses whether a CPA firm can provide statutory audit services in a foreign market directly or through setting up a subsidiary or a branch in the foreign country. It also covers discussions about the cross-border transfer of audit working papers. Research has been performed related to the U. S. , U. K. , Australia, Singapore, Hong

Kong, Japan, Germany and France, as representative territories.

**Audit services performed locally by a foreign CPA firm** – Statutory audit is a sovereign right of a nation and is extensively regulated in all territories. Generally, there are legal requirements for the statutory audit services to be performed by locally registered / licensed CPA firms which are at least majorly owned by residents of the home country. As such, it is rare for the statutory audit service to be performed by an overseas CPA firm. For foreign companies listed in a local stock exchange, some exchanges permit overseas CPA firms, subject to meeting specified requirements and registering with the local regulator, to issue an audit report as part of the listing requirement under their local regulations. E. g. in U. S. the audit of a U. S. listed foreign issuer company can be performed by a CPA firm which is registered with the PCAOB and subject to its oversight and inspection requirements even though it is an overseas CPA firm. In practice, the audit service is normally performed by a CPA firm from the country where the major operations of the U. S. listed foreign issuer are located, given such CPA firm has local knowledge to perform the audit and can perform the audit more effectively. In Europe, under the ruling of EU, an overseas CPA firm is allowed to issue audit reports for a foreign company who is listed in a European stock exchange, subject to certain oversight requirements and provided the regulatory environment of the territory of the overseas firm is equivalent to that in the E. U ( "EU Equivalent"). In China, the statutory audit opinion must be signed by Chinese CPAs. Currently China does not allow foreign companies to be listed in the local stock exchange, and thus there is no relevant rule regarding whether an overseas CPA firm can provide audit service for a domestically listed foreign company.

**Establishment of a local branch or subsidiary by a foreign CPA firm** - Most of the CPA firms in the world are in the legal form of a partnership (either a limited liability partnership or a general partnership). Since partners are individuals, it is not possible for a CPA firm to have subsidiaries. In addition, due to the legal requirements for providing statutory audit as mentioned above, a branch of a foreign CPA firm will not meet such requirements and therefore would not be allowed to provide statutory audit service. Furthermore, legal liability considerations would deter any foreign CPA firm from opening a branch. As such, it is very difficult for a CPA firm to expand its business into a foreign market through setting up a foreign subsidiary or branch. Where the legal form of corporation is allowed for CPA firms, most countries request the shareholders of CPA corporations to be natural persons who are locally qualified CPA individuals; as such, it is difficult for a CPA corporation to provide audit service in a foreign market by setting up a foreign subsidiary or branch. It is also observed that the global practice for expanding a CPA firm's business in overseas markets is through networks of locally owned firms, which are separate legal entities with no ownership connection to each other. These network firms are connected through network standardized quality and branding. They share the same brand name and follow the same internal control policies. There are also internal quality review programs being implemented among the network firms to ensure uniform service quality among member firms and thus maintain the brand's reputation.



**Administration of audit working papers** - Audit working papers are the property of the CPA firm. As such, audit working papers are stored by the CPA firms in their home territory and not transferred across borders, although most of the territories researched do not have specific rules or requirements to preclude or limit such transfer. Usually, auditors include in their engagement letters a clause that confirms the audit working papers are the property of the auditor and no access/transfer is granted except as required by Law or auditing standards. Based on auditing standards, in a group audit arrangement where the overseas subsidiary is material to the group, the group auditor is required to obtain audit comfort over the subsidiary and thus they might need to review the subsidiary's auditor's audit working papers. In such situation, there's usually a channel available for the group auditor to review such audit working paper, and generally, there are no impediments to complying with these auditing standards.

**Recommendation:**

As statutory audit is a regulated service in all territories, it is extremely difficult for a Chinese CPA firm to expand its statutory audit practice to the overseas market either directly or through setting up subsidiaries or branches. As such, China CPA firms should follow the common practice in the world's CPA profession to create China branded network firms in overseas markets based on the overseas regulatory requirements in order to expand their business in overseas markets. How to establish and develop a global network with China brand and ensure the network firms' quality would be a key study point for Chinese CPA firms. Large global CPA firms such as Big-Four have extended their networks in China by establishing local CPA firms which are registered with local regulators according to local rules. However, these local firms share the same brand name, information system and internal control etc. to ensure globally consistent service quality.

(C) The "Negative List" approach for accounting services



Research has been performed to identify whether the "negative list" approach can be used to regulate the CPA profession for providing international services and common "negative list" clauses in cross-border service trade agreements. "Negative list" means a list of "disallowed" activities in the local market. Under such approach, a foreigner is allowed to perform all activities as a local citizen except for those specified on the "negative list". It was first used in the North American Free Trade negotiations, when North American countries including the U. S commit to free trade and removal of trade barriers unless specific exclusions are negotiated. With the negative list approach, opening and market access are the main objective of the negotiations. Nowadays, more and more countries start to use the negative list approach in cross-border Free Trade Agreements ("FTA") and in the control over foreign direct investments ("FDI"). In the service industry, including accounting professional services such as statutory audit, there are emerging trends to adopt the negative list approach in cross-border service trade agreements.

Based on the project team's research, the most representative negative list approach used in the cross-border accounting and auditing services is the FTA between Hong Kong and certain EU countries. The project team summarised the "List of Reservations" in accounting and auditing services between Hong Kong and Iceland, Switzerland as well as Norway. In the FTA between U. S. and Korea, both countries agree to establish a "Professional Services Working Group" which consists of representatives from each country to facilitate the cooperation in professional services, including auditing services. The commitments by various territories in the WTO trade in service agreements also provide information of certain reservation terms. Study over the "list of reservations" or "restrictions" will help identify the focus points of different territories during the negotiation for market opening so as to develop a high-quality "negative list".

The Chinese government started to use the negative list approach in managing cross-border service trade agreements in recent years in selective areas/zones. Specifically the approach is being used both within borders for the policies and regulations in the pilot free trade zones in mainland China and across borders for the free service trade agreements with Hong Kong and Macao. Furthermore, the Chinese regulators are also considering increased utilization of the negative list approach in other cross-border investment agreements, such as the one between China and U. S..



**Recommendations:**

- The negative list approach can facilitate cross-border trade negotiations through encouraging free trade and national treatment to foreign suppliers. This is important for accounting and auditing sector as the demand for global co-ordination of accounting and auditing services is increased given more and more companies expand their operations worldwide. The Chinese government should promote the negative list approach in the cross-border service trade agreement negotiations with other territories to achieve more effective opening of the market, and thus to promote the global co-ordination in the CPA profession.

- Accounting/auditing professional service is an emerging sector in China. Such service, especially the statutory audit service, should be highly regulated. If regulators fail to promptly discover the newly emerging business activities which need to be "restricted" and update the negative list in time, it may lead to "market abuse" of the negative list. Chinese regulators are suggested to pay close attention to the emerging business activities of the accounting/auditing professional services and the regulatory measures of other territories, so that they could set supervision policies in a timely manner to regulate the emerging business activities and update the "negative list" when necessary. This would help Chinese regulators to effectively govern the accounting/auditing professional service sector.

- The controls over foreigners and foreign CPA firms to practice in local market should be properly reflected in the negative list in the respective cross-border agreements. As statutory audit is a sovereign right of a nation, it is extensively regulated in all countries given the importance of such services to a nation's overall economy. The negative list used in the accounting/auditing professional service sector should reflect the necessary restrictions, especially on the statutory audit, in a clear manner to ensure consistency with other relevant regulatory rules.

- Comparative study shows that the "restrictions" specified in the negative list of the accounting/auditing professional service sector by the Chinese regulators are few, which means that the Chinese market is open to an exceptionally great extent in the world. This reflects the commitments made by China when joining the WTO. It is necessary to perform detailed analyses of the pros and cons from the practices so as to identify a balance between extending the market-opening and protecting sovereign rights.



## B. Competitiveness of accounting services in China

Based on a review and analysis of the rules and practices regarding opening-up of accounting services, it is noted that in the territories reviewed, various requirements are in place to mitigate the risks and challenges for opening up the local accounting services market. As such, continuous improvement of the local CPA profession is required to build a concrete foundation for further expansion of the profession across borders. In this regard, six topics have been identified to cover most of the current concerns of China and policy debates relating to improving the local CPA profession.

The project team performed detailed study and analysis on the six topics respectively to identify the key existing issues and make relevant recommendations. Specifically the six topics are:

- Practicing rules and regulations for CPA profession
- Mandatory rotation of CPA firms for performing statutory audit services
- Government purchase of professional services from CPA firms
- Audit of financial institutions
- Professional indemnity insurance for CPA profession
- Joint audit

(A) Practicing rules and regulations for CPA profession[①]

This topic talks about the practicing rules that regulate the audit services of the CPA profession to ensure an effective oversight. Research has been performed over U. S. (four representative states – New York, Illinois, California and Texas), U. K., Australia, Canada, Singapore and Hong Kong as representative territories for global practices. Given the importance of the audit part of the CPA profession to a country's capital market and overall economy, it is an extensively regulated profession in all the countries researched. The study focused on the four key regulatory elements, which are licensing/registration requirements for CPAs and CPA firms, allowed legal forms of CPA firms, quality control and inspection on CPA practices, and disciplinary actions on CPAs and CPA firms.

**Licensing/registration requirements** - All territories have implemented licensing/registration requirements for CPA individuals and/or CPA firms for performing audit services to ensure that only suitably qualified professional individuals and firms engage in audit services. Requirements for CPA firms are carried out in different ways across countries. Specifically, in U. S., U. K., New Zealand and Singapore, CPA firms need to register with recognized authorities to be appointed as the statutory auditor. Similarly in China and Hong Kong, an auditing license is required for firms engaging in statutory audit services. The authorities that regulate the registration or licensing will

① i. e. those that wish to perform audit services

第一部分

evaluate the CPA firms' fitness and properness, including expertise, skills, and other related aspects required for performing statutory audit services. Detailed requirements may vary between authorities, but there is normally a requirement on the qualification of the majority of the firms' principals (typically the partners and directors). The registered/licensed firms are then subject to on-going oversight by the respective authorities.

Requirements for CPA individuals engaging in statutory audit services are always in the form of issuance of practicing certificates (e. g. in U. K. and Hong Kong) or registration with recognized authorities (e. g. in Australia and New Zealand). Such requirements are only for individuals who are responsible for an audit and sign the audit opinion usually in the CPA firm's name. CPA individuals holding practicing certificates or registered as statutory auditors are subject to the respective authorities' oversight. Additionally, all CPAs need to obtain sufficient Continuous Professional Education (CPE) to maintain their recency and qualification.



**Legal form** - Most of the territories allow for different types of legal form of a CPA firm. It can be set up as a partnership, sole proprietorship or corporation. In U. S. , U. K. , Germany and Singapore, partnership is permitted in the form of a limited liability partnership. In China, under MOF regulation, CPA firms are required or strongly encouraged to change legal form from limited liability to a special general partnership. All the CPA firms with securities business permit have completed such legal form transition.

**Quality control/inspection** - In each territory, independent auditor oversight bodies are established to perform various on-going quality control activities and inspections over the audit practices mostly following the 11 core principles for independent audit regulators developed by the International Forum of Independent Audit Regulators (IFIAR). This globally recognized set of principles covers the regulator's structure, operation and inspections and addresses the common concerns regarding the CPA profession's audit quality control such as independence and competence. As suggested by the IFIAR principles, a "risk-based" approach is always adopted by each country's audit regulator. CPA firms that conduct audits for "public interest entities" and have a large volume of audits are normally inspected more frequently. It is also noted that there are efforts made by the government to ensure different regulatory bodies are coordinating and communicating with each other to exchange information, better allocate resources and avoid duplication of inspection efforts. By contrast, in China, MOF, together with the provincial Finance Bureaus and CICPA carry out systematic inspections of the CPA firms on a regular basis to review the quality of the firm's practice. However, in addition to the CICPA and MOF inspections, some other regulatory bodies carry out extended inspections on CPA firms. Specifically, CSRC carries out inspections of CPA firms who provide audit service to listed companies in China; CBRC carries out inspections of CPA firms who provide audit service to banks in China; and CIRC carries out inspections of CPA firms who provide audit service to insurance companies in China. This approach may create possibilities of duplicated inspections.



**Disciplinary actions** – There are a range of penalties and sanctions for violations noted during inspections for both CPA individuals and CPA firms. These normally include fines, censure, suspension/restriction of services for a recommended period of time, and practicing certificate or registration or license being withdrawn (or not reinstated) for a certain period of time. Some regulators may also require a CPA firm to obtain an independent review and report on one or more engagements, and / or engage someone to design policies to effect compliance.

**Recommendations:**

- China should consider having regulators from different sectors and at different levels integrate their individual inspection programme into one systematic inspection programme for oversight over the auditors to efficiently utilize the government resources and avoid duplicate inspections. An analysis on the attributes of each representative country's respective key regulations against the IFIAR's core principles was made to help us see a spectrum of possible regulatory approaches. The integrated inspection programme should be in compliance with the IFIAR principles.

- China could consider varying inspection approaches between CPA firms based on the firms' risk profile such as size, revenue, previous inspection results, number of public interest entity and other regulated clients. If a firm is deemed as having higher quality, the firm can be inspected less frequently or less intrusively. By contrast, if a firm is providing lower quality services, the firm should be subject to more regular and more in-depth regulation.

- Disciplinary actions need to be concentrated on the CPA individuals instead of the CPA firms, which is due to three main considerations: i) for small CPA firms, if the disciplinary actions are against the CPA firm, the audit partner can terminate the CPA firm and set up another firm to continue the practice (This can be mitigated by having a licensing system that precludes the setting up of a new firm by an individual who is not "fit and proper"); ii) for large CPA firms, given reputation is very important for the firm, if the disciplinary actions are against the CPA firm but not the individual, there will be a long and costly dispute process as the CPA firm will do its best to defend itself; iii) it's much more difficult and time consuming to prove a systemic defect in a big firm's control system than a defect in a single audit engagement. As such, it would be more effective and efficient to discipline CPA individuals on individual audit engagements. To concentrate such regulation and disciplinary actions for CPA individuals are considered a good practice and it has been introduced in some countries with good results, such as Australia and New Zealand.

- Based on a review of the staffing of foreign regulators, including the staff's capabilities and experience, we realized that sufficient and competent staffing ensures the effectiveness of the regulatory activities. Due to certain constraints such as historical reasons, currently some of the Chinese audit regulators are not as well equipped as CPA firms in terms of staff's competence. Consequently, the regulatory activities are sometimes focused on less important areas, but not on the audit quality. Additionally, the roles and responsibilities for different departments within the regulatory bodies are currently not appropriately established and need to be amended to match the functions and competence of each department.

(B) Mandatory rotation of CPAfirms for performing statutory audit services

Global practice has been analysed for mandatory rotation requirements for CPA firms regarding statutory audit services and the consequences of such requirement. Study has been carried out over the following territories: U. S. , U. K. , EU, Singapore, Japan, Hong Kong China, Australia, Brazil, India, Netherlands and Turkey. These are considered good representatives of the global practices. It is noted that U. S. regulators held lengthy debates over the mandatory rotation requirement for audit firms and Congress voted to prevent the PCAOB from imposing mandatory rotation in July 2013 due to the obvious disadvantages arising from the mandatory rotation of firms. In U. K. , after a long debating process, the Competition Commission, not a regulator of the profession, persuaded law makers not to introduce mandatory rotation. In order to enhance competition (not audit quality), mandatory tendering should be introduced where a CPA firm has completed 10 years of service. The incumbent is permitted to re-tender. In Singapore the Monetary Authority of Singapore cancelled mandatory rotation for domestic banks in 2008 due to the negative effects identified to both the banks and the auditors from the mandatory rotation requirement.



While debate over mandatory rotation of CPA firms does continue, in the major financial centers, the debate has finalised. Supporters hope that mandatory rotation can avoid the threat of intimidation between auditors and clients which can impair independence of the auditor due to long-term familiarity. Some people also believe that mandatory rotation can improve market competition and thus can reduce the market concentration. By contrast, opponents believe that mandatory rotation of CPA firms will damage audit quality and corporate governance, especially when the rotation tenure is over a short period, The key disadvantages of mandatory rotation are as follows:

- Costs, timing and burden on management
- Undermining existing corporate governance arrangements
- Reduced choice
- Reduced quality
- Limited industry specialization

- Global environment
- Effects on the audit profession
- Market interference

**Recommendations:**

- Due to the disadvantages associatedwith the mandatory rotation of CPA firms, China regulators should continue with and re-inforce mandatory rotation of CPA individuals instead of mandatory rotation of CPA firms. This can avoid the independence issue between auditor and his/her client due to long term familiarity and avoid the disadvantages brought by mandatory rotation of CPA firms at the same time. Currently, China has implemented mandatory rotation of the signing CPA for listed companies. The regulators can consider further refining the mandatory rotation policy and improving the regulatory control over signing CPA rotation.
- For special industries (e. g. state-owned enterprises and financial institutions) where mandatory rotation of CPA firms is currently adopted, the regulators can consider extending the rotation tenure in the short run (e. g. extending the mandatory rotation tenure to 10 years), thus to avoid the various disadvantages from compulsory rotation by short tenure. In the long run, along with China's overall economic reform, the Chinese regulators can consider improving the decisive function of market in the allocation of economic resources by promoting a strong corporate governance environment, in which the independent non-executive directors should function effectively. Supervision mechanism should also be strictly set up to ensure CPA firms implement robust independence controls to maintain their independence. With such control environment and procedures in place, China can consider lifting the mandatory rotation requirements for CPA firms and focusing on mandatory rotation of CPA individuals and other governance requirements over independence.



(C) Government purchase ofprofessional services from CPA firms

Thistopic reviews the practices of governments purchasing professional services from CPA firms and analyzes the benefits and challenges of such practices to find possible approaches China can consider adopting for opening up the public sector professional services to CPA firms. Study has been performed on U. S. , U. K. , Australia, Singapore, New Zealand and Hong Kong as these are the major developed economies in the world and China can learn from these mature practices. Research results show that all these territories' governments purchase professional services from CPA firms and there is a set of public sector auditing standards in place, for government bodies, government agents and not-for-profit organizations.

Benefits for government purchasing professional services from CPA firms are as follows:

- It can help increase transparency and enable local scrutiny of the public bodies.
- It will reduce the auditing authorities' burden for conducting all the government audits.
- The CPA firms may also bring in good practices from the business sector, especially for the non-audit services such as management consultancy services. This practice may further improve the management skills and transparency of government entities.

Challenges for government purchasing professional services from CPA firms are as follows:

- It may raise questions and increase the difficulty for the government's budget control due to the possibility that one service will cost much more than a similar one as a result of the market competition. However, the Department for Communities and Local Government (DCLG) in U. K. argued that the outsourcing of the Audit Commission's in-house practice, in the long term will represent a considerable saving to the taxpayer because the centralized arrangements of local governments' audit are inefficient and can't benefit from a market competition mechanism.

- Government's practices are always associated with sensitive information. Purchase of professional services from CPA firms will grant them access to such information and thus there may be a need for additional protection of such information.

- Given the objectives of audits on the public sector and the private sector are very different from each other, CPA firms may lack enough understanding and expertise in dealing with government activities. As such, it requires a high level of monitoring and oversight on the relevance and related quality of audits performed by CPA firms in relation to government entities.

Additional challengesin China:

- Currently in China, CPAfirms have quite limited involvement in the public sector practices which are mostly conducted by the National Audit Office. Comparing the audits performed by CPA firms and by the National Audit Office, similarities have been noted in terms of independence and professional ethics requirements, etc. However, given the audits performed by CPA firms and by the National Audit Office focus on different areas (e. g. audits performed by CPA firms focus on the true and fair presentation of financial statements while audits performed by the National Audit Office additionally focus on the compliance of the public sector entities), CPA firms mainly opine on financial information while the National Audit Office mainly opines on the compliance of the public sector entities (e. g. compliance on usage of government grants). As such, differences exist between the audits performed by CPA firms and by the National Audit Office in audit purpose, audit strategy, applicable audit standards, monitoring and oversight, etc. Additionally, the National Audit Office also performs certain special audits on the public sector entities such as audits on accountability of the entity's top management, audits on the budget execution, and audits on cash flow of specific projects, etc. Such differences require the development of a set of public sector audit standards applicable to CPA firms in order to regulate CPA firms' participation in public sector audits in terms of scope, approach, and code of practices, etc.

- The existing public sector auditing standards need to be further developed and specified. Currently in China, the regulations and standards for government audits are more like general principles rather than detailed practicing standards for auditors to comply with when performing specific audit procedures. As such, if it is planned to have CPA firms largely engage in the public sector audits, a detailed set of uniform auditing standards for CPA firms is required, and CICPA has already started working on these standards.

- Currently in China, a series of reform and development of the government accounting standards is being promoted. The third plenary session of the 18th CPC[①]Central Committee set out the requirement for developing and implementing an accrual-basis comprehensive government accounting and financial reporting system. However, according to the current "Accounting Standards for Government Entities", most government entities are using cash-basis accounting with some exceptions where accrual basis accounting is adopted for some special businesses and events. As such, the existing government accounting standards and financial reporting framework need to be reformed and MOF is actively promoting the reform.



- There is a need to develop the talent pool for government accounting and auditing practice, and to improve the expertise in government accounting and auditing standards. On one hand, the government financial statements' preparers need to keep themselves updated and familiar with the evolving government accounting standards and financial reporting framework, and the managing personnel need to also have adequate knowledge of government auditing standards. On the other hand, there must be sufficient training provided to the CPA firms and the CPA individuals for government accounting and auditing standards if CPA firms are going to be largely involved in the government audit.

- Auditors from CPA firms may encounter difficulties in performing certain audit procedures in relation to government entities due to lack of authority.

- Although in short term. CPA firms, on average, probably have a bit higher cost base than the National Audit Office's in-house auditors in China, in the long run, government purchase of services would help save the overall public sector audit cost by a considera-

① Communist Party of China

ble amount. Reform may therefore be required in the current government budget management to assume the financial burden of such services.

- Since it's a new approach for government to purchase services from CPA firms in China, a transparent and fair bidding mechanism is yet to be established. In addition, what kind of CPA firms are qualified to perform audit to government bodies would be an important consideration in such mechanism.

Recommendations:

- It would be a good idea for CPA firms to become engaged in the public sector so as to increase the transparency of government's financials, improve the government accountability, ensure public scrutiny of government entities and promote a clean and transparent government. We can anticipate that in the near future, there will be significant demand from the government for professional services from CPA firms, such as the audit services of government entities' financial statements to be prepared on accrual basis and under the new government accounting system which China is now actively developing. As such, China should support and encourage government purchase of professional services from CPA firms with sufficient supervision in place.

- The government needs to develop a standard procurement system for government purchase of professional services. Such a system may include which department is responsible for the procurement, procurement approach (e. g. public tendering or direct appointment), publication of tendering documents, items to be included in the tendering documents, required information of CPA firms, assessment criteria for CPA firms, on-going monitoring of appointed CPA firm's performance, etc. Other countries' practices relating to these aspects can be utilized as references.

- If government plans to outsource some work to professional service firms, it needs to recognise the cost structure of the professional service firms. Such costs need to be appropriately incorporated into the government budgeting system, while the government can decide whether the cost should be centrally managed or allocated to the entities receiving the services.

- China should promptly develop and implement the accrual-basis comprehensive government accounting and financial reporting system in accordance with the requirements set by the third plenary session of the 18th CPC Central Committee. At the same time, standardization and specification of auditing standards and guidance in relation to the public sector is critical to making the auditors accountable and is a precondition for successful government purchase of professional services from CPA firms. As part of China's audit standards system, such standards and guidance need to be presented in a detailed way to eliminate confusion and can make reference to the generally accepted standards in the private sector to the largest extent, with additional specifications for the special areas in public sector audits, such as compliance. This provides a framework under which all parties can operate knowledgably.



- China needs to promote the development of the talent pool for government accounting and auditing practices. First, the government should enhance the training to its key accounting personnel to equip them with adequate knowledge of government accounting standards, competence in preparation of accrual-basis financial statements, and to some extent understanding of government auditing standards and practices. Additionally, the CPA firms and CPA individuals who provide professional services to government entities should be familiar with the accounting and auditing standards and practices for public sectors and have relevant qualifications and practical experiences, especially when providing services to some special industries (e. g. social security funds). The regulators can also consider adding requirements for public sector accounting and auditing knowledge and skills in the CICPA exam and continuing education for CICPA members. At the same time, the CPA firms should enhance relevant internal training for government services.

- Aswith other audits, a high level of monitoring and oversight needs to be provided by the recognized regulatory authority, MOF. Other relevant bodies, such as the National Audit Office, can also exercise oversight on the audits it governs. Additionally, MOF and the National Audit Office should further enhance communication and coordination with regard to the development of public sector auditing standards for CPA firms so as to have CPA firms effectively supplement the government auditors in the audit practices for government entities.

(D) Audit of financial institutions

Research has been performed by the project team to discuss the role of the statutory auditor in the regulatory system of financial institutions and ways to improve the quality of the statutory audits for financial institutions. The research focused on the following countries: U. S., U. K., Singapore and Australia, as these countries are the major financial centers in the world. The research result shows that most financial institutions are public interest entities and financial institutions in most countries operate in a heavily regulated environment. Regulation structures differ in each territory, but typically involve prudential regulation, consumer protection and market stability. The purpose is to promote a stable and dynamic financial market and prevent financial crises. Along with the internationalization of Reminbi and marketization of interest rates in China, more and more challenges are emerging in audits of financial institutions in China.

**Statutory auditors play an important role in financial market regulation** - Governments have attempted to eliminate or mitigate financial crises by regulating the financial sector directly. One major goal of regulation is transparency: making a company's financial situations publicly known by requiring regular reporting under standardized accounting procedures. Another goal of regulation is to make sure institutions have sufficient assets to meet their contractual obligations, through reserve requirements, capital requirements, and other limits on leverage. Auditors play an important role in the government regulation as follows:

- Transparency - throughperforming high quality statutory audit over financial statements for financial institutions, auditors can help enhance transparency of the related financial information;

- Asset sufficiency -through performing compliance audit over the reserves, capital and other leverage ratios[①] to ensure the asset sufficiency of the financial institutions.

**Lessons learned fromthe recent financial crisis** - The recent financial crisis tell us that specialisation should be enhanced for the statutory auditors of financial institutions on the following areas to address the higher risk areas in the audit:
- Utilization of IT technology in audits of financial institutions
- Credit analysis and impairment review over financial assets
- Fair valuation and use of valuation experts
- Consolidation and the treatment of special purpose vehicles
- Internal control and fraud risk
- Disclosure



To fulfil the special requirements in auditing financial institutions, the CPA firm must have sufficient audit experience, professional audit teams and industry specialists and experts, such as computer system experts, actuarial experts, valuation experts etc. Furthermore, as big financial institutions have very large numbers of transactions and complex operations, the audit team must have sufficient size and sufficient staff members. As a result of these special requirements, most financial institutions in the world tend to select big CPA firms to provide professional services for them.

**Recommendations:**
- **Sufficient education** - There should be sufficient education for both the management of the financial institutions and the auditors in relation to the abovementioned higher risk areas to ensure the financial institution's financial reporting is "transparent and adequate". Education should also be conducted to potential investors in the market to ensure they can read and understand the financial statements properly and thus make informed investment decisions

---

① This compliance audit is not required to be performed by the financial institution's statutory auditor and financial institutions are permitted to engage another qualified CPA firm to perform the audit. However, in practice, as the statutory auditor can normally perform the compliance audit more efficiently than other CPA firms, these audits are normally performed by the statutory auditor.

based on the audited financial information and other information.

- **Talent pool** – China CPA firms should develop the talent pool for providing audit services for financial institutions and increase the size of the professional teams in order to meet the requirements for audit of big financial institutions. China MOF always promotes fostering of accounting and auditing talents in China and has introduced various training plans for accounting elites in China. China CPA firms can take advantage of such training programmes to plan their own talent pool programme so as to further improve their capability in auditing financial institutions.

- **Regulatory inspection** - Regulatory inspection can help ascertain the quality of the statutory audit work performed. Given the importance of financial institutions to the nation's economy, regulators can consider further improving the regulatory inspection of the statutory auditor of the financial institutions in terms of frequency and coverage to ensure a stable and robust financial control system is in place. Regulators can make the inspection programme transparent to the public by providing information on the selection method used, the coverage of the inspection etc. This can help further improve the public confidence and build up market trust. The government inspection should concentrate on the auditor's experience, their ability and the quality of the audit work performed. In additional, under certain circumstances, especially when the financial institutions under audit are not willing to comply with respective regulations, for the benefit of public interest, there should be a channel for the auditors to communicate such violations with the regulators directly.

- **Disciplinary actions** - A proper control environment cannot exist without proper disciplinary actions which could be in the form of public notice, fine or restriction of the service scope for the CPA firm. E. g. banning the affected CPA firm and the partners from providing auditing service to new financial institution clients for a period of time. Furthermore, the issues noted in the audit of the financial institutions may reflect that there are non-compliance issues within the underlying financial institutions. There should be a communication channel available for the issues to be communicated to the relevant regulators of the financial institutions so that appropriate actions can be taken to ensure market stability. In fact, the above regulatory control is applicable to all regulated industries, such as the nuclear industry. In some territories, a tripartite meeting arrangement exists whereby the regulator can call meetings with the financial institution and its auditors together to discuss accounting and control issues.

(E) Professional indemnity insurance for CPA profession

The project team has reviewed global practices regarding compulsory professional indemnity insurance requirements for CPA firms providing statutory audit service in the local market, the obstacles for CPA firms to purchase appropriate indemnity insurance from the market, as well as how to overcome such obstacles. Research has been carried out for the following territories: U. K., Germany, France, Australia, Singapore, U. S. and Hong Kong. These are major representative economies in the world. Research results show that most territories have a compulsory minimum level of insurance coverage for CPA firms / CPA individuals required either by law or by accounting professional bodies. In most of the territories, such as Singapore and Hong Kong, the compulsory indemnity insurance only applies to the CPA firms with limited liability legal form, i. e. Limited Liability Partnership or Limited Liability Company where applicable. Such requirement does not extend to the general partnership CPA firms where the liability is unlimited and is joint and several. It is also noted that there is no adequate available insurance for Big-Four CPA firms in the commercial insurance market to cover all the needs. As such, Big-Four CPA firms have set up their own captives globally (a self-insurance mechanism among their network member firms).

**Measures taken to support the professional indemnity insurance to CPA firms in various territories** - To ensure that there are insurance policies available to the practicing members at reasonable cost, efforts have been put in by either the government or the accounting professional bodies in each country. In U. S. and U. K., the accounting professional bodies negotiated with the insurance companies to agree on a standard insurance policy, which is available to all members of the accounting professional body; in Australia, the law has set up a maximum liability cap for the audit profession so that the insurance company can measure the risk exposure and thus provide a better insurance coverage to the public accountants. Lloyd's, the world's specialist insurance market where different insurance providers come together to share the risk from providing certain type of insurance for particular coverage also provides a good example on how to diversify the professional indemnity insurance risk for the CPA profession.

**China's achievement in this area** - In China, the professional liability insurance for CPA firms is relatively new. In late 2011, CICPA Shanghai initiated a group tendering process for the Shanghai CPA firms to purchase professional indemnity insurance from the insurance providers. The result of the tendering negotiation is a win-win situation for both the CPA firms and the insurance companies. The CPA firms have a better coverage at lower cost, which can provide a reasonable level of protection for the CPA firms; on the other hand, the insurance companies who win the bid can have their business increased significantly as more CPA firms are willing to buy the insurance policy from the winning insurance company as a result of the tendering. In addition, both parties benefit from the spreading of risk. In late 2014, MOF also issued an exposure draft that sets up requirements for CPA firms in purchasing professional indemnity insurance and invites for public feedback. It is expected to be officially announced in 2015.



**Recommendations:**

- The Chinese regulators should encourage all CPA firms in China to take proper risk management measures and set up robust risk control system. Along with the transformation to special general partnership for CPA firms in China, compulsory professional indemnity insurance requirement should be introducedto CPA firms which don't have sufficient indemnity risk reserve in order to better protect the investors' interests.

- CICPA Shanghai's practice for group negotiation of the insurance policies with insurance companies is a good practical example for

CPA firms to obtain insurance at reasonable cost. Such a pooling arrangement spreads risk and contains premium cost to acceptable levels. This could be copied to other areas in China and thus extend the insurance coverage for CPA firms. In addition, some global insurance members join together as syndicates to insure risks at global insurance markets, such as Lloyd's. China's regulator may consider obtaining information from such global insurance markets about global insurance practice and underwriter practices which could be useful for arranging global insurance protection for CPA firms in China.

(F) Joint audit

This topic mainly reviews the joint audit practices in the European market and analyses the impact of a mandatory joint audit system. Study has been performed mainly for France as it is the major economy in the world which has compulsory joint audit requirement. Although a group audit arrangement can involve more than one audit firm, there are significant differences between the two types of audit arrangements in the way the work is carried out and how the audit report is issued. In the case of joint audit, all the participating CPA firms must agree the split of work between themselves and jointly sign the audit report while under the group audit arrangement, the group audit report is signed by the group holding company auditor alone. Our study shows that the perceived advantages from joint audits (reduced market concentration; improve audit quality) are not achieved in practice and furthermore, the following **disadvantages** have been observed in practice:

- results in higher audit cost
- doesnot improve audit quality and may even result in poorer audit quality, such as an imbalanced allocation of the work or important areas falling between the joint firms
- possibly results in more concentration and less choice
- restricts the audit committee's decision with regards to the best approach for auditing the accounts of the company

**Recommendations:**

- Based on the current situation of China's audit market, introduction of joint audit does not appearto be an economical approach since it

第一部分

is very likely to create additional financial burden for the capital market and the unclear benefits which may be outweighed by the financial burden for a long period of time.

- Joint audit is not a practical approach for China given the existing significant gaps and divergences between the accounting firms in terms of size, resources, expertise and audit methodology, and the joint audit's inherent limitation on the clarity about the respective responsibility of audit firms.
- The potential benefits a joint audit is thought to bring with regard to independence and audit quality may be achieved by alternatives such as reinforcement of independence compliance, and / or strengthened supervision.
- Although joint audit may not be suitable for Chinaat the current stage, it could be possible to have experienced CPA firms participate in the audit of financial institutions as component auditors. CPA firms other than the "big-4" in China can accumulate experience from auditing of small to medium sized financial institutions and gradually participate in audits of big financial institutions as component auditors. Over a period of time, they will be able to play a more important role in such audits.

## C. Cross-border accounting regulation and cooperation

The studies and analysis performed on the previous sections and topics indicate the existence of differences in many respects relating to the rules and practices of the accounting profession between China and other countries, which may lead to accounting regulatory conflicts for cross-border transactions such as monitoring activities of companies listed in overseas capital markets. However, the globalization of business and accounting services calls for effective cross-border regulatory cooperation to resolve the existing regulatory conflicts and protect the investors' interests in the global markets. As such, the project team has done research on the existing international cooperation approaches and the key challenges China encounters in the international cooperation activities to find a possible solution to the cross-border regulatory conflicts.

In Chapter 10 -Cross-border accounting regulation and cooperation, research has been performed for the following countries: EU, U. S. Australia and New Zealand as these are major economies in the world and Australia and New Zealand have implemented cross-border cooperation for their territories. Research results show that there are two typical international cooperation approaches in terms of cross-border inspection, namely the EU approach and the US approach.

Under the EU approach, the European Commission (EC) adopted the "Equivalence Decision" recognising the equivalence of the audit oversight systems in ten third countries. EU member states and the recognised third countries can rely on each other's inspection of audit firms under such approach and as a result, no onsite inspection by the regulators from EU member states is necessary.



Under the US approach, the PCAOB performs onsite inspection of overseas CPA firms who must be registered with them if they issue audit opinions on U. S. issuers. This can be done either by PCAOB alone or by PCAOB together with local regulators, such as ASIC in Australia. This approach relies on extra-territorial legislation being effective and the ability to carry out inspections overseas from U. S.. This model is almost unique to U. S. and has several disadvantages.

Recommendations:

- In resolving cross-border regulatory conflicts and achieving effective cooperation, it is fundamental that the approach adopted can protect local investors' interests, while each country's sovereignty and concern over the security of economic information are also respected. Mutual understanding and assistance need to be enhanced to establish a systematic international cooperation mechanism. All competing influences that impact such mechanism need to be considered and balanced to achieve the overall equilibrium. Specifically, we need to focus on the cross-border coordination but recognition must also be given to the various differences between territories. Additionally, we need to attach equal importance to both standards set-up and implementation enforcement.

- China should consider seeking more communication and cooperation with EU to promote the mutual reliance and assistance concept to resolve the existing international regulatory conflicts. Under this concept, when a foreign regulator notes any potential defects from an audit of a Chinese company listed overseas conducted by a Chinese CPA firm, the foreign regulator can communicate its findings with the independent regulator in China and request it to conduct further inspections and/or investigations. The results of the inspection / investigation as well as the disciplinary actions against the auditor should be thoroughly communicated to the foreign regulator where the company is listed. Under certain circumstances, joint inspection can be arranged to achieve the regulatory purpose.

- The China-US cooperation conflicts originate from the inherent conflict between the US inspection approach and the territorial legislation authority, and China is aware of the disadvantages of the US approach. However, if such conflicts are not properly resolved soon, US-listed Chinese companies' image would beunnecessarily impaired and the opening-up of China's accounting services would also be impacted. As such, China may consider taking the initiative to obtain mutual understanding of the existing conflicts and difficulties by holding round table discussions and/or dialogues and call for collective efforts to resolve the conflicts. China also needs to reinforce the supervision and oversight over the Chinese companies on overseas capital markets by means of indirect listing. By doing such, China will demonstrate to the world its confidence and determination to resolve the existing cross-border regulatory conflicts. This will also provide the basis for the next step multi-level cross-border regulatory cooperation. In May 2015, MOF issued "Provisional Regulations on Cross-Border Auditing Business of Accounting Firms" which represents a significant move China has undertaken towards the objective of resolving the conflicts.

- China needs to take a more active role in the international activities of cross-border regulatory cooperation. As one of the strongest economies in the world, China's participation in world-wide activities is necessary. China should consider participating or actively holding periodic round-table discussions with other countries to discuss cross-border regulatory cooperation issues / conflicts and finding out possible solutions with collective efforts of other countries. China can also consider taking initiatives to negotiate and sign memoranda of understanding or bilateral agreements with other countries for cross-border regulatory cooperation activities. Additionally, China can better utilize platforms of the large international organizations such as International Organization of Securities Commissions (IOSCO) and International Forum of Independent Audit Regulators (IFIAR). Through those platforms, China can learn from best practices of audit regulatory activities in other countries and obtain global recognition of China's audit oversight system. Also participation in such international discussions and experience sharing activities can increase China's influence in the establishment of global regulatory standards.

- China may consider doingfurther research and analysis of global regulations and practices, and advising on amendments of China's regulations in response to global trends. China should also learn the best global practices and take a lead to fix the issues identified by other countries and global organisations, and remove misunderstandings that the international organisation has against China, so as to improve China's image and increase the investors' confidence in the globe.

# 第二部分

# THE SECOND PART

# 第一章　境外人士成为执业注册会计师



执业注册会计师是指在一个国家取得了注册会计师资格，能够在该国/地区开展法定审计服务并签署法定审计报告的专业人士。执业注册会计师能够提供的服务种类很多，比如代理记账服务、纳税申报服务、审计服务、非审计鉴证服务、咨询服务等等。其中，最为常见也是受到最多监管的便是法定审计服务。在这里，有必要对法定审计服务与其他服务加以区分：法定审计是一个国家主权管理的体现，其服务在各国均受到严格监管，而其他类型的服务一般受到的监管有限。因此专业人士要想提供法定审计所需要取得的资格与提供其他服务需要取得的资格有很大不同。

法定审计是指根据国家法律规定，必须执行的带有强制性的审计。例如，中国外商投资企业法、公司法等均规定外商投资企业或上市公司每年必须接受中国注册会计师的审计。法定审计最主要的作用是利用独立的第三方对公司财务报表进行审计，增强财务信息的可信度，为监管者、税务机关、银行、股东、债权人、债务人、管理层、员工、市场上潜在的投资人以及其他利益相关者提供决策所需要的可靠财务信息，从而维护资本市场秩序乃至整个国民经济的稳定。如果一个国家的法定审计失控，审计质量无法保证，导致财务信息不真实，这样各利益相关者就无法利用经审计财务信息作出正确的决策。由此可见对法定审计进行监管，确保法定审计服务市场的秩序是非常必要的。因此各国政府也对法定审计实行高度监管，对于境外人士在本国提供法定审计服务存在多项管理措施。本章重点讨论境外人士在各国/地区法律法规约束下，能否取得当地执业注册会计师资格并在当地提供法定审计服务。

## 一、国际经验

项目组调查研究了美国（主要选取纽约、伊利诺伊、德克萨斯及加利福尼亚四州作为代表）、英国、澳大利亚、新加坡、德国以及中国香港的相关法规与实践。在被调查的国家/地区中，美国的规定与其他国家/地区略有不同，以下进行详细介绍。

图 1 是在美国和其他国家成为一个执业注册会计师的路径简要图解。本书将各国/地区执业注册会计师的“职业道路”分为五步，以下也将按照这“五步”对成为执业注册会计师进行详细介绍。

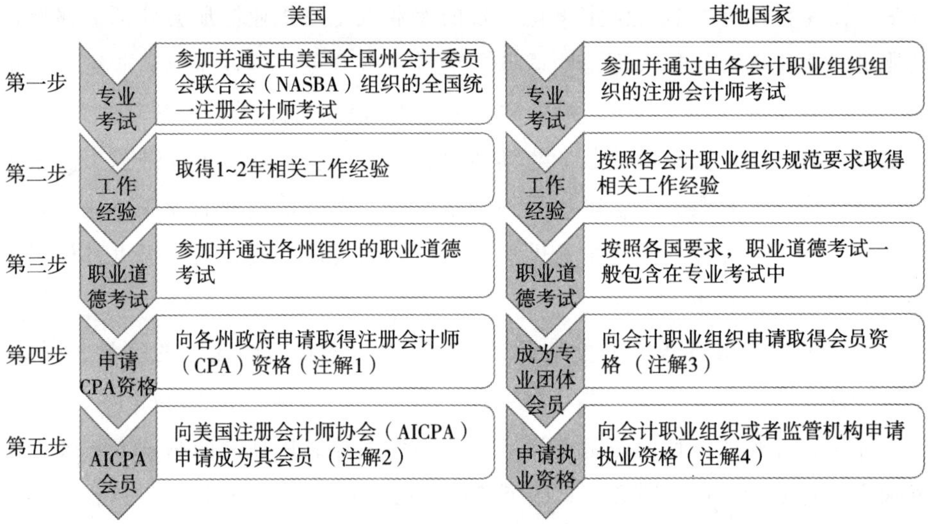


**图 1　执业注册会计师的“职业道路”**

注解 1：美国执业注册会计师资格由各州政府负责登记注册。符合资格的申请人向各州政府提出申请注册后成为美国注册会计师，即可在美国签署法定审计报告。

注解 2：在美国各州取得 CPA 资格的注册会计师即可签署法定审计报告，无需成为 AICPA 会员。但取得 CPA 资格的注册会计师可以向 AICPA 申请成为 AICPA 会员。因此在美国 CPA 不一定是 AICPA 会员，但是 AICPA 会员一定是 CPA。

注解 3：取得会计职业组织会员资格的会计师可以提供代理记账、纳税申报、公司财务等非法定审计服务，但是不能提供法定审计服务。

注解 4：想要提供法定审计服务的会员需要额外申请并取得“执业执照（practicing license）”。在英国及香港，执业执照是由会计职业组织根据法律授权颁发的；在澳大利亚、德国及新加坡，执业执照是由政府相关部门颁发的。

以下详细分析在美国及其他国家如何成为当地注册会计师并提供法定审计服务，对境外人士有哪些额外限制或者境外人士成为当地注册会计师可能面临的困难等。各个国家有共性的方面也有存在差异的方面。

## （一）通过专业考试

首先，要成为一个执业注册会计师，申请人必须拥有相关知识及技能，例如关于会计、审计、税务、法律、职业道德等方面的专业知识。因此各国都采用考试的形式对候选人进行相关知识的测试。具体考试科目及考试安排在各个国家/地区存在一定的差异。例如，英国的特许公认会计师公会（ACCA）有14门考试科目，ICAEW 有16门考试科目（具有相关会计专业文凭的考生可以申请免考一定的科目），但其对考生的学历背景要求很低，一般不需要有大学文凭，通过2门 A Level[①] 考试的人即可参加，没有会计或审计相关学术背景的人也可以参加考试。美国的专业考试由美国全国州会计委员会联合会（NASBA）统一安排，只有4门考试科目，但其要求考生拥有美国大学相关学士学位，并且其学位课程中必须包含一定时间的会计及商业相关课程。对于外国大学的学术背景，需要经国际高等商学院协会（AACSB）[②]或者美国商学院联盟（ACB-SP）[③] 认证为与美国大学学历等同方可参加考试。澳大利亚、香港及新加坡的要求也都与美国类似。澳大利亚与美国类似，要求考生最低拥有澳大利亚大学与会计专业有关的本科学历。对于国外的学历，澳大利亚一般只认可新加坡南洋理工学院或者新加坡管理大学的相关文凭。新加坡要求考生必须拥有新加坡大学相关专业文凭，对于国外大学的文凭，必须经过美国伊利诺伊州考试委员会（Illinois Board of Examiners）认证为等同于 AACSB 或者 ACBSP 同等学位的学历背景方可参加考试。香港要求考生必须拥有与会计专业相关的大学学士学位，对于外国大学取得的会计相关学士学位，需要满足 HKICPA 的认证要求或者考生可以参加经 HKICPA 批准的转换课程，来达到 HKICPA 的认证要求。除了对学历的要求，香港还要求考生必须参加一个为期14个星期的认证课程（Quali-

---

① 英国教育体制下的等级水平，相当于中国的高中。

② The Association to Advance Collegiate Schools of Business International，是全球首屈一指的商学院和会计项目非政府认证机构。

③ Association of Collegiate Business Schools and Programs，是以教学为核心的商业学校和课程而设立的重要的官方认可的协会。

第二部分

fied Program, or "QP") 后方能参加考试。各国对于考生一般都没有国籍限制，任何国家的考生都可以参加考试。英国的 ACCA 及 ICAEW，澳大利亚及新西兰的 CAANZ，香港的 HKICPA 等都在全世界范围内设立了很多考试地点，方便外国考生参加考试，这也与推广培训课程、提升协会国际影响力有关。目前美国的注册会计师考试除在美国本土以外，在日本及中东地区也设有考点，并正考虑在南美洲开设考点。

综上所述，各国/地区考试目的都是为了保证注册会计师申请人有相关知识及技能，对参加考试的考生一般没有国籍要求，境外人士可以与本国人一样参加注会考试。但考试都使用相关国家的官方语言，因此考生需要掌握当地语言才能够参加考试。对于考生的专业背景要求，各国对考生在外国取得的学历经过认证后一般可以豁免考生拥有本国相关学历的要求。这样，一般而言，境外人士在掌握当地语言的前提下，想要参加一个国家/地区的注会考试一般都不存在障碍。



### （二）取得相关工作经验

考试通过后，下面一个要求就是拥有相关工作经验。除美国以外，其他国家/地区对于取得会计职业组织会员资格的相关工作要求与取得法定审计资格的工作要求不同。以下先介绍取得会计职业组织会员资格的工作经验要求。美国对于取得会计职业组织会员资格与取得法定审计资格的工作要求没有区别，所以这里统一介绍。

表 1 概述了各国/地区对于成为会计职业组织会员的工作经验要求：

各国对于工作经验性质要求大同小异。一般都需要与会计、审计、税务、咨询等专业相关。对于工作地点要求，美国虽然没有明确要求其相关工作经验必须在美国完成，但是各州一般都要求申请人拥有"社会保险号码"，对于境外人士来说，这就要求申请人必须有资格在美国工作，通常需要拥有工作签证。其他国家没有要求这种相关工作经验必须在本国完成，对于在外国取得的相关工作经验，如果满足相关会计职业组织对培训雇主的要求或者经过相关会计职业组织的个别认证，也可以满足要求。

表 1　　会计职业组织会员的工作经验要求

| 国家/地区 | 会计职业组织/州政府 | 工作经验要求① |
|---|---|---|
| 英国 | 英格兰及威尔士特许会计师协会 | 450 天工作经验（工作培训），通常需要 3 到 5 年完成。工作性质应该与以下一个或几个方面相关：<br>• 会计<br>• 财务管理<br>• 审计/鉴证<br>• 破产<br>• 税务<br>• 信息科技 |
| | 英国特许公认会计师公会 | 拥有 3 年相关工作经验，并且在 20 个工作表现目标中完成 13 个目标② |
| 美国 | 加利福尼亚州 | 2 年相关工作经验，包括使用会计、鉴证、制表、管理建议、财务咨询、税务或者咨询技能的任何服务。对于签署鉴证报告的人来说，他们需要拥有不少于 500 个小时的鉴证工作经验 |
| | 德克萨斯州 | 1 年非常规会计工作经验，包括在会计师事务所取得的客户服务经验以及其他领域取得的会计工作经验，例如商业领域、政府部门、律师事务所、教育领域或者实习期间取得的工作经验（需要经额外批准） |
| | 伊利诺伊州 | 1 年相关工作经验，包括在政府部门、商业机构、学术领域及会计师事务所取得的工作经验 |
| | 纽约州 | 1 年相关工作经验，包括在注册会计师事务所、政府部门、非政府领域及教育机构取得的工作经验 |
| 澳大利亚 | 澳新特许会计师协会 | 在澳大利亚特许会计师的监督下完成，或者在其他经许可的国际会计联盟成员的监督下完成至少 3 年全职（或者等效的兼职）工作经验 |
| 新加坡 | 新加坡特许会计师协会 | 根据申请人不同的途径，取得 3～6 年相关工作经验 |
| 香港 | 香港会计师公会 | 根据申请人不同的资历背景，取得 3～6 年相关工作经验 |

第二部分

① 为申请注册会计师资格前获取的累计工作经验。

② 20 个具体工作目标参见 ACCA 官方网站 http://www.accaglobal.com/us/en/student/practical-experience/performance-objectives.html。

### （三）通过职业道德考试

为规范会计师行业，各国/地区都制定了复杂的会计师职业道德规范要求。职业道德考试是为了保证会计师了解这些道德规范要求。在美国，按照各州要求，申请人一般在完成专业笔试后，需要通过一个由各州组织的职业道德考试。这种考试通常可以通过计算机网络完成。新加坡要求申请人完成一个为期 3 天的职业道德与专业操作培训课程。其他国家/地区一般将职业道德考试作为专业考试的一部分来进行。

### （四）申请 CPA 资格（美国）或成为会计职业组织会员（其他国家/地区）

1. 美国

在美国，申请人完成上面三步以后，就可以向其所希望执业的州政府相关部门申请注册会计师资格了。美国各州对申请人的身份要求不同，有些州要求申请人必须是美国公民，目前阿拉巴马州、夏威夷州及路易斯安那州有这样的要求；还有个别州虽然没有要求申请人必须持有美国国籍，但是其要求考生必须是该州居民，例如爱达荷州、堪萨斯州和密苏里州。美国其他大多数州对申请人没有公民或居民要求。

取得美国注册会计师资格的会计师就可以在其所在州执业，进行会计、税务、咨询等相关服务或者提供法定审计服务并签署法定审计报告。这里值得强调的是美国对于提供法定审计服务的注册会计师没有额外的资格认证要求。这和其他国家做法是不同的。对于跨州执业（即在一个州取得注册会计师资格的会计师到另外一个州提供审计服务），各州一般对于临时执业都存在一些灵活的安排。对于长期执业一般都要求执业人提出申请完成一定的注册程序方可。通常情况下，申请人会在他们居住和工作所在州申请并注册成为美国注册会计师。

2. 其他国家/地区

在项目组调查的国家/地区中，除美国以外其他国家/地区在完成上面三步之后就可以申请成为会计职业组织会员。这些职业组织会员可以在公司财务岗位任职，也可以提供代理记账、代理报税、税务咨询等各种与会计专业相关的服务。会计职业组织对其会员都有后续教育要求及安排，会员必须满足每年一定时间的后续教育才能够继续保持会员资格。同时，这些会计职业组织也通过发布职业道德准则要求、独立性准则要求以及会计/审计相关指南等约束其会员，同时安排了定期检查，保证会员的资历及操守满足这些要求。这样，会计职业组织的各项纪律及安排已经基本能够满足对提供法定审计服务以外的会计师的监管要求，因此，对从事这些职务或服务的人员，各国一般没有额外的监管要求。

如果一个会计职业组织会员希望提供法定审计服务并签署法定审计报告，他/她则必须申请额外的“执业资格”，职业组织会员的资格并不能够满足签署法定审计报告的要求。在第五步中我们将详细介绍申请执业资格的要求及条件。

### （五）成为 AICPA 会员（美国）或申请执业资格（其他国家/地区）

1. 美国

在美国各州登记注册取得注册会计师资格的人可以向 AICPA 申请成为其会员。AICPA 对美国 CPA 没有额外的考试或准入要求，但是成为其会员后就要满足其会员要求，包括后续教育、职业操守、独立性等等。如前所述，在美国各州登记注册的美国注册会计师即可提供包括法定审计服务在内的各种服务，因此不需要成为 AICPA 会员而提供这些服务。美国各州政府对于在本州登记的注册会计师也有不同的后续教育及其他相关要求。

在项目组调查的国家/地区中，英国、澳大利亚、新西兰、新加坡及香港都需要会计职业组织会员额外申请一个“执业执照（practicing license）”或者通过额外的注册程序才能够对法定审计报告签字。这个执业执照或注册程序可能是政府授权会计职业组织颁发或者执行的（如英国），也可能是由政府相关监管部门颁发或者执行的。以下将对各国/地区执业执照及注册程序申请及资格要求进行详细讨论。

2. 英国

英国公司法授权下，ICAEW 负责向注册会计师颁发英国审计执业执照。申请人必须满足 ICAEW“审计资格”要求，具体要求如下：

（1）通过 ICAEW 的额外三门考试，包括技术整合案例分析、商业报告技术整合以及税法。

（2）拥有满足 2006 年公司法要求下的额外 2～3 年工作经验，具体要求为：

①取得 ICAEW 会员资格前与取得会员资格后的工作经验中，有不少于 3 年的工作是在经批准的培训环境中进行的，其中，至少 2 年是在英国会计师事务

所中完成；

②取得 ICAEW 会员资格前与取得会员资格后的工作经验中，至少有 240 天是在 ICAEW 授权培训雇主单位（均为英国会计师事务所）进行的；

③在上述 240 天的工作经验中，至少有 120 天从事的工作是 2006 年公司法要求下的法定审计服务，其他时间可以是法定审计服务也可以是与法定审计服务性质类似的其他审计服务，这些服务性质应该满足 ICAEW 和职业监管局的定义；

④审计服务工作必须在拥有英国执业注册会计师执照的人监督下，在 ICAEW 授权培训雇主单位完成。

3. 澳大利亚

澳大利亚要求法定审计师必须由 ASIC 登记授权，成为注册的“公司审计师”才能够在澳大利亚提供法定审计服务。成为澳大利亚法定审计师必须满足以下条件：

（1）继续教育：每年接受至少 120 个小时关于职业发展的继续教育，继续教育活动必须能够提高审计师的专业技术水平或者专业服务水平；

（2）满足质量保证要求；

（3）按要求购买职业责任保险；

（4）拥有处理纠纷的能力。

另外，澳大利亚要求其公司审计师必须是澳大利亚居民。

4. 新加坡①

新加坡要求注册会计师必须向 ACRA 申请，取得执业执照后方可在新加坡提供法定审计服务。申请人需要在申请前五年拥有不低于 2500 个小时的、满足条件的审计工作经验，其中一半以上的时间需要在新加坡完成。符合条件的工作经验应该满足以下要求之一：

（1）审计管理层职位；

（2）审计质量检查职位；

（3）审计技术支持职位。

---

① 具体要求可以从以下 ACRA 网站中找到：https：//www.acra.gov.sg/components/wireframes/howToGuidesChapters.aspx？pageid＝1676#2093。

5. 中国香港

香港法定审计报告必须由取得执业资格的香港注册会计师签署。取得执业资格需要满足以下条件：

（1）至少4年全职工作经验，其中至少1年是在取得香港注册会计师资格（非执业资格）后进行的。如果全部的工作经验都是在取得香港注册会计师资格后完成的，那么相关工作经验要求可以缩短为30个月。不管是哪种情况，工作经验中大部分必须是进行审计相关工作，其中至少1年需要在香港完成。

（2）是香港常住居民。

（3）通过了香港法律和税法考试。

（4）没有破产记录。

（5）满足HKICPA的继续教育要求。

以上分析显示，在除美国以外的其他国家/地区，会计师必须经过额外的授权申请程序才能获得法定审计报告的签字权并提供相应的法定审计服务。各国/地区对这种额外的“签字权”资格要求各有不同，但是大多需要会计师拥有本国审计工作经验或者为本国居民，以保证执业注册会计师拥有充足的“本地知识”及“本地经验”。此外各国还通常对这种有签字权的执业注册会计师有强制保险要求。本书第八章对会计师职业责任保险进行了详细分析。

会计师除了通过以上途径取得会员资格以外，还有一种途径是通过会计师组织之间的互认。以下将对不同会计职业组织间的互认安排进行详细分析。

根据考察，世界上主要的会计职业组织都与其他职业组织存在一定程度的“互认”安排，这种互认可以是考试科目的豁免，或者是会员资格的直接互认。研究发现，世界上主要会计职业组织的互认安排都比较相似。下面就以香港会计师公会为例进行分析。香港会计师公会与世界上主要会计职业组织签署了以下两种不同的互认协议：

第一种：会员资格互认协议，是指会员不需要经过额外的考试，只要满足一定条件就能够取得香港会计师公会会员资格。这种安排包括以下会计职业组织：

- 澳大利亚及新西兰特许会计师协会（CAANZ）
- 英格兰及威尔士特许会计师协会（ICAEW）
- 苏格拉特许会计师协会（ICAS）
- 加拿大特许会计师协会（CICA）

- 爱尔兰特许会计师协会（CAI）
- 津巴布韦特许会计师公会（ICAZ）
- 美国注册会计师（US CPA）
- 英国特许公认会计师公会（ACCA）

第二种：考试互免协议，是指会员需要额外通过香港会计师公会的考试方能取得香港注册会计师资格，一般需要额外考试的科目为香港法律和税法。这种安排包括以下会计职业组织：

- 澳大利亚会计师公会（CPA Australia）
- 英国特许管理会计师公会（CIMA）
- 中国注册会计师协会（CICPA）
- 英国国际会计师公会（AIA）

这些不同程度的“互认”安排是根据双方会计职业组织对成为会员的资历要求测评结果进行衡量的。这种对会计职业组织的测评是一个非常复杂的过程，包括对双方会计职业组织所在环境的会计、审计制度的分析，对职业组织道德标准要求的分析，对相关国家税务及法律体系的分析，对会员学术背景要求分析，对考试科目安排及其覆盖深度、广度的分析，对工作经验具体要求的分析等等。这种测评一般是由希望缔结互认协议的双方聘请独立的第三方专业评估机构（一般来自第三国）来进行的，通常测评所需时间也长达1～2年。简单来讲，根据测评结果，如果双方会计职业组织在各方面要求基本等效，那么一般情况下会以会员资格互认的形式缔结协议。如果非等效，则双方会基于具体项目进行协商，可能安排考试互免的协议方式。

值得一提的是，这种会计职业组织之间的互认安排都仅限于会员资格层面。通过互认协议取得一个国家会计职业组织会员资格的会员无法在当地签署法定审计报告。想要取得法定审计报告签字权的会员必须按照相应的额外监管要求，满足一定的条件并进行额外的注册登记。如上文介绍，在美国，申请人必须满足美国相关州的监管要求，向各州监管机构进行申请，成为注册会计师后方可签署法定审计报告；在其他国家/地区，申请人要取得“执业执照”或者登记成为“公司审计师”后方可签署法定审计报告。

一些欧盟成员国之间的互认协议存在一些特殊安排，这些安排包括法定审计签字权的互认。由于各欧盟成员国之间很多会计审计准则以及法律制度都得到了统一，这样的安排就显得比较合理。举例来说，英国和德国允许欧洲经济区（European Economic Area，EEA）内各国的审计师和会计师事务所在本国提供法定审计服务，但德国额外要求签字会计师通过一项能力测试，该测试包括笔试和面试，内容主要涵盖法定审计相关法律规定、经济法、税法以及德国注册会计师（Wirtschaftsprüfer）行业的监管规定。

（六）小结

如前所述，法定审计对一个国家资本市场及社会经济的稳定具有重要影响，各国对法定审计也都实行严格监管。世界上大部分的国家/地区将法定审计签字权与注册会计师其他服务资格分开进行管理，注册会计师在取得了会计师资格后需要额外取得针对法定审计的“执业执照”或者登记注册为公司审计师，方能提供法定审计服务并签署法定审计报告。这种“分类管理”方式的优势主要表现在以下几个方面：

1. 政策制定

法定审计相比注册会计师提供的其他服务风险更大、影响更深。将法定审计签字权与其他服务资格分离可以使准则制定者能够针对拥有法定审计签字权的会计师制定更高标准的政策要求，以确保法定审计服务质量。而这些政策要求不会影响到其他注册会计师，也不会带来不必要的合规成本。例如，英国及澳大利亚都要求拥有“审计执业资格”的注册会计师购买职业责任保险，而对于其他注册会计师则没有这种要求。

2. 监管成本及有效性

法定审计签字权分离后，监管者可以将监管力度更多地投入到那些拥有“执业资格”的注册会计师身上，而对于其他注册会计师则可以相对缩小资源投入。这样既可以节省监管成本，又能够提高监管的有效性，是一举两得的做法。

3. 会计职业组织的规模及影响力

法定审计签字权分离后，会计职业组织可以适当降低其入门标准而不必担心该举措会影响该国家/地区的法定审计质量。降低其入门标准有利于扩大本国会计职业组织的规模及影响力。例如，英国的ACCA在全世界范围内广泛招纳会员，针对不同国家的会员，允许选择当地税法及公司法进行考试，这样激励不同国家考生的积极性，也因此使得ACCA会员目前达到了17万人，遍布180个国家。由于拥有众多的会员，ACCA每年可以收取相当规模的会员费，这些资金可以用来支持 ACCA 在会计审计领域进行专业研究，同时也提升了 ACCA 在国际会计审计界的影响力。但是扩大的会员规模并不会影响到英国法定审计质量。如前所述，要想取得英国法定审计资格，ACCA 会员必须额外满足一系列的要求，因此法定审计仍然限制在可控范围之内。

4. 国际间合作

将法定审计签字权分离出来，有利于会计职业组织与国际上其他会计职业组织的合作。会计职业组织可以与其他国际性会计职业组织签订互认协议，扩大国际交流及国际影响力，同时不必担心对本国法定审计的影响，因为法定审计签字权并不会直接赋予那些签有互认协议的会计职业组织的会员。

## 二、中国实践



根据财政部和中注协的规定，对参加中国注册会计师职业资格考试的考生没有国籍或者居民要求，任何国家的考生都可以报名参加考试。此外，为方便香港及海外考生，中注协在香港及欧洲都设立了考点。考生必须拥有大专以上学历，参加 6 门专业知识考试及 1 门综合考试，考试科目包括会计、审计、财务成本管理、税法、经济法以及公司战略与风险管理六门科目。全部考试需在计算机上完成，这要求考生拥有中文计算机输入技能。除中文试题以外，各科考试均设置 5 分的英文作答附加分题，鼓励考生使用英文作答。

通过考试的考生需要取得 2 年以上从事独立审计业务工作实践经验，即可向中注协申请取得中国注册会计师协会会员资格，并同时取得法定审计报告的签字权。此外，从事非审计工作的考生通过考试以后，可以向中注协申请成为非执业会员，非执业会员没有法定审计报告的签字权。

另外，中注协目前没有与世界上其他会计职业组织签订会员资格互认协议，仅与英格兰及威尔士特许会计师协会及香港会计师公会签订了部分考试科目互免协议。取得互免资格的考生仍然需要参加并通过税法及经济法专业考试及综合阶段考试。

## 三、有关建议

第一，中国应考虑聘请第三方专业评估机构对其会员资格进行分析，并与外国知名会计职业组织，如美国注册会计师协会（AICPA）、英国特许公认会计师公会（ACCA）、澳新特许会计师协会（CAANZ）、澳洲会计师公会（CPA Australia）等进行比较，按照比较结果适时、适当安排建立会员互认制度或者部分考试科目互免制度。中国政府也可以考虑进一步拓展与香港会计师公会（HKICPA）及英格兰及威尔士特许会计师协会（ICAEW）的互认安排。这样会帮助中国注册会计师更容易成为国外会计职业组织会员，并在国外工作。此举也会吸引更多的海外优秀人才成为中国注册会计师，并在全球范围增强中国注册会计师协会的国际影响力。通过互认协议授予的会员资格并不会必然授予其在本国签署法定审计报告的资格，这也是互认协议的常规做法。监管机构可以考虑设立额外的执业资格要求或类似手段来限制执业许可，这样就可以更好地对有签字权的注册会计师进行监督管理。

第二，随着越来越多的中国公司在海外设立机构或进行兼并收购，越来越多的国际公司来中国设立公司，中国应与外国会计职业组织或会计监管机构安排更多的交换项目，来增加本国注册会计师的国际经验，此举能够帮助中国注册会计师接触海外实务、获得海外经验，这些注册会计师回国后，就拥有了更开阔的视角和良好的国际关系网络，从而可为中国公司吸引外资和海外投资活动提供更好的服务。另一方面，此举也会帮助经验丰富的中国注册会计师走出去，将中国的专业经验和知识带到国外，以便其他国家更好地了解中国的实务。例如中注协可以安排与国外具有影响力的会计职业组织互换一部分会员到对方国家的会计师事务所进行学习工作。这些会员因此能够取得国外相关审计经验，并同时可能在国外工作期间取得满足在国外申请法定审计报告签字权的资格要求。这有利于帮助中国的注册会计师向海外发展。

第三，中国可以考虑将注册会计师资格与法定审计报告签字权分离，建立签字注册会计师管理制度。取得注册会计师资格的会员需要满足额外的要求方能取得法定审计报告签字权。这样有利于监管机构对具有法定审计报告签字权的会计师进行单独管理，提高监管有效性。此举将有效避免对所有注册会计师进行“一刀切”的管理，有利于针对非法定审计服务的注册会计师制定更加灵活的政策措施，吸引更多的注册会计师会员。法定审计报告签字权分离也有助于中国与国外会计职业组织在互认协议中进行更加灵活的安排。

中国可以考虑在某些国际化程度较高的地区（如香港）设立注册会计师培养基地。中国香港作为一个国际性金融贸易都市，吸引了大批国际性人才。中国可以考虑在香港设立中国会计师人才培养基地，培养拥有中国知识及实践经验的国际型会计及审计人才，为推动中国会计行业发展储备力量。中国也可以考虑进一步完善注册会计师考试制度，吸引港澳台及海外考生参与中国注册会计师考试，根据这些考生的特点给予一定的灵活安排。例如有人提出中国注册会计师的机考制度使得部分港澳台及海外考生由于不熟练中文输入而难以顺利通过考试，对于这些考生给予手写考试的选择将会大大提高考生的积极性。

# 第二章 境外会计师事务所开展法定审计业务



如本书前面章节所述，法定审计在全世界各国均受到严格监管。对于境外会计师事务所及员工在本国提供法定审计服务存在诸多管理措施。本章重点围绕以下几个关于境外会计师事务所的监管问题展开：

- 境外会计师事务所能否为本国注册成立的公司提供法定审计服务，对于这样的服务有何等限制性措施；
- 境外会计师事务所能否为在境外成立、在本国上市的公司提供与上市有关的审计服务，对这样的服务有何等限制性措施；
- 境外会计师事务所能否在本国设立分支机构（含法律形式上的分/子公司或非法律形式上的成员所），并通过该分支机构在本国提供法定审计服务；
- 审计工作底稿能否跨境转移，各国法律法规对其是否存在一定的限制性措施。

## 一、国际经验

项目组主要调查了美国、英国、澳大利亚、新加坡、德国及中国香港的相关政策措施及实际操作情况，同时也参考了法国、日本及印度的有关做法。

### （一）对于境外会计师事务所执行法定审计的相关要求

调查显示，除美国以外，其他国家/地区普遍限制境外会计师事务所对在本国注册成立的公司提供法定审计服务。这样的限制通常为法律明文规定，或者通过一些隐含的限制性措施实施。在欧盟地区，根据欧盟相关指令的要求，欧盟成员国之间存在一定的互惠政策。以下将对各主要国家/地区的做法进行详细讨论：

1. 美国

美国与世界上其他国家的做法存在差异。首先，美国仅对特定公司存在法定审计要求，而其他国家大多数的做法为要求全部[①]在本国注册成立的公司提供法定审计报告。在美国需要进行法定审计的公司包括美国证券交易委员会（SEC）发行人（包括权益发行人和债务发行人，即存在上市股票或公开发行债券的公司）及在SEC注册的证券经纪人及承销商。其次，美国允许满足一定条件的会计师事务所，不论是在美国注册成立的事务所还是在美国境外注册成立的事务所，在PCAOB登记注册成为“PCAOB登记事务所”。PCAOB登记事务所可以为任何需要在美国提交法定审计报告的公司提供法定审计服务，不论这个被审计公司是在美国注册成立还是在美国境外注册成立。目前在PCAOB登记注册的会计师事务所总数超过1000个，它们来自88个国家/地区，其中大约47个来自中国大陆。[②] 在PCAOB登记注册的要求之一是会计师事务所要接受PCAOB的质量检查。与欧洲做法不同，PCAOB要求境外会计师事务所接受PCAOB的“现场检查”。需要指明的是，PCAOB是法定的独立审计监管机构，其职能类似于中国财政部，但监管对象和范围小于中国财政部。本书在第九章对跨境监管进行了详细讨论及分析，在此处不作进一步的讨论。

根据美国的监管要求，理论上任何一个在PCAOB登记注册的会计师事务所都可以为任何一个SEC发行人或在SEC注册的证券经纪人及承销商提供法定审计服务。但是在实践中，由于审计师[③]需要对被审计客户主要运营的市场有充足的了解并拥有相应的审计技能，这包括对被审计客户销售及采购市场的了解，对相关地法律及税务要求的掌控等。实际上只有被审计客户主要运营市场的当地审计师拥有这些技能，而来自被审计客户所在国以外的审计师通常无法拥有这些知识。另外，来自被审计客户所在国以外的审计师还面临着跨境审计需要

① 一般国家对“休眠公司”，即没有业务活动或业务活动极少的公司免除法定审计要求。但这样的公司只是个别现象。

② PCAOB登记注册会计师事务所信息可以从以下网址中查找 http://pcaobus.org/Registration/Firms/Pages/RegisteredFirms.aspx。

③ 本章所称审计师，均指提供审计服务的会计师事务所。

的额外签证费用、差旅费用等，这些都导致其无法与来自被审计客户本国的审计师相竞争。例如，如果一个在美国上市的公司的主营业务在中国（不论其注册地在美国、中国或者其他国家），则中国的审计师由于拥有相应审计技能及成本竞争优势，通常为其提供审计服务。而一个主要运营业务都在美国本土的美国上市公司，其审计通常由来自美国本土的审计师提供。从这个意义上讲，PCAOB 对审计师选择的开放性规定，更多具有理论或象征意义。

2. 英国

除个别情形外，英国法律要求所有在英国注册成立的公司接受年度法定审计。根据英国公司法的规定，为在英国注册的公司提供法定审计服务的会计师事务所，其全部主管合伙人（即事务所的所有人）必须是拥有英国执业资格的会计师或者是来自欧洲其他成员国（EEA 地区）的执业注册会计师，会计师事务所须同时拥有英国执业资格。前面章节讨论了会计师如何取得英国执业资格，其中一个前提条件是必须获得在英国具有执业资格的事务所中的相关工作经验。这样的要求导致在英国通常只有在英国本国注册成立的会计师事务所或者来自其他欧洲成员国的会计师事务所能够为英国公司提供法定审计服务。



3. 澳大利亚

与英国一样，澳大利亚要求绝大多数在澳大利亚注册成立的公司接受年度法定审计。对澳大利亚公司进行法定审计的注册会计师必须在澳大利亚证券和投资委员会（ASIC）注册并得到执业许可，ASIC 具有类似中国工商总局的企业登记注册职能。而得到执业许可的前提条件之一是这个会计师必须是澳大利亚居民①。澳大利亚公司法规定会计师事务所的控制权必须掌握在那些在澳大利亚拥有执业许可的会计师手中。这样的规定导致在实际操作中，只有来自澳大利亚本国的会计师事务所才能够为澳大利亚的公司提供法定审计服务。

4. 新加坡

新加坡法律也要求绝大多数在新加坡注册成立的公司接受法定审计。提供法定审计服务的会计师事务所必须按照会计师法的规定在新加坡会计与企业管制局（ACRA）注册登记并取得执业资格。取得执业资格的前提条件之一是该会计师事务所不低于 2/3 的所有权掌握在具有新加坡执业会计师资格的会计师

---

① 这里的居民与永久居民概念不同，凡是在澳大利亚取得长期居住权的个人均满足这个条件。例如拥有长期工作签证的个人可以满足这个条件。

手中，并且这个会计师事务所的主管合伙人必须在新加坡居住。这样的要求导致只有在新加坡注册成立的会计师事务所才能够为新加坡公司提供法定审计服务。

5. 中国香港

香港公司法要求全部在香港成立的公司，除个别休眠公司以外，都要进行法定审计。提供法定审计的事务所必须取得香港会计师公会颁发的执业资格证书。取得这个资格证书的前提条件之一是该会计师事务所的合伙人必须取得香港会计师公会颁发的执业资格证书，而香港会计师取得执业资格的前提条件之一是该会计师必须是香港居民。通常情况下，只有香港的会计师事务所能够为香港公司提供法定审计服务。

以上调查分析显示，除美国以外，其他主要国家/地区的法定审计服务均不能由境外会计师事务所提供。在美国，虽然法律允许在 PCAOB 注册的境外会计师事务所提供法定审计服务，但由于审计技能及成本的限制，在实际操作中，在 PCAOB 注册的境外会计师事务所一般只为在外国的美国上市公司提供与上市报告相关的法定审计服务，一般不会为那些主营业务在美国本土的公司提供法定审计服务。



### （二）对境外会计师事务所向外国上市公司提供法定审计服务的要求

世界上一些主要的资本市场已经对外开放，允许外国公司在本国资本市场挂牌上市，美国称这样的公司为“外国私人发行人”（以下统称为 FPI）。与本国公司的法定审计不同，这些 FPI 注册在外国，主营业务也在外国。由外国审计师对这些 FPI 执行审计工作不涉及“跨境审计”，而是由审计师在外国对这些 FPI 进行服务。一国政府是否接受境外审计师对这些 FPI 执行审计并发表审计意见用于上市地公告是近年来热门讨论的话题之一。世界上允许外国公司直接挂牌上市的资本市场主要集中于美国和欧洲（主要为卢森堡、伦敦及法兰克福），以下将围绕这两大主要资本市场进行详细讨论。

1. 美国

如前文所述，美国允许在 PCAOB 登记注册的境外会计师事务所对 FPI 执行审计工作并用于上市公司财报披露等用途。这样的会计师事务所必须接受 PCAOB 的“直接检查”。

2. 欧盟

根据欧洲议会和欧盟委员会共同发表的对法定审计的指引第 45 章规定，对于在欧盟成员国上市的外国公司，各成员国应该允许满足一定条件的境外会计师事务所提供与上市报告要求相应的法定审计服务，并对这些会计师事务所及其注册会计师进行登记，登记的会计师事务所及其注册会计师要接受上市地欧盟国家的质量检查。但是如果这些境外会计师事务所在近三年里接受了注册国的检查，并且注册国的检查及质量控制体系是欧盟所认可的，则欧盟成员国将依赖这些会计师及会计师事务所在本国的检查结果，不再进行重复监管。目前中国对于会计师的质量检查体系已经通过了欧盟认可，所以中国的会计师事务所在满足一定的条件下，可以不必接受欧盟成员国的直接检查。

综上所述，美国和欧盟均允许境外会计师事务所对 FPI 执行与上市财报有关的法定审计服务。不同的是，美国要求对这些执行审计的会计师事务所进行现场检查。而欧盟遵循“互认”原则，如果外国的监管体系能够满足欧盟标准，则不必进行现场检查。



### （三）境外会计师事务所在本国设立分支机构并提供法定审计服务

上文讨论了境外会计师事务所能否直接在本国提供法定审计服务。以下将分析境外事务所能否通过在海外成立分/子公司、或者成员所的方式在海外提供法定审计服务。

对于合伙制会计师事务所，不论是无限责任普通合伙制还是有限责任合伙制，由于合伙人是自然人，这就使得合伙制会计师事务所无法拥有子公司。在有限的、允许合伙制会计师事务所的合伙人为公司的国家，例如英国，其合伙人也必须满足一系列的条件，例如这个公司必须拥有英国法定审计执业执照或者其他被认可的欧洲国家的法定审计执业执照。在这些条件要求下，只有英国或者其他被认可的欧洲国家的会计师事务所有可能在英国开设子公司。由于各国对于提供法定审计服务的会计师事务所都有严格的审批及注册要求，境外会计师事务所的分所通常都无法满足这些注册要求而取得当地法定审计资格，因此会计师事务所的分所通常也仅限于在同一国家的不同地区开设的分所。

允许有限责任公司制会计师事务所的国家/地区对成立分公司或者子公司也存在诸多限制。例如，在新加坡，会计师法规定有限责任公司制的会计师事务所的股东必须是自然人（即不能是另外一个公司），这也就决定了公司制会计师事务所不可以是另外一个公司的子公司。在香港，会计师公会条例也有类似的规定。在英国，会计师事务所可以成立分公司或者子公司，但是这些分/子公司要取得英国执业资格方能在英国提供法定审计服务。通常只有欧洲经济区国家的外国公司有可能通过设立分/子公司的形式在英国发展，其他国家/地区的会计师事务所则很难满足这样的要求。在美国，各州立法对于会计师事务所登记的要求不同，但大多数都要求其拥有权掌握在本州注册的会计师手中。这也就使外国公司在美国成立的分/子公司很难取得当地会计师执业资格。

世界上绝大多数的会计师事务所都是通过成立网络所（也称为成员所）的形式向海外发展的。网络所是法律上各自独立的个体，通常是由一批熟悉本地市场及拥有相关经验及资格的合伙人建立起来的。通过协议，每个国家的成员所均可以共享品牌、专业技术、软件、培训体系以及成员所之间的便捷协作，并遵守同样的内部控制政策。目前包括“四大”在内的大型会计师事务所均在全球范围内建立了成员所网络，这些网络所在各自国家/地区范围内提供法定审计服务，并互相配合，通过集团审计指引和集团审计报告等形式，为跨国集团公司提供统一标准下的审计服务。为了确保统一的服务质量，网络所之间还开展内部质量检查以维护品牌声誉。



### （四）审计工作底稿的管理

工作底稿是会计师事务所的财产。审计师职业道德要求其对客户信息保密，除非经客户允许或者是在监管机构依法要求情况下，不得将客户有关信息提供给任何第三方。按照各国监管要求，会计师事务所有责任在一定年限内保留其审计工作底稿，并在本国有关监管机构要求时提供工作底稿信息。由于以上要求，会计师事务所一般不会将工作底稿转移出境。会计师事务所在他们的业务约定书中通常都会包含这样的条款，约定审计工作底稿是审计师的财产，除法律或者审计准则要求情况下，不得对外提供或转移。以下将讨论当外国监管机构未进行跨境监管而要求提供工作底稿时，或者在集团审计的安排下当外国母公司审计师要求提供审计工作底稿时对工作底稿的共享安排。

1. 外国监管要求

目前国际上存在跨境监管需求的国家主要是美国。由于存在众多在美国上市的外国公司，同时 PCAOB 允许在 PCAOB 注册的境外会计师事务所对其提供法定审计服务，按照 PCAOB 的要求，这些会计师事务所需要接受 PCAOB 的现场检查。这就出现了跨境监管问题。对于欧洲国家来说，如前面所述，对于监管体系得到欧盟认可的国家的会计师事务所，在满足一定的条件下，欧盟国家可以依赖该事务所本国监管者对其的监管，而不需要直接对其进行检查，因此就不存在跨境监管问题。本书第十章对跨境监管进行了详细讨论。本章仅就工作底稿跨境转移问题进行探讨。

由于 PCAOB 的检查通常为现场检查，即 PCAOB 会派人进入到被检查的会计师事务所现场进行检查，因此通常不需要被检查的会计师事务所将其工作底稿运送出境。对于 PCAOB 的现场检查，世界上部分国家已与 PCAOB 签订了备忘录，允许 PCAOB 对本国会计师事务所就执行美国上市公司审计项目的工作底稿进行现场质量检查。这样的国家包括澳大利亚、新加坡、加拿大、韩国、日本、英国、德国、法国、挪威、瑞士、西班牙、芬兰、荷兰、瑞典、丹麦等。

2. 集团审计安排

跨国集团的审计通常由不同的会计师事务所共同完成。这些会计师事务所可能来自共同的事务所网络，或者来自不同的事务所网络，如由子公司的审计师对子公司提供审计服务，并向集团审计师出具按照集团审计要求的审计报告；集团审计师依赖子公司审计师的工作，对包含子公司在内的集团合并财务报表发表审计意见。在这样的安排下，集团审计师已经得到客户许可接触子公司的信息，从而子公司审计师不需要对集团审计师进行保密。通常集团审计师会从子公司审计师处获得审计报告及其他一些重要事项报告，在必要情况下，集团审计师可能需要检查子公司审计师的工作底稿。这就可能涉及工作底稿共享问题。

调查显示，一般情况下，集团审计师会利用电子信息技术，在远程直接检查子公司审计师的工作底稿，或者集团审计师会来到子公司审计师工作现场进行工作底稿检查。调查显示，一般国家监管机构的监管措施会保障集团审计师能够有渠道在分支机构所在国，或在集团审计师所在国，对这些审计工作底稿进行审阅，在通常情况下，不会存在障碍。

综上所述，会计师事务所直接到外国提供法定审计服务、拓展相关业务的途径壁垒重重。除美国外，其他国家基本上通过法律要求限制境外会计师事务所在本国执行法定审计业务。即使在美国，由于市场的选择，法定审计也都是由被审计客户所在主要市场的当地会计师事务所执行的。同时，根据 PCAOB 的要求，在 PCAOB 登记注册的会计师事务所必须接受 PCAOB 的直接检查，以确保其审计质量。

由于在世界范围内，会计师事务所大多以合伙制形式存在，而大多数国家对在本国执行法定审计的会计师事务所都有所有权要求及对其主管合伙人有本国相关工作经验的要求。这就使得会计师事务所很难通过直接在国外成立分公司或者设立子公司的形式进行海外扩张。另外，在新加坡及香港法律都明文规定，有限责任公司制会计师事务所的股东必须是自然人，法律责任的归属问题也使会计师事务所很难在外国开设分公司或子公司。

纵观世界上大型会计师事务所的发展，包括“四大”在内，他们都是以网络所的形式向海外扩张的。如前所述，网络所的优势主要表现在以下几点：

（1）本地知识及经验。大多数网络所都是由本土会计师在本地成立的会计师事务所，拥有充足的本地知识及经验，能够有效地在本土进行各种服务；

（2）法律许可。如前所述，世界上大多数国家都对境外会计师事务所在本土提供法定审计服务有各项管理措施。由于网络所是由本土会计师按照当地法律成立的会计师事务所，能够满足当地法律的各种限制性要求；

（3）规模效应。网络所通过资源共享，达到规模效应的目的。共享的资源通常包括员工培训、信息系统、质量标准、道德标准、专家支持等等；

（4）品牌效应。网络所最大的优势在于享有共同品牌并能够利用品牌的声誉吸引客户；

（5）增加影响力。当网络所在世界范围内形成一定的规模时，即可能对行业产生重要影响，这包括对会计、审计准则的解释及运用；对行业职业道德的规范等等；

（6）全球统一服务。网络所通过执行全球统一的操作流程及标准，能够为客户提供全球统一化的服务。这对于大型跨国企业来说是尤为重要的；

（7）人才培养。网络所能够为员工提供在各网络所直接互换及学习的机会，便利的人才交流安排利于培养国际化人才以提高整体服务水平；

（8）特殊专家培养。网络所能够集中更多的资源来培养专业人才，例如会计及审计行业专家、精算专家、税务专家、评估专家、计算机系统专家等等，以供各网络所共享；

（9）全球专业技能。随着国际贸易的发展，审计师通常需要对其客户对外贸易涉及的国家/地区的相关法律、税法等进行了解。网络所为审计师获取这些知识及信息提供了便捷的途径。

网络所是由在法律上独立的会计师事务所组成的，主权分散。因此如果管理不善，也易出现一定的弊端：

（1）不易统一管理。由于主权的分散，各网络所在法律上不存在依附关系，这也就给网络所的统一管理带来了困难；

（2）难以建立统一的质量标准。同样由于网络所主权分散并可能缺乏统一管理，这样很难制定统一的质量标准并确保所有的网络成员所都执行统一的质量标准；

（3）品牌声誉管理。如果没有统一的质量标准及严格的内部控制措施来维护这一标准，网络所就无法建立起一个高质量品牌的形象，也就无法打造品牌声誉。而且如果网络所中的个别会计师事务所出现质量问题，就会影响整个网络所的品牌声誉。美国“安然”事件后全球安达信网络的崩塌即是一个例子。

克服以上网络所弊端的方法就是要在网络所之间建立起严格的内部控制机制，确保各网络所按照统一的质量标准进行商业操作，维护品牌声誉。



## 二、中国实践

中国财政部一直以来对法定审计服务的监管给予高度重视，注重借鉴国外经验并结合中国国情进行改革和创新。中国政府对于境外事务所在中国开展审计业务也有各种相关政策。与其他国家类似，境外会计师事务所不能以在中国成立分所或者子公司的形式，从事审计业务。从 1992 年起，“四大”开始陆续进入中国。中国最初允许这些“外资所”以中外合作的方式在中国设立会计师事务所并提供法定审计服务。至 2012 年，“四大”中外合作会计师事务所的合作期限陆续到期，财政部也相应出台了《中外合作会计师事务所本土化转制方案》，要求“四大”进行本土化转制。目前，“四大”已经全部完成了特殊普通合伙制转制并且正在按照中外合作会计师事务所本土化转制方案中“过渡期”的要求将合伙人的比例进行调整。过渡期截止到 2017 年底，届时，“四大”大多数合伙人均须拥有中国注册会计师资格并符合财政部《会计师事务所审批和监督暂行办法》的要求。同时，特殊普通合伙制会计师事务所的首席合伙人必须有中国国籍。

以上要求在实质上与除美国以外的其他大多数国家做法一致，是为了保护审计市场的稳定和秩序，确保审计师拥有中国审计经验及相关的知识技能。

境外会计师事务所可以通过临时执行审计业务的方式在中国临时开展业务。临时执业是指境外会计师事务所接受外国委托方的委托，对中国内地设立的子公司或其他相关机构临时执行审计业务。为防范在跨境审计服务中，境外会计师事务所违规入境执业及由此可能产生的权责问题，对于境外会计师事务所临时入境开展审计业务和与中国公司境外上市有关的跨境审计服务，财政部也作出了相关具体规定。

对于审计工作底稿共享的问题，对于属于临时执业范畴的，中国政府允许中国子公司审计师为集团审计目的向海外母公司审计师提供其审计工作底稿信息，以满足集团审计要求。中国财政部及证监会近期也与 PCAOB 就跨境监管问题开展进一步磋商，探索可行的监管合作模式。

中国的以上各项监管要求体现了对境外会计师事务所在中国执业进行全面的管理和监督，对于法定审计的管控也体现了中国的国家主权管理，在本质上与国际惯例一致。



## 三、有关建议

根据以上的分析，各国对于法定审计服务都进行了严格监管，会计师事务所很难直接跨境到外国市场提供法定审计服务，也无法通过成立海外分/子公司而在海外市场拓展其法定审计业务。这样，中国注册会计师事务所要想做大做强，扩展海外业务，就应遵循国际注册会计师行业惯例，按照国外监管要求，在海外市场设立网络所，以便拓展海外业务。

1. 拓展国际网络所的契机

成立海外网络所并不是盲目的。会计师事务所应该根据自身能力及商业机会有计划地进行海外扩张。随着越来越多的中国公司向海外并购，发展海外业务，服务这些中国公司的会计师事务所可以随着这些中国公司一步一步进入海外市场。这样就保证了会计师事务所初次进入海外已经拥有了客户，并且可以逐步在当地发展其他客户。换言之，中国企业和资本“走出去”的重点地区，包括正在兴起的“一带一路”，都将是中国会计师事务所构建国际网络的重点地区。

2. 维护品牌声誉

网络所最大的“资产”便是它的品牌声誉。通过这种品牌声誉，网络所才能够在海外市场上赢得客户，拓展业务。同时网络所通过提供高品质的服务，进一步维护其品牌声誉并扩大品牌影响力。所以网络所成功的关键是保证一贯的高水平服务质量。会计师事务所首先要提高其自身的服务质量，建立客户信誉度，打造良好的品牌声誉，这样才能够为其海外网络所发展业务打造基础。要保证所有网络所都能够按照同样的标准提供服务，会计师事务所网络所应该制定统一的质量标准体系，包括服务指南、员工培训、操作流程、内部控制系统、职业道德标准等等。“四大”会计师事务所内部均制定了统一的质量标准体系，其全球成员所必须遵守。这些质量标准体系可能比外部法律法规要求更加严格，以此来保证“四大”全球统一的服务质量。

3. 保证服务质量

为了保证整个网络的服务质量，会计师事务所需要建立严格的内部质量检查制度，以保证其统一的服务品质并进一步维护品牌声誉。通常这种质量检查在成员所之间定期进行，每个提供外部服务的网络所合伙人在 3 ~5 年内都会被抽查一次。质量检查依照网络所内部统一的质量标准要求进行。并且网络成员所内部也制定统一的标准对存在质量问题的合伙人进行处罚。这些措施能够有效的保证网络所成员按照统一的标准提供服务，进而维护品牌声誉。

本书将在下面章节进一步讨论了如何提升会计服务的竞争力。注册会计师事务所只有在提高自身竞争力的前提下才能够进行海外扩张，有效地与海外的会计师事务所进行竞争，在国外市场上占有一席之地。

# 第三章 会计服务市场开放负面清单管理模式



负面清单是指一系列不被允许的活动的清单，列明了企业不能投资的领域和产业。那些没有被包含在负面清单里的活动就是“允许的活动”或外资享有国民待遇的事项。以负面清单为基础的管理模型遵循“法无禁止即可为”的原则。而“正面清单”是指被允许的活动的清单，与正面清单相反，那些没有被包含在正面清单中的活动就是“禁止的活动”。负面清单概念首先被用在北美自由贸易谈判中，以美国为首的北美各国同意除个别单独讨论的领域以外，在各自国家全面放开自由贸易，取消贸易壁垒。在以负面清单模式为基础的自由贸易谈判中，市场开放和市场准入是谈判各方的核心目的。现在，越来越多的国家开始将负面清单概念用于双边贸易协定和控制外商投资当中。包括会计审计专业服务在内的服务业中，例如法定审计服务，也开始使用负面清单方法进行双边服务协定谈判。本章主要讨论负面清单能否被有效地使用在注册会计师行业国际服务贸易协定当中以及这种服务贸易协定中常见的“负面清单”条款。

## 一、国际经验

从很多方面来讲，会计很可能是这个世界上最国际化的专业领域之一。商业的全球化促进了会计服务在全球范围的合作。随着跨国公司的全球化发展，大型的会计师事务所也必须放眼全球以提供全面的服务。复杂的商业交易（包括国际并购及扩张），为在国际证券市场上市准备的财务报表以及纳税申报资料都增加对高质量并满足多重监管要求的会计专业服务的需求，以确保商业交易能够平稳高效地推进。这样，对会计专业服务领域的市场开放需求相比其他服务领域就显得更为强烈。实际上，世界上已经有很多国家开始使用负面清单方法来进行贸易协定，一些国家也开始参照负面清单的概念对会计及审计专业服务领域作出了相关规定。

根据调查，世界上在会计审计服务领域较有代表性的负面清单应当属于香港与欧盟部分国家在自由贸易协定中使用的负面清单。表 2 总结了冰岛、瑞士及挪威在与香港签署的自由贸易协定中对会计审计服务领域的保留性限制措施：

**表 2　　针对会计审计服务领域的保留性限制措施**

| 国家 | 保留性限制措施 |
| --- | --- |
| 冰岛 | 提供审计服务的专业人士必须在冰岛居住或者是其他欧洲经济体或欧洲自由贸易体成员国或法罗群岛的公民 |
| | 必须拥有经相关注册会计师公会批准的与会计审计相关的硕士学位，并且通过特殊考试 |
| | 会计师事务所多数投票权必须由欧洲经济体或欧洲自由贸易体成员国或者法罗群岛认证的会计师或者会计师事务所持有 |
| | 审计服务必须由经认可的注册会计师及会计师事务所提供，冰岛经济事务部会发布拥有在冰岛执业许可的审计师及会计师事务所的清单，审计服务必须由清单中的审计师及事务所提供 |
| 瑞士 | 会计师事务所中至少有一名合伙人在瑞士居住或者在瑞士拥有注册的办公地址 |
| | 外国文凭只有经过认证与瑞士学历等同并且瑞士与取得文凭的国家签有互认协议的时候方可生效。而且审计师必须掌握一种瑞士官方语言 |
| 挪威 | 只有在挪威登记注册的会计师能够在挪威提供审计服务 |
| | 会计师事务所必须是在挪威成立的公共有限责任公司，私人有限责任公司或者普通合伙公司 |
| | 会计师事务所必须在挪威拥有营业地点。其经理人必须是挪威注册会计师 |
| | 审计报告必须以挪威语言出具 |
| | 注册会计师必须在挪威永久居住，并且在过去 5 年中至少 2 年在挪威执业 |

在美国与韩国的自由贸易协定中，双方同意成立一个由双方代表组成的“专业服务工作小组”，协助进行以下与专业服务相关的事项（包括审计服务在内）：①提供双方与专业服务领域有关的准则信息及取得相关专业服务资格及证书的要素信息；②开发双方能够共同使用的准则及通用的专业服务资格要求，并就双方资历互认提供建议。

调查研究显示，对于外商投资领域的管控及双边服务协定的谈判始于正面清单。正面清单就那些谈判涉及的领域作出承诺，对于那些没有涉及的领域则没有任何承诺。正面清单列举出那些被允许的领域或开放措施，没有被列举的则是不被允许的。由于商业活动的复杂及多样性，要想列举所有商业活动领域或者将某个特定商业活动领域内的所有开放措施全部一一列举既有难度又效率低下。更重要的是，在正面清单方法下，当一个新兴活动出现的时候，这个活动就自动被排除在市场准入之外，直到通过双边谈判，将这个新兴活动被特别纳入正面清单当中。正面清单模式很难适应现代商业活动复杂多变的特性和经济全球化下贸易自由化的快速发展需求。各国监管者需要寻求一个能够提高双边贸易及服务谈判有效性的方法来刺激本国经济发展。这样负面清单法就应运而生了，它能够提高贸易壁垒的透明度及增进市场开放的谈判效率。

统计数据表明，在使用负面清单方法的国家/地区，出口服务贸易被大大加强了。例如，在北美自由贸易协定下，北美洲成为世界上最大的自由贸易区域，目前涵盖了4.5亿人口，每年生产并提供17万亿美元产品及服务。从这个自由贸易协定签订之日起，美国和其他协定国之间的贸易数据得到了大幅增长。截至2012年，美国出口到北美贸易协定国的非公共部门商业服务达到了886亿美元，相比2011年增长了5.4%，相比2002年增长了109%，相比1993年（在北美自由贸易协定签署之前）增长了223%。2012年美国从北美贸易协定国进口的非公共部门商业服务达到了449亿美元，相比2011年增长了6.1%，相比2002年增长了52%，相比1993年（在北美自由贸易协定签署之前）增长了171%。

台湾地区于1988年宣布了针对外商直接投资的负面清单政策。在这个政策下，除清单上列明的领域以外，外商投资可以自由的在其他全部领域进行。在这一政策刺激下，1989年台湾外商直接投资达到了24.18亿美元，将近1988年的六倍。

使用负面清单的一个潜在问题是对于新兴商业活动没有任何限制。由于在双边谈判中无法预测未来将可能产生的全部商业行为，在负面清单方法下，这些新兴商业行为就可能是不受任何限制的。这就要求监管者对新兴商业行为进行密切关注，针对那些需要受到限制的行为及时更新负面清单。

各国的世贸组织承诺表也提供了部分限制性措施信息。对此进行分析，有助于各国在市场开放磋商谈判中找到彼此的利益关切点，制定更高水平的负面清单。

表 3 对世界主要国家在世界贸易组织的承诺中针对会计审计专业服务领域的一些限制作出了总结：

表 3　针对会计审计专业服务领域的限制性措施

| 国家/地区 | 限制性措施 |
|---|---|
| 澳大利亚 | 只有自然人能够注册成为提供审计或者清算服务的专业人士。事务所中至少一名权益合伙人必须是澳大利亚居民 |
| 日本 | 审计服务必须由自然人通过会计师事务所提供，会计师事务所必须在日本拥有营业地点。会计师事务所按照日本法律规定必须拥有 5 个或以上合伙人，必须全部都是日本注册会计师 |
| 马来西亚 | 必须由在马来西亚登记注册的合伙公司或者马来西亚公司提供服务，其中外方投资占比不得超过 30%。审计师必须在马来西亚登记注册拥有执业许可，并且必须是马来西亚居民。取得审计资格的考试语言为英语 |
| 新加坡 | 公共会计师必须是新加坡居民，或者会计师事务所中至少一名合伙人必须是新加坡居民 |
| 中国香港 | 法定审计必须由取得香港注册会计师资格的个人通过个人独资事务所或者合伙制事务所提供 |

## 二、中国实践

中国政府在近年开始对于特定区域使用负面清单方法进行双边服务贸易管理。

对负面清单模式的运用体现在对内和对外两个方面。对内主要是运用在国内自由贸易试验区的政策措施管理。2015 年 4 月，国务院公布了上海、天津、广东、福建四个自贸区的负面清单。会计审计领域为“担任特殊普通合伙会计师事务所首席合伙人（或履行最高管理职责的其他职务），须具有中国国籍。对外主要体现在与港澳的双边服务贸易自由化协定中。2014 年 12 月，内地与港澳分别签署了《内地与香港（澳门〈关于建立更紧密经贸关系的安排〉关于内地在广东与香港（澳门）基本实现服务贸易自由化的协议》，其中会计审计服务领域的负面清单为：“取得中国注册会计师资格的香港/澳门居民可在广东省担任合伙制会计师事务所合伙人，会计师事务所的控制权需由内地居民持有；

担任合伙人的香港/澳门居民需每年在内地居住且在该会计师事务所执业 180 天以上；担任合伙人的香港/澳门居民应按规定投保职业责任保险。”

此外中国监管机构也在考虑进一步加强负面清单在其他双边投资协定中的使用，如中美双边投资协定。

以上负面清单显示了中国政府开放会计服务领域的决心与态度。

## 三、有关建议

负面清单方法可以通过增强自由贸易及对外国人实行“国民待遇”来增进双边服务协议谈判的有效性。这对于会计审计服务行业是尤其重要的。随着越来越多的公司向国外发展业务，会计审计专业服务也需要在全世界范围内放开。中国政府应该鼓励在与其他国家/地区的服务贸易协定中使用负面清单的方法实现更高水平的开放，从而增强在注册会计师专业服务领域的全球合作。



正如前文所述，使用负面清单的一个潜在问题是对于新兴商业行为的管控。由于会计审计专业服务在中国是一个新兴产业，而这种专业服务，尤其是审计服务是一个需要高度监管的领域，如果监管者没有能够及时发现需要被限制的新兴商业行为或没有能够及时更新负面清单，这可能会导致负面清单被商业滥用的现象。中国的监管者需要密切关注在会计审计专业服务领域的新兴商业行为及其他国家/地区监管者的管控措施，以在必要的情况下，及时对新兴商业活动制定相关管控政策并且更新负面清单，以达到对会计专业服务领域的治理需要。另外，负面清单需要清晰易懂，并且与其他监管法律法规保持一致，这样才能够避免产生歧义。

本书分析了各国对于境外人士及境外会计师事务所在本国执业的管理及限制并且提出了与中国监管有关的建议。这些政策措施都应该反映在双边协定的负面清单当中。由于法定审计是一个国家主权管理的体现，对于一个国家的经济来说具有至关重要的影响，各国政府也都在这一领域制定了严格的管控措施。因此针对于会计审计专业服务领域的负面清单应该明确反映以上管控措施，以确保相关政策的一致性。

对比研究分析可以发现，中国会计审计领域的负面清单是极少的，开放程度在全球首屈一指，这与当初中国加入 WTO 的承诺密切相关。认真总结正反两方面的经验，对于中国既扩大开放又有效维护国家利益是十分必要的。

# 第四章　注册会计师行业监管法规

## 一、国际经验



### （一）注册会计师行业现行的监管法规和规定介绍

前文中提到中国会计服务的开放及因此带来的注册会计师行业的全球化都呈现出必然的趋势，中国注册会计师行业需要持续不断地发展壮大，提升竞争能力，为这一行业向国际发展奠定坚实的基础。同时，我们也注意到开放可能带来的风险和挑战。这就要求我们对注册会计师行业实施严格的监督。

注册会计师行业提供的审计服务，其透明度和担负的责任对一个国家资本市场和整体经济都至关重要，因此，世界各国对注册会计师行业都进行了严格的监管。本书探讨的正是对注册会计师提供审计服务方面现行的监管法规和规定。我们的研究主要围绕美国（主要为四个代表州—纽约、伊利诺伊、加利福尼亚和德克萨斯）、英国、澳大利亚、加拿大、新加坡和香港这几个国家/地区展开，研究重点集中在四项监管要素上：对注册会计师个人和会计师事务所的资格认证/注册要求、会计师事务所的法律形式、注册会计师服务的质量控制和检查以及对注册会计师个人和会计师事务所的纪律处罚。

1. 注册会计师/会计师事务所资格认证/注册要求

在本项目研究的所有国家/地区，为确保从事审计服务的个人和事务所具有恰当的执业资格，开展审计业务都需要进行资格认证或注册，而这些认证/注册要求可分为对注册会计师个人的要求和对会计师事务所的要求两种。

（1）对注册会计师个人的要求。如前文中提到的，在很多国家/地区，成为会计职业组织的会员并不等同于获得法定审计师资格（此处的法定审计师是指审计项目的负责人，其将代表事务所签署审计意见）。在这些国家/地区，法定审计师的资格认证通常通过授予执业资格或者要求在公认的监管机构注册这两种形式来实现。具体来说，在英国和香港，注册会计师需要获得额外的执业资格（Practicing Certificate，PC）才可以签署法定审计意见；澳大利亚则要求注册会计师在监管机构注册成为公司法定审计师（Registered Company Auditor，RCA）。不论哪种形式，注册会计师获取此类法定审计师资格都需要满足一些额外的条件（具体条件参见之前的报告），并经过监管机构的评估和认可，而拥有执业资格或注册成为法定审计师的注册会计师个人都须接受监管机构的监督。除此之外，所有的注册会计师都需要获得足够的后续职业教育（Continuous Professional Education，CPE）以保证其专业资格的持续有效性。



（2）对会计师事务所的要求。关于注册成立会计师事务所的要求，各国的做法不一。具体来说，在美国，所有为美国上市公司提供审计服务的会计师事务所（包括美国当地的事务所和外国的事务所）都需要在公众公司会计监督委员会（Public Company Accounting Oversight Board，PCAOB）登记注册。目前，美国的绝大多数会计师事务所都已在 PCAOB 注册，并接受 PCAOB 的定期检查。此外，在某些州（如德克萨斯和伊利诺伊），根据州立法，事务所在本州从事会计服务（特别是鉴证类服务）或将事务所命名为“CPA”事务所，需要从该州的监管机构取得相关的营业执照。同样地，在英国，根据《2006 年公司法》第 1212 条的规定，会计师事务所需要在公认的监管机构（Recognised Supervisory Body，RSB）进行注册，成为注册的法定审计单位（Registered Auditor），方可提供法定审计服务。目前，英国共有 5 家这样的监管机构，均为公认的会计职业组织，如英格兰及威尔士特许会计师协会（Institute of Chartered Accountants in England and Wales，ICAEW）。亚洲市场方面，新加坡具有与英国类似的注册要求，而香港则要求事务所从香港会计师公会（HKICPA）取得审计执照，才可开展法定审计服务。这些负责会计师事务所注册的监管机构会评估事务所是否满足提供审计服务的条件，包括拥有的资格情况、专业知识和能力、声誉等等。各监管机构的具体要求可能存在差异，但通常要求绝大多数事务所主管人员（一般为合伙人和总监）具备专业资格。例如，英国要求注册成为法定审计师的会计师事务所满足其注册机构的一系列规定，这些规定通常要求绝大多数事务所主管人员具备该机构的会员资格。此外，会计师事务所经过注册或认证后就接受注册机构的持续监督和检查。

关于会计师事务所的法律形式，大部分国家/地区允许会计师事务所采取不同的法律形式，事务所可以是合伙、独资或者公司制。实践中，合伙制是最常见的法律形式，美国、英国和新加坡还进一步允许会计师事务所设立为有限责任合伙制，类似于中国的特殊普通合伙制。

2. 对注册会计师/会计师事务所服务的质量控制/检查

对注册会计师行业实施有效监管是确保和提升审计质量的重要举措，同时也能够促进完善财务报表体系，提高市场投资者信心。在我们研究的国家/地区，并不存在一套统一的监管模式，各国/地区的监管者都需要结合当地的市场特性、法律环境等等因地制宜，制定最适合本国/地区的监管体系。然而，我们也注意到，各个国家/地区的监管模式中存在一些共同的元素，这些元素也正是“独立审计监管机构国际论坛”（International Forum of Independent Audit Regulators, IFIAR）制定的“审计监管核心原则”（Core Principles of Audit Oversight, IFIAR Principles）所提倡的。IFIAR是一个独立的国际组织，它将世界各地的独立审计监管机构聚集在一起，讨论研究有关审计监管的相关事宜。



IFIAR的这套核心原则在国际上被普遍认可，其涵盖独立审计监管体系的三个方面，即监管机构的组织结构、经营管理和检查活动，同时也针对注册会计师行业审计服务质量控制的常见问题，如独立性，提出了解决方案框架。在这一部分，我们就围绕这套原则在各国/地区的实践情况进行研究，研究结果帮助我们了解一系列可行的监管方案。

（1）关于组织结构的原则。

原则一：审计监管机构应服务于公众利益，其权利义务应在立法中进行明晰且客观的规定。

原则二：审计监管机构应保持独立性。

原则三：审计监管机构应透明且负责。

这三项原则讨论的是审计监管机构的权力与职责，以及对审计监管机构的独立性、透明度和责任要求，详细分析如下：

①权力与职责。我们注意到，IFIAR核心原则所指的审计监管是针对公众利益实体（Public Interest Entities, PIEs）的审计工作的监管，然而，各个国家/地区对公众利益实体的定义不尽相同，同时由于受到成本和资源调配的制约，

审计监管机构的监管范围也有所差别。有些国家/地区重点监管对上市公司的审计，有些国家的监管则覆盖更广泛的范围，其中，美国和英国的做法比较典型。美国对上市公司和证券交易公司有法定审计要求，为这些公司提供审计服务的会计师事务所则须在 PCAOB 登记注册，接受 PCAOB 的监管。而在英国，法定审计要求覆盖的范围较美国更为广泛，除上市公司外，私营企业、慈善机构、退休基金、保险公司、银行及投资基金等等都需要进行法定审计。如前文提到的，在英国这些公司的审计由在公认的监管机构注册的“法定审计师”来完成，而英国的财务报表委员会（Financial Reporting Council，FRC）统一监管法定审计师。各国/地区审计监管机构的具体的职责范围在各国/地区的立法中都有明确的规定，同时立法也赋予审计监管机构实施监管必需的权力，使得监管机构能够通过检查和处罚等方式确保会计师事务所遵守监管机构对法定审计师的规定以及审计准则、独立性准则和其他相关职业准则的要求。



②独立性。IFIAR 的核心原则指出，审计监管机构应保持独立运营，履行职责和行使权力不受政治上的干涉和商业利益的影响，这是设置审计监管机构组织结构应遵守的一项根本原则，但 IFIAR 并未限制组织结构的具体形式。举例来说，美国国会依法单独设立了 PCAOB 这一非营利组织，负责审计监管工作。PCAOB 共有 5 名委员，其中 1 名是主席，由美国证券交易委员会（Securities and Exchange Commission，SEC）任命，一并征询财政部部长和联邦储备委员会主席的意见，5 名成员中须有 2 名注册会计师。此外，IFIAR 核心原则的独立性要求还涉及监管机构的资金来源，原则指出：“审计监管机构应拥有稳定且充足的资金来源，来保证监管活动的实施，同时该资金来源不受注册会计师或会计师事务所的影响。”在我们研究的国家/地区，审计监管机构的资金来源形式多样，主要包括中央政府资助（如澳大利亚）、向被检查的会计师事务所收费（如新加坡）、向被审计的公司征收年费或其他费用（如美国、加拿大）、向会计职业组织及被审计公司征收税费（如英国）。

③透明度及责任。为保持透明度和履行责任，各个国家/地区的审计监管机构都会针对其年度监管情况和主要发现进行某种形式的报告。各地有关检查结果的报告在报告的详细程度和形式方面存在差异。有些国家/地区对检查结果作整体情况报告（如澳大利亚、加拿大、新加坡），此类报告通常包括针对整体注册会计师行业的主要检查发现、监管机构的主要活动、采用的监管方法等等。其他一些国家/地区在针对整体情况报告的基础上，还会针对个别会计师事务所

作出检查情况报告（如英国、美国）。具体地，在美国，PCAOB 向每一个被检查的事务所出具书面的检查报告。而同样地，在英国，FRC 对大型的事务所出具单独的检查报告，对其他为上市公司提供审计服务的小型事务所出具联合检查报告。

（2）有关经营管理的原则。

**原则四**：审计监管机构应具备全面的监管力度。

**原则五**：审计监管机构应具备充足的监管人力资源，同时确保监管人员独立于注册会计师行业，并具备恰当的胜任能力。

**原则六**：审计监管机构应保持客观性，避免利益冲突，并具备恰当的保密安排。

**原则七**：审计监管机构之间及审计监管机构与相关的第三方之间应具备恰当的合作安排。

这四项原则针对审计监管机构的运营管理方面，主要包括三个要素：监管力度；监管人员的独立性、胜任能力、客观性及保密安排；监管合作。

①监管力度。监管力度通常通过纪律处罚的权力来保证，足够的监管力度应保证检查发现的问题能够得到妥善解决。在我们研究的国家/地区，我们注意到由监管机构执行纪律处罚或者由监管机构以外的机构负责纪律处罚都是可行的选择。举例来说，在澳大利亚和新加坡，负责纪律处罚的组织独立于监管机构。具体地，在澳大利亚，依据《2001 年公司法案》的规定，独立于澳大利亚证券和投资委员会（Australian Securities and Investments Commission，ASIC）的"公司审计师及清算人纪律惩戒委员会"（Companies Auditors and Liquidators Disciplinary Board，CALDB）负责对注册的公司审计师的违规情况作出裁决，实施处罚决定，而违规情况则是由 ASIC 向 CALDB 通报。换言之，即检查权与处罚权相分离。但在其他的一些国家/地区，比如加拿大、英国和美国，纪律处罚的权力就掌握在审计监管机构自己手中。当然，不管纪律处罚的机制建立在监管机构内部还是外部，该机制下通常建立有一个检举的渠道，鼓励相关人员向监管机构举报发现的违法行为。

②独立性、客观性、胜任能力及保密安排。在我们研究的国家/地区，各地的监管机构都为监管人员制定了一套职业道德和行为规范，用来规避利益冲突、强化客观公正及确保保密性。此外，为保证独立性，有些国家的监管机构要求监管人员与会计师事务所保持独立的关系。具体来说，在新加坡，如果监管人

员曾经供职于某个会计师事务所，该人员不允许参加该事务所的检查。类似地，在美国，PCAOB 的 5 名委员及其雇员不能受雇于任何一家会计师事务所或是与事务所存在关联关系，同时，PCAOB 的监管活动不能受到任何会计职业组织的任何形式的控制。为保证监管人员具备评估会计师事务所内部控制系统的胜任能力，审计监管机构需向监管人员提供恰当的职业培训，确保其具备或取得充足的审计和财务报表相关的经验。举例来说，英国要求其审计监管人员具备至少 7 年的实践经验（该经验须是获得相关专业资格后取得的）、熟练掌握国际财务报表准则（IFRS）、拥有英国上市公司或其他重要实体的审计经验，并有信心和能力在检查过程中质询事务所的资深合伙人。

③监管合作。随着注册会计师行业和会计服务的全球化进程，越来越多的会计师事务所在提供跨境服务时需要接受外国监管机构的监管。那么，各国监管机构之间需要建立有效的跨境监管合作机制，从而保护国际资本市场上投资者的利益。目前已存在多种监管合作形式，如双边协议、信息交换谅解备忘录、相互协助、联合检查，等等，针对跨境监管合作，我们将在后面的报告中进行详细的论述。除跨境监管合作外，境内的不同监管者之间（如审计监管机构与证券监管机构）的合作也十分重要。例如，澳大利亚的“财务报告委员会”由 18 位分别来自不同监管机构的成员组成，这些机构包括澳大利亚财政部、ASIC、澳大利亚证券交易所，成立该委员会的目的就是协调各监管机构之间的信息交流与合作，建立恰当的沟通渠道，优化资源调配，避免重复检查。

第二部分

（3）有关检查活动的原则。

原则八：审计监管机构应至少对为公众利益实体提供审计服务的会计师事务所实施定期检查。

原则九：审计监管机构应确保检查活动以风险为导向。

原则十：审计监管机构应制定有效的检查程序，确保检查同时涵盖会计师事务所整体及个别审计项目。

原则十一：审计监管机构应建立有效机制，向会计师事务所报告检查结果，并确保其完成相应整改。

检查活动是审计监管体系中最重要的组成部分，IFIAR 原则指出了检查活动的四项关键要素，分别为检查频率、风险导向、同时涵盖事务所整体及个别审计项目的检查方案以及检查结果报告。

①检查频率。检查频率的设定是风险与资源平衡的结果。在我们研究的国

家/地区，审计监管机构设定的检查频率大约为每年一次至每6年一次不等，我们也注意到在绝大多数国家/地区，检查频率也因事务所的规模和市场份额大小而异。基本上，一个会计师事务所的审计客户（尤其是公众利益公司）越多，该事务所接受的检查越为频繁。具体而言，在澳大利亚，前四大事务所（即“四大”会计师事务所）每18个月被检查一次；接下来10家事务所每2年半被检查一次，这10家事务所约审计5%的上市公司；剩余的约72家小型事务所被检查的频率较低（平均约3年一次）。同样地，在加拿大，审计100家以上上市公司的事务所每年被检查一次；上市审计客户在50～99家的事务所每2年至少被检查一次；上市审计客户为50家以下的事务所每3年至少被检查一次。在美国，PCAOB对审计100家以上上市公司的事务所每年检查一次，对审计100家以下上市企业的事务所则每3年检查一次，该频率同时适用于为美国上市公司提供审计服务的境外事务所与美国当地的事务所。欧洲市场方面，欧盟要求其成员国对为公众利益实体提供审计服务的事务所至少每3年检查一次，对其他提供法定审计服务的事务所至少每6年检查一次。根据这一要求，欧盟各成员国分别设立了各自的检查频率。例如英国，“四大”会计师事务所每年被检查一次；其他审计上市公司的主要事务所每3年被检查一次；其他事务所根据其规模每6年至少被检查一次。亚洲市场方面，新加坡对审计公众利益公司的事务所每两年检查一次，对其他事务所每4年检查一次。在香港，“四大”会计师事务所每年被检查一次；对其他审计大量上市公司的事务所每3年进行一次全面检查，并在3年期间内进行一次中期检查；其余审计上市公司的事务所每3年至少被检查一次；对剩余事务所依据其风险情况随机抽取进行检查。



②风险导向。检查方案以风险为导向是IFIAR原则推崇的一个核心理念，上文介绍的各国/地区检查频率的制定也恰恰体现了这一理念。除此之外，在绝大多数国家/地区，风险导向的理念贯穿整个检查过程，比如选择检查的审计项目、确定检查重点等等。美国PCAOB的检查方案就是一个“风险导向”的典型案例。在美国，PCAOB对具体审计项目的检查不是随机抽取，也不是指针对部分会计师事务所选取审计项目检查，而是通过对一系列风险因素的分析，选取可能存在困难和复杂问题的审计项目进行检查。这些风险因素既与被审计公司相关，比如公司的性质（比如所处行业和市值）、可能遇到的审计问题以及公司是否在新兴市场拥有重大经营等；也与承接审计的事务所相关，比如事务所主要上市审计客户的类型和范围、以前年度的检查结果、事务所内部风险控

制和检查的发现等。此外，检查人员还会考虑负责审计项目的合伙人以往被检查的情况。另外一点值得指出的是，总体上 PCAOB 的检查重点集中在具有最大资本市值的公司的审计项目上。类似美国的做法在其他国家/地区也屡见不鲜，比如澳大利亚、加拿大、英国、新加坡和香港，其监管机构对审计项目和检查重点的选择都基于对风险的评价，通过考虑各项风险因素，识别出高风险的行业、公司、事务所和审计项目合伙人等领域。

③同时涵盖事务所整体及个别审计项目的检查方案。在所有我们研究的国家/地区，审计监管机构的检查方案均同时涵盖事务所整体及个别审计项目。对事务所整体的检查主要针对事务所的内部质量控制体系，比如对合伙人的业绩考核、独立性政策、客户承接与续接程序、事务所内部检查程序等，此类检查通常包括访谈和检查内部文档等等。对个别审计项目的检查则是通过审阅审计工作底稿来实施。此类检查会根据对该项目的风险分析确定重点检查的审计领域，与审计意见相关的重大审计判断以及获取的审计证据的充分性、恰当性通常都是重中之重。此外，这两个层次的检查实际上是相辅相成的。一方面，对事务所内部质量控制体系的检查结果会影响监管人员对该所个别审计项目检查的选择，另一方面，如果监管人员在对某一具体审计项目检查时发现了过失，监管人员就会进一步调查这些过失是否是由于该事务所内部质量控制体系存在系统性漏洞造成的。



④检查结果报告。IFIAR 原则要求审计监管机构将检查过程中发现的事务所内部控制体系以及具体审计项目中存在的潜在问题或批评意见向事务所报告。在我们研究的国家/地区，这一要求均被有效地执行，但检查报告的公开化程度有所不同。绝大多数国家/地区并不公开针对单家事务所的检查报告，但可能定期公告整体审计市场的检查情况。举例来说，澳大利亚定期公告一份针对整体审计市场检查结果（包括主要观察结果、发现等）的报告，但对单家事务所的检查报告仅与被检查的事务所作一对一的沟通；英国每年对外出具公开年报，报告当年监管机构的主要活动和检查发现，而对单家事务所的检查报告，除大型事务所（如“四大”）的报告予以公开外，其他报告均不予以公开；加拿大对单家事务所的检查报告也不公开，除非事务所自报告日起 180 天内未能针对报告提出的问题和缺陷进行整改，此时监管机构可考虑将报告中的相关部分公开。与绝大多数国家/地区做法不同的是美国，在美国，PCAOB 对所有被检查的事务所出具单家检查报告，并刊登在 PCAOB 的网站上。但是，有关该事务所

内部控制体系的检查结果不包含在公开的报告内，除非该事务所自报告日起12个月内未能完成有效的整改。

3. 对注册会计师/会计师事务所的纪律处罚

如前文所述，保证监管和纪律处罚的力度对实施有效监管十分重要。在我们研究的国家/地区，我们注意到各地针对检查发现的违规行为均制定了各种处罚措施，常见的处罚措施包括取消法定审计资格、暂时或永久性地吊销执业资格或行业禁入、经济处罚、公开训诫或批评等等。有时，监管机构（如美国的PCAOB）还会要求事务所聘请独立的第三方对其某一个或几个审计项目进行检查并出具检查报告，或者请专人设计事务所内部管理政策以确保其符合行业要求。处罚的强度由监管机构依据相关法律规定和实际情况决定。总体上看，处罚强度与违规行为的严重程度和影响成正比。具体而言，以美国PCAOB网站上公告的处罚决定为例，通常事务所漏缴年费将被处以一定金额的罚款，但如果事务所未能遵守审计准则的规定执行审计工作，导致财务报表的重大错报未被发现，那么该审计项目的负责人（包括项目主管合伙人、关键合伙人、质量复核合伙人）就可能受到暂时停止执业的处罚。同时，如果监管机构发现该审计项目的问题也反映了事务所内部质量控制体系的漏洞（例如事务所在内部检查中未发现该问题），则事务所整体也可能受到一定的处罚，如被公开批评。

我们也注意到，各个国家/地区的纪律处罚有针对注册会计师个人的，也有针对会计师事务所的，具体对谁进行处罚取决于违规行为到底是由于负责具体审计项目的注册会计师个人的过失还是事务所的整体缺陷。仍以美国PCAOB的规定为例，PCAOB规定若注册会计师个人或者会计师事务所被查出存在违反PCAOB法规或其他相关职业准则的情况，PCAOB可对其分别或同时处以相应的惩罚。具体来说，如果注册会计师个人（审计项目负责人等）在执行审计程序、出具审计报告时有违规行为或是未妥善履行其职责，该注册会计师个人将会受到处罚；如果会计师事务所未能按照PCAOB规定的内部控制要求对其注册会计师个人实施合理的监督，事务所也将受到处罚。这里提到的合理监督是指事务所建立适当的内部质量控制体系，该体系符合相关规定，也能够合理预防或发现其注册会计师的违规行为。此外，我们也注意到，有些国家（如澳大利亚）较为注重对注册会计师个人的处罚，这主要是因为证明一个事务所的系统缺陷比证明单个审计项目的过失要困难得多，且耗时费力，因此处罚注册会计师个人要更有效率。

### （二）对注册会计师行业现行监管法规和规定的分析

基于以上研究，我们了解到世界各地都采取了各种措施对注册会计师行业实施有效监管，提升审计服务质量。接下来，我们针对以上了解到的各国监管情况来作进一步的分析和讨论，我们的分析将围绕以下几个方面展开：

1. 法定审计师①资格管理

尽管会计服务市场和注册会计师行业在全球化背景下不断开放、加速融合，但鉴于法定审计对当地经济的重要性，各国的法定审计市场仍然是被高度保护和严格监管的。正因如此，前文研究的法定审计师的资格认证/注册要求才应运而生，目的就是要确保参与法定审计的事务所和个人具备足够的专业知识、技能和经验。我们注意到，有的国家/地区对注册会计师个人有认证/注册要求，有的对会计师事务所有认证/注册要求，有的则对二者都有认证/注册要求。然而，我们也注意到，这些要求，不论是对事务所的还是对注册会计师个人的，实质上针对的都是审计项目的负责人，即事务所的合伙人或总监。这样做的好处是将有限的监管资源集中在对审计市场具有最重大影响的群体上，这样在保证监管有效性的同时也提高了监管效率。换言之，对合伙人、股东的监管是重中之重，抓住了这个“牛鼻子”，就抓住了审计质量控制的关键和要害。



2. 有效监管的特征

通过将各国/地区的审计监管实践对照 IFIAR 核心原则逐一对比分析，我们总结了有效监管的一些共性特征，这些特征包括但不限于：

（1）监管机构独立于会计职业组织；

（2）赋予监管机构的权力与其目标配比；

（3）监管机构保持足够的透明度，并能够参考会计职业组织及其他资本市场参与者的信息；

（4）监管机构拥有充足的监管人力资源，监管人员具备恰当的胜任能力；

（5）监管机构的资金来源充足且稳定；

（6）能够与国内外其他相关监管机构协同合作、信息互换；

（7）能够实施全面的检查，并保证处罚力度。

若能实现以上特征，具体的监管方式方法、监管机构的组织形式等可以因

---

① 法定审计师包括提供法定审计服务的会计师事务所及注册会计师个人。

地制宜，无需拘泥于某种特定模式。

3. 全面且统一的检查方案

由于检查是审计监管体系中最重要的部分，各国/地区都制定了一套全面的检查方案。这些方案通常全面而彻底，覆盖检查过程的方方面面，包括检查范围、检查频率、检查策略与方法、检查结果报告及后续跟踪等等。同时，我们还注意到，在我们研究的国家/地区，通常只有一个监管机构主管审计监管工作，行使监管权力。此外，政府对确保不同监管机构间进行合作与交流也作出了努力，通过建立有效的沟通渠道，各监管机构就可以协同彼此，互通信息，从而实现更好的资源配置，避免重复检查。

4. 风险导向的检查方式

尽管检查是审计监管体系中最重要的部分，但是，由于受到有限的监管资源的制约，监管机构无法实现对全体会计师事务所和注册会计师个人实施定期检查，同时全面检查也不是一种高效的方式。因此，在我们研究的国家/地区，监管机构都采用了“风险导向”的检查方式，通过对一系列风险因素进行评估，选取具有高风险特征的会计师事务所和审计项目进行检查，这些风险因素既包含与事务所相关的方面，比如其审计客户规模大小和以前年度检查结果，也包含与被审计公司相关的方面，比如其所处行业和财务状况的稳定程度。

5. 纪律处罚的重心

全面的检查之后，适当的纪律处罚是保证检查发现的问题和缺陷被妥善整改的有效手段。由于纪律处罚常常涉及争议和诉讼，监管机构应当考虑将处罚的重心放在注册会计师个人还是会计师事务所。现如今，一些会计师事务所的规模已经相当庞大（如“四大”），与这些大型的事务所打官司会非常耗时费力，同时也可能对整体审计市场产生重大不良影响。基于我们的研究，我们发现澳大利亚将处罚集中在对注册会计师个人的管理上，这一选择正是考虑到证明单个审计项目的缺失相比证明事务所整体的系统缺陷要容易的多，处罚个人将更为快捷有效。此外，这种做法也能够在处罚个别合伙人的同时保证事务所整体的正常运行。

## 二、中国实践

与其他国家/地区一样，中国的注册会计师行业受到广泛且高度的监管，中国的审计监管体系也被欧盟认可与欧盟的监管体系等效。为进一步分析中国在注册会计师行业监管方面的现状和面对的挑战，我们针对本书第一部分中提到的四项监管要素将中国与其他国家逐一比较分析。

### （一）注册会计师/会计师事务所资格认证/注册要求

中国目前针对注册会计师个人获取审计报告签字权没有额外的执业资格要求，但会计师事务所在中国开展法定审计服务，必须取得执业许可。此外，中国的法定审计报告需由两名注册会计师签署，合伙会计师事务所出具的审计报告，应当由一名对审计项目负最终复核责任的合伙人和一名负责该项目的注册会计师签名盖章；有限责任会计师事务所出具的审计报告，应当由会计师事务主任会计师或其授权的副主任会计师和一名负责该项目的注册会计师签名盖章。



### （二）会计师事务所法律形式

历史上，中国允许会计师事务所设立为公司制或合伙制。目前，根据有关规定，财政部鼓励大中型会计师事务所从有限责任公司形式转制为特殊普通合伙制形式，中国所有的证券资格会计师事务所已经完成了转制。转制的目的是从源头上强化注册会计师的执业责任约束，促使其增强风险意识，不断提升执业质量。

### （三）对注册会计师/会计师事务所服务的质量控制/检查

中国目前尚未加入 IFIAR，但是中国现行的审计监管体系在很多方面也体现出前文提到的有效监管的特征，比如监管机构的独立性、透明度、责任划分以及执行全面且以风险为导向的检查方案。然而，我们也注意到中国现行的检查方案也存在一些可以进步的空间。中国目前由财政部门（包括财政部和地方财政厅局）和中注协对事务所进行系统的定期检查，但除此之外，中国证监会对为中国上市公司提供审计的事务所进行延伸检查，同时，银监会、保监会、审计署在对其管辖的银行、保险公司、国有企业实施专项检查时也通常需要为这些企业提供审计服务的事务所配合检查。我们注意到，近几年，一些监管机关在避免重复检查方面作出了努力，如财政部、证监会、中注协经过协商，对具有证券期货业务资格的会计师事务所的检查调整为每三年一次，在同一年度内不重复检查，减轻了会计师事务所的负担。但是，由于各监管机关在各省都设有派出机构，地方监管机构针对驻地企业的检查通常会扩展到外部审计师，所以同一分所或同一审计业务在同一年有可能被不同的监管机构检查。此外，检查所涉及的方面可能重复，上述各类延伸检查的存在为这种重复创造了可能性。比如财政部、证监会、中注协对总所的检查都包含事务所的质量管理制度，同时地方监管机关对设立在当地的分所的检查也涵盖了事务所质量管理制度，但通常总所与各分所执行的质量管理制度是统一的。

### （四）对注册会计师/会计师事务所的纪律处罚

与其他国家/地区一样，中国也针对注册会计师个人和会计师事务所制定了一系列纪律处罚，比如罚款、暂停执业资格等等。我们注意到，中国目前有超过 8000 家会计师事务所（含分所），其中大量的事务所规模较小，通常仅由几名注册会计师组成，而另一部分事务所，虽然数量很少，但单家规模较大，全国范围内员工数以千计。在这样的情况下，若监管机构将纪律处罚集中在对事务所的管理上，就可能面临两项挑战。首先，由于在新设立事务所的控制上通常不会特别检查新设事务所合伙人曾供职的事务所是否受到过处罚，小型事务所的合伙人在事务所受到处罚后，可以通过关闭现有事务所并设立新所的形式继续执业，因此，对此类事务所实施暂停执业资格的处罚可能是无效的。其次，与大型事务所打官司，证明其系统缺陷难度大、耗时长、成本高，对此类事务所实施处罚效率低，效果差。



## 三、有关建议

基于上述研究和分析，我们对于注册会计师行业监管法规和规定有以下四点建议：

（1）针对审计师的检查，中国可以考虑将各部门和各级的监管机构的检查结合起来，形成一个统一的系统化的检查方案，以便有效地利用政府资源，避免重复检查。对各国审计监管机构的各项安排比照 IFIAR 原则逐一进行的分析可以帮助我们了解一系列可行的监管方案。

（2）中国可以考虑对事务所进行分类监管，由监管机关依据过往检查经验和监管实践，以事务所的规模、收入、质量控制考核结果、公共利益公司及其他被监管的客户的数量等为分类依据，对不同类别的事务所采取不同的监管措施。事务所的质量越高，对该所的监管力度与检查次数可以相应减少；反之，如果一家事务所质量下降，则降低其级别，加强对其监管力度。

（3）纪律处罚的重心应从事务所转向注册会计师个人。此建议基于三条考虑：①对于小型事务所，如果纪律处罚主要针对事务所，那么事务所的合伙人就可以选择关闭该事务所，再重新设立一个新所继续从业（除处罚个人外，该项风险还可以通过建立适当的注册会计师个人及事务所从业资格认证/注册要求体系来进行控制，通过认证注册过程将曾有不良行为记录的会计师及事务所剔除在外）；②对于大型事务所，鉴于声誉对其事务所至关重要，如果纪律处罚是针对事务所而不是个人，事务所就会聘请律师竭尽全力来维护自身声誉，这就将导致一个冗长且昂贵的诉讼过程；③证明大型事务所的质量控制系统缺陷比证明单个审计项目的缺陷更为耗时费力。因此，处罚负责单个审计项目的会计师个人要更为有效和快捷。将监管和纪律处罚集中在对会计师个人的管理上不失为一种更好的手段，而且这种做法的有效性在某些国家已经得到了验证，比如澳大利亚。



（4）中国审计监管机构有必要进一步提升胜任能力。对比国外监管机构，由其监管人员配置和能力、经验等可看出，只有监管机构处于更胜一筹的地位，才能推动监管工作取得实效。由于历史原因等多方面条件的制约，中国一些监管机构同会计师事务所相比仍存在本能欠缺，导致监管工作偏离执业质量这一核心而停留在其他次要层面；同时，也存在监管机构内部权责配置不当等问题，需要结合职能定位、胜任能力等加以调整完善。

# 第五章　会计师事务所强制轮换

自国际金融危机以来审计质量在很多国家/地区日益受到重视，也有更多的人针对审计轮换展开了大量研究。本书主要对全球各主要市场的审计强制轮换要求进行总结，以及分析强制轮换会计师事务所存在的问题。审计强制轮换有两种方法，一种是轮换签字审计师及主审计师，即“换人”；另外一种是轮换会计师事务所，即“换所”。由于轮换审计负责人的方法对会计师事务所及被审计公司干扰较小，同时能够避免由于审计客户与审计师过分熟悉而带来的对审计师独立性的顾虑，所以这种轮换审计负责人的方法已为大众广为接受并且多国监管机构也在使用这种方法对审计行业进行规范。而轮换会计师事务所的方法在市场上则存在较多争议。所以本书重点讨论会计师事务所轮换的问题。在以下篇幅中，如果没有明确指出，轮换是指轮换会计师事务所。



## 一、国际经验

### （一）轮换要求

目前，国际上大约有 30 个国家在实施不同形式的会计师事务所轮换，其中，中国强制要求某些特定公司轮换会计师事务所，是全球范围内实行强制轮换的最大市场。在意大利，所有的公司每九年必须选择更换会计师事务所。在法国，对于实行联合审计的公司，会计师事务所每次任期为 6 年，但是可以无限期续任。最近一段时期开始实行强制轮换要求的国家包括巴西、荷兰和土耳其。个别国家先前采取了对会计师事务所的强制轮换政策，但随后又废除了这个政策，这样的国家包括加拿大、捷克共和国、新加坡以及韩国。

表4总结了全球主要市场对于会计师事务所强制轮换的要求。根据这些信息，我们看到，尽管多年来会计师事务所轮换一直都是全球范围备受关注的重点话题，但是在成熟的经济体中只有少数监管者实施了强制轮换事务所的要求。

表4 会计师事务所强制轮换要求

| | 强制轮换 | 强制招标 | 没有要求 |
|---|---|---|---|
| 美国 | | | √ |
| 英国 | | √[①] | |
| 欧盟 | √ | | |
| 新加坡 | | | √ |
| 中国香港 | | | √ |
| 日本 | | | √ |
| 澳大利亚 | | | √ |
| 加拿大 | | | √ |
| 捷克 | | | √ |
| 韩国 | | | √ |
| 意大利 | √ | | |
| 巴西 | √ | | |
| 印度 | √ | | |
| 荷兰 | √[②] | | |
| 土耳其 | √ | | |
| | | | |
| 中国 | √ | | |



## （二）轮换范围

在存在强制轮换或招标的国家/地区，监管者通常关注的是那些公众利益实

① 英国目前要求上市公司按照财务报告委员会发表的企业治理守则进行招标。这个守则是按照“遵守或者解释”的原则进行的。上市公司如果不能遵守守则要求就需要在其年报中对此进行解释。英国竞争及市场管理局于2014年12月针对欧盟提出的强制轮换会计师事务所的要求发表征求意见稿，搜集各界对强制轮换的意见及建议。英国至今没有针对强制轮换出台新的法律法规。

② 由于国会需要进一步的审核，执行期限延迟到2016年1月1日（原为2013年1月1日）。

体。表 5 总结了在实行强制轮换的国家中，对轮换范围的要求：

表 5　　会计师事务所强制轮换范围

| | 所有公司执行强制轮换 | 个别公司执行强制轮换 |
|---|---|---|
| 英国 | | • FTSE350[①]公司<br>• 信贷机构<br>• 保险服务公司 |
| 欧盟 | | • 在欧盟成员国上市的公司<br>• 信贷机构（无论是否上市）<br>• 保险服务公司（无论是否上市） |
| 巴西 | | • 上市公司、银行及保险公司 |
| 印度 | √ | |
| 荷兰 | | • 在欧盟成员国上市的注册于荷兰的公司<br>• 在荷兰注册的银行，信贷机构以及保险服务公司<br>• 财政部指定的实体 |
| 土耳其 | √ | |
| 意大利 | √ | |
| | | |
| 中国 | | • 国有企业<br>• 金融机构 |

大多数针对强制轮换的研究和调查都是以平衡对公众利益实体的监管力度与他们的合规成本为目的的。如本书所述，每个国家都对其实行的监管要求有着各自的解释，对监管力度与合规成本之间的平衡有各自的理解，每个国家也都对公众利益实体有着不同的定义。

通常情况下，强制轮换的要求仅限于在相关国家/地区注册或者上市的公司。对于这些公司的子公司或者合营公司来说，除非他们自身满足强制轮换的要求，他们是不在监管范围内的。

## （三）现任会计师事务所是否可以参与轮换

在实行强制招标而不是强制轮换的国家，例如英国，现任审计师可以参与

① 在英国的上市公司中按照市场资本额排名前 350 的公司。

对下任审计师的招标。除现任审计师的参与以外，强制招标与强制轮换在其他方面的要求是基本一致的。

### （四）任期

在存在强制轮换或招标规定的国家/地区，轮换或招标期限规定一般为5～20年之间。表6总结了各国对于招标或者轮换期限的最长任期要求：

表6　　会计师事务所强制轮换期限

| | 最长任期 |
|---|---|
| 英国 | • 每10年进行重新招标<br>• 两年内转换为欧盟管制，见以下欧盟要求 |
| 欧盟 | • 10年后轮换<br>• 成员国可以允许最高20年的任期，前提是至少每10年进行重新招标<br>• 前任审计师重新聘用需经过4年冷却期 |
| 巴西 | • 上市每5年轮换，银行及保险公司每4年轮换<br>• 如果公司设立了审计委员会，可以延长至10年<br>• 3年冷却期 |
| 印度 | • 每10年轮换<br>• 5年冷却期 |
| 荷兰 | • 每8年轮换<br>• 2年冷却期，将按照欧盟规定修改为4年 |
| 土耳其 | • 7年后轮换<br>• 3年冷却期 |
| | |
| 中国 | • 一般每5年轮换<br>• 特定情况下可延长至10年，但签字会计师需要实行5年轮换 |

中国当前轮换期限的要求（通常为5年，仅在特定情形下能够延长）相比其他国家的任期偏短。

### （五）国际上对轮换的态度与争议

前面所总结的各国关于审计轮换及招标政策是经过了相当一段时间才形成的，国际金融危机也对这些政策的发展起到了推进作用。轮换的主要目的是为了保证审计质量，避免由于审计失败而引发资本市场动荡以及可能发生的经济危机。围绕着这一目的，国际市场上对轮换能否真正提高审计质量存在着众多争议。下面我们就支持与反对轮换的观点进行分析。

市场上支持轮换的理论认为，轮换能够保证审计师的独立性，从而提高审计质量，以下是对具体观点的分析：

1. 避免会计师事务所与客户过于亲密

强制轮换被认为能够防止由于审计师与客户长期合作而产生过于亲密的关系，从而提高审计师的独立性及客观性。

2. 降低审计师对客户的经济依赖

强制轮换被认为能够减少审计师对客户的经济依赖而增强审计师的独立性。由于需要与客户保持长期合作关系而带来的商业压力可能使审计师在执行审计工作中缺乏精准与独立[①]。

对于像“四大”这样的大型会计师事务所来说，由于他们有众多的客户，对单个客户经济依赖风险相对较低。对于中小型会计师事务所来说，对单一大客户的收费可能会占其收入的比例较高，这样就可能存在经济依赖问题。

3. 降低审计市场集中及系统风险

一些利益相关者认为，轮换能够给小型会计师事务所带来更多的商业机会，因此可以降低审计市场的集中度。欧盟在其绿皮书[②]中阐述，他们担心审计市场上由于市场高度集中带来的潜在系统风险，如果“四大”会计师事务所之一倒闭将严重影响投资者信心，从而造成对整个金融市场的影响。

4. 引入新视角

有些利益相关者认为新任审计师能够使用新视角来看待审计项目从而比现任审计师更有可能发现问题。另外，由于知道不久就会有新的审计师对现任审计师的工作进行审核，这也促使现任审计师在工作中保持良好的职业怀疑态度。这些都有利于提高审计质量。

---

① 在全部主要国家的审计准则中都规定了审计师需要在承接新客户之前衡量其独立性，对审计收费的依赖是独立性衡量的一项重要指标。所以即使没有强制轮换要求，经济依赖也会得到控制，因此不存在问题。

② 欧盟委员会绿皮书：“审计原则：从危机中取得的教训”，发表于2010年10月13日。这是欧盟委员会自2008年开始于美国并蔓延至整个欧洲的金融危机后，探讨如何尽快恢复市场秩序，发挥审计对稳定整个经济的作用而发表的一篇文章。该文章在正式发表之前经全球各主要会计师协会提出意见，例如美国的AICPA就这篇报告给予很多反馈意见。

## （六）强制轮换的问题及弊端

反对强制轮换的观点认为，以上所述的强制轮换的好处从理论上讲是合理的，但是在实践中存在很多弊端，这些弊端往往使得强制轮换在理论上的优势很难得以实现；相反地，轮换可能导致审计质量的下降，导致实行轮换的最终目的无法实现。下文对强制轮换的问题及其弊端进行了分析：

1. 增加时间以及成本及审计风险

反对轮换的人认为，新任会计师事务所学习曲线较为陡峭，结果导致新任审计师在项目初期效率低下。尽管事务所对过渡期管理有着规范的管理流程，事务所和客户还是会不可避免地产生额外成本。单独就英国来说，事务所转换成本预计约为 3 千万英镑①②，还不包括管理时间投入在内的机会成本。竞争委员会还发现在英国，即使审计费用在轮换协商时被降低了，但大约在 3 年后又会回升至原来的水平 。对欧盟绿皮书回复者中③，反对轮换的人士大多认为轮换“会增加额外成本”。



还有观点认为，在某些特定情形下，强制轮换给公司带来的额外成本会加倍。例如，在重要交易或者商业并购中途更换审计师会格外复杂并且成本高昂。在市场动荡的时候，强制轮换也会对公司造成严重损害。实际上，新加坡的银行监管机构——新加坡金融管理局，在 2008 年国际金融危机顶峰期取消了对本土银行强制轮换会计师事务所的要求。新加坡金融管理局认为该次危机是金融市场有史以来的空前灾难，并认为银行管理层有必要专注于商业运营④。同时它也指出了在非常时期审计连续性的好处。银行审计强制轮换制度自 2008 年取消后未再恢复，并且新加坡的三家本土银行也自管制改革后一直未更换审计师。

2. 降低审计质量

众多反对审计轮换制度的意见普遍认为，没有证据表明轮换能够提高审计质量。在对欧盟绿皮书的回复中，33% 的人认为轮换会导致审计质量降低，所

---

① 竞争委员会报告，“大公司审计市场调查：对英国大公司法定审计的调查报告”，发表于 2013 年 10 月 15 日。

② 毕马威 英国，“毕马威对竞争委员会的回复”。

③ Goethe 大学的法兰克福，就欧盟对绿皮书“审计原则：从危机中取得的教训”咨询结果的分析，发表于 2011 年 11 月 21 日。

④ 新加坡金融管理局声明，“暂时取消会计师事务所强制轮换要求”，发表于 2008 年 10 月 21 日（于 2014 年 6 月 23 日进行了修订）。

以反对轮换。实际上，研究表明强制轮换会降低审计质量，特别是当这种强制轮换年限规定较短时影响更加明显[①]。相反地，如果一个审计师不会在短时间内就被迫轮换，该审计师则有更多的时间对被审计单位及其行业进行了解；获得相应的审计专长并且能够对审计风险作出更好的判断，从而提高审计质量。较长审计任期可以使审计师有更多的机会更好地了解公司的运营流程，并且展示他们的审计经验、技术专长以及良好的审计质量，从而赢得客户的信任，这样当审计师对管理层提出质疑时就更具影响力。比如当一项交易的会计处理方法不明确而管理层或者管理层聘请的外部顾问建议采用不恰当的会计处理方法时，审计师的质疑就更能够得到管理层的尊重。

### （三）损害现行公司治理制度

有些利益相关者认为，与其强制轮换会计师事务所，不如由审计委员会对审计师的独立性以及审计质量进行评估并向股东会提议是否应该更换审计师。公司治理的一个基本原则是要求公司的管理层与治理层分开，由治理层对管理层进行监督并向股东提出治理意见，包括是否更换审计师。治理层以其对公司的了解，综合考虑更换审计师的利弊，从而作出对公司、对股东最有益的决策。强制轮换，即无论审计师质量及独立性如何，都要定期轮换，而无关治理层的决定，则会削弱治理层的决策能力。治理层职能的部分丧失不利于公司建立一个良好的治理环境，也不利于独立董事行使他们的治理职能。在美国，国会于2013 年 6 月投票反对 PCAOB 实施强制轮换，在其中一项通过的法案中监管者重申了立场：“为公司聘任外部审计师应当是董事会职权，而非由监管者决定”。

### （四）过度市场干预

审计市场在近几十年来经过了大量整合，整合的结果是在大部分成熟市场上，绝大部分的上市公司都是由一些大中型事务所来审计。欧盟委员会在其绿皮书中将此作为重点议题，提出了这样一个问题：是否可以通过刺激中小型事务所发展或者通过将大型事务所进行分拆来消除市场过于集中所带来的风险。

---

① M. Cameran，A. Prencipe 和 M. Trombetta 所著，“审计期限和审计更换：强制轮换真的能够提高审计质量吗？”，Bocconi 大学和 IE 商学院，2010 年；与 Soo Young Kwon，Youngdeok Lim 和 Roger Simnett 所著，“强制会计师事务所轮换与审计质量：韩国审计市场的证明，”发表于 2010 年 11 月 19 日。

Goethe 大学的一项研究显示，71% 受访者认为当前审计市场的集中化是由于市场自身推动力的作用（即市场需求）造成的，只有 2% 的人认为应该将大型事务所进行分拆。因此欧盟在这个问题上观点明确：“当前审计市场结构是由于客户需求所引起的，干预该种结构的做法是不合理的。”

两位提出 HR1564 提案（阻止 PCAOB 实行强制轮换要求的国会提案）[①] 的共和党国会议员也显然不支持联邦政府实行过度监管，干预市场。该提案最终在国会上通过并取得了不同党派的支持。

对于中小型事务来说，强制轮换审计师制度也没有为其带来利益。主要原因在于他们缺少对上市公司的审计经验以及应对大型审计项目的能力，因此这些大型审计项目还是在少数大型事务所中进行轮换。

### （五）增强审计市场集中度



在对欧盟绿皮书的反馈意见中，11% 的人认为，对事务所实行强制轮换会造成未来市场更加集中，所以反对强制轮换。

在很多重要金融市场上，对于复杂的跨国集团公司来说可以选择的会计师事务所是非常有限的。由于“四大”有全球网络以及相关审计经验，这些复杂的跨国公司大多选择“四大进行审计。在大多数市场上，中小型事务所业务范围有限，可能不具备对这类跨国公司进行审计所需要的经验、专业知识以及全球资源。因此，在本来就有限的可供选择的事务所中，强制轮换的要求会严重限制这类跨国集团可以选择的会计师事务所数量。

### （六）对特殊行业的影响

强制轮换会让那些对审计服务存在特殊行业技术要求的公司难以寻求适合的会计师事务所，这会有损审计质量并增强特定市场的集中度。

审计师在审计期间获取与被审计单位有关的特殊行业知识及经验，投入大量资源来获取并保持在这些特殊行业的专长并保持在特殊行业较高的审计质量。但是并不是所有的事务所都有着同样的行业专长，特别是在那些存在复杂的监管要求及会计处理的特殊行业中，如果公司无法寻求具有足够行业专长的事务所进行审计，审计质量将大打折扣。

---

① 1564 提案“审计诚信与工作保护法案”，2013 年 7 月 8 日。

（七）在全球环境下难以实施

有观点认为，强制轮换在复杂的全球背景下极难实施。例如，一家跨国集团在全球范围内拥有多家子公司或分支机构，其中有数家被要求不同年限的强制轮换。在这种情况下，在任何一个子公司或者分支机构面临强制轮换时，该集团就要将全球范围内的公司进行审计师变更（为了能够在全球范围内使用单一审计网络并享受其带来的效率），或者为该子公司或分支机构在有关规定区域选择不同的事务所。任何一种方法都会给集团审计带来成本和效率的影响，同时增加了审计风险。不同的国家在强制轮换上有不同的要求，这不仅仅体现在轮换期限、冷却期，还体现在公司所属类别及所适用的政策上。越多国家采取强制轮换措施，对于跨国集团和事务所来说问题就越复杂。

（八）对于审计行业的不利影响

部分利益相关者，尤其是事务所本身，提出轮换会给审计行业带来挑战：无论审计质量如何，审计师都需要定期更换。那么，事务所为了吸引并留住合格的审计人员，需要增加聘用及续聘成本。如果轮换导致需要变更工作地点，那么这种成本就会更加高昂。由于事务所每次都需要按照新的审计项目要求委派合适的审计团队，其本身也面临着服务能力的不确定性等问题。这种不确定性也对规划和强化审计师职业管理带来困难。这些将会降低审计行业的吸引力，不利于事务所吸引及保留人才，并最终导致整体审计质量的下降。



## 二、中国实践

中国对签字会计师和会计师事务所都有强制轮换的要求。目前针对上市公司及证券公司执行强制轮换审计师的要求，针对银行及国有企业执行强制轮换会计师事务所的要求。具体监管政策总结如下：

（一）对签字会计师的强制轮换的范围和要求

依据中国证券法和中国注册会计师法的规定，2003 年中国证监会和财政部联合出台《关于证券期货审计业务签字注册会计师定期轮换的规定》，目的在于提高某些领域的注册会计师的独立性。受管制的实体，被定义为“相关机构”，是指上市公司，寻求 IPO 首次上市的公司以及金融机构，包括从事期货、证券业、股票交易、证券投资基金、证券投资基金管理公司以及结算的公司等。具体轮换要求如下：

（1）签字会计师不得连续超过 5 年为上述机构签发审计意见，期满后需要至少 2 年的冷却期后方可续聘。

（2）当两个签字会计师同时到达 5 年期限限制，其中一个审计师可以延长 1 年审计年限。

（3）在上市公司完成首次发行后，审计师最多还能继续为其发表审计意见 2 年。

（4）上市公司需要在每年年报中披露其签字会计师。

### （二）对会计师事务所的强制轮换的范围和要求



1. 财政部关于金融企业会计师事务所轮换的规定

根据 2010 年印发的《金融企业选聘会计师事务所招标管理办法（试行）》，金融企业指获得金融业务（包括证券、保险业务）许可证的政策性银行、邮政储蓄银行、国有商业银行、股份制商业银行、城市商业银行、农村商业银行、农村合作银行、信用社、新型农村金融机构、信托投资公司、金融租赁公司、金融资产管理公司、财务公司、保险公司、证券公司、期货公司、基金管理公司，以及金融控股公司、融资性担保公司、金融监管部门所属的从事相关金融业务的企业等。

监管要求规定，金融企业每 3 年需要对会计师事务所进行招标，金融企业连续聘用同一会计师事务所（包括该事务所的相关成员单位）原则上不超过 5 年。连续聘用会计师事务所的起始年限从该会计师事务所实际承担金融企业财务报表审计业务的当年开始计算。截至 2010 年 12 月 31 日，如果金融企业连续聘用同一会计师事务所年限已经达到或超过 5 年的，最长可延缓 3 年更换，但连续聘用年限最长不得超过 10 年。签字注册会计师连续承担同一金融企业审计业务不超过 5 年。

2. 财政部及国资委关于国有企业会计师事务所轮换的规定

财政部及国资委于 2011 年印发《关于会计师事务所承担中央企业财务决算审计有关问题的通知》，规定审计国有企业的事务所连续任期不得少于 2 年但不得超过 5 年。在中国排名前 15 并且拥有优良执业记录的事务所，经国有企业申请以及国资委批准，可以适当延长审计期限，但最长不得超过八年。国有企业每 3 年必须进行一次审计师招标。

经财政部和证监会审核批准可以对 H 股上市公司进行审计的会计师事务所并完成了特殊普通合伙制的组织形式转变，经国有企业要求以及国资委批准后，可以从特殊普通合伙组织形式的工商登记完成日起，将轮换年限延迟 2 年，但整体连续审计期间不得超过 10 年。

事务所在完成连续 5 年任期后，满足以上规定，经批准可以继续为国有企业提供审计服务的应当更换审计合伙人和签字注册会计师。

作出以上规定主要是为了避免由于审计师的独立性问题而引发的审计质量缺陷。然而在实际操作中，部分专业人士认为强制轮换也带来了一系列的顾虑和挑战，尤为突出的是对审计质量带来的不利影响：

为了在轮换和招标中胜出，会计师事务所耗费了大量人力物力进行项目策划及撰写标书。这些事务消耗了事务所的部分资源，相对削减了执行审计项目工作的人力物力资源。

由于审计轮换期限相对较短，审计师没有充足的时间对被审计客户的行业特点及其运营情况进行了解，也无法在短期内培养出大量的有经验的行业专家来进行项目审计。

由于审计轮换期限较短，事务所就没有动力为提高审计质量在项目前期进行大量投资。因为这些投资只有在长期审计过程中通过审计经验的积累，提高后期审计效率而得到回报。由于审计轮换期限较短，审计师无法等到这些投资回报就被迫轮换了。

从注册会计师个人发展的角度，由于无论审计质量好坏，审计客户在短期之内都会被轮换，在这样的项目上即使有突出的表现也不能够给注册会计师个人带来职业发展的最大利益。因此注册会计师可能也没有动力去对这些客户进行深入的了解和付出。

此外，在中国还存在一个值得关注的现象，就是当一个审计客户被轮换到另外一个会计师事务所的时候，部分之前的审计团队核心人员会被新任会计师事务所高薪聘任，继续对这个审计客户提供审计服务。这样就导致该审计服务还是由相同的团队提供，只是更换了签字的会计师事务所和签字合伙人。这与轮换签字合伙人的实质效果并没有很大的不同，但是新任会计师事务所为了能够聘任到之前的审计团队人员，通常都需要提供更好的薪资报酬，因此事务所的人力成本上升了，但是却没有给被审计的公司带来额外的利益。

## 三、有关建议

正如前文所述，从美国和欧盟就强制轮换讨论的结果看来，利益相关人士似乎并不认为强制轮换或者强制招标能够提高审计质量。实际上，前文所述及的 Goethe 大学研究显示，73% 受访者不支持限制审计年限的做法。在美国，94%的人反对 PCAOB 在 2011 年提出的强制轮换议题。在新加坡，由于强制轮换对银行及审计师带来了负面影响，金融管理局于 2008 年废止了对于本土银行的强制轮换要求。尽管欧盟最终确定了强制轮换会计师事务所的要求，但其成员国在本国法律中可以选择将轮换任期延长至 20 年。有迹象显示欧洲的几个重要资本市场（如英国）都会选择延长轮换期限的安排。



由于强制轮换会计师事务所，特别是当这种轮换期间较短时会给审计师及被审计单位带来极大的不利影响，我们建议：

### （一）加强对轮换签字注册会计师（“换人”）的要求，以代替轮换会计师事务所（“换所”），同时建立良好的公司治理环境来确保审计师独立性及维护审计质量

在中国通过采用轮换项目负责人和签字注册会计师的方式，同时采取措施建立一个良好的公司治理文化及治理环境，对审计市场进行管控。在良好的公司治理环境下，公司的董事能够履行其治理职责，保护投资人及股东的利益并作出对公司最有利的决策。有了这样的前提条件，董事能够依据公司的实际情况判断更换签字注册会计师是否对公司有利，以及用什么方式来更换签字注册会计师。事实上没有一个政策能够适合所有公司的不同需求，因此应该由公司的董事按照各自公司的需求作出适当的决策。

目前，中国财政部、证监会及银监会等都先后提出了与公司治理相关的要求及规范。例如，2002 年，证监会颁发了《上市公司治理准则》，以推动上市公司建立和完善现代企业制度。2010 年，财政部、证监会、审计署、银监会和保监会联合颁发了企业内部控制配套指引，包括《企业内部控制应用指引第 1 号——组织架构》等 18 项应用指引、《企业内部控制评价指引》和《企业内部控制审计指引》。这些配套指引从各个方面要求企业建立良好的治理结构，完善

企业治理制度。十八届三中全会通过的《中共中央关于全面深化改革若干重大问题的决定》进一步要求建立并完善金融企业治理结构。这些规范及指引主要从以下几个方面入手来建立公司治理环境及治理机制：

1. 增强董事会的有效性

董事会成员应当客观、具有相关经验及能力并且保持多样化；对董事会成员的绩效进行披露；对董事会成员进行持续教育。

2. 提高监管职能

董事会应监督公司治理要求的执行情况并采取必要的惩治措施；上市条例应该强调公司治理要求；寻求跨国监管合作及信息互换。

3. 成立专门委员会

董事会应根据公司实际情况下设专门委员会，对专门问题进行讨论并提出意见。这可能包括风险委员会、薪酬委员会、审计委员会及委任委员会等。

4. 股东的权利及义务

应加强股东参与，例如对董事会的选聘应加强信息披露及透明度等。

以上这些措施及要求与国际上对公司治理的要求在原则上一致。中国监管者应该进一步加强对上市公司及国有企业的治理要求，提升其内部治理水平。

### （二）在过渡期间适当延长现行会计师事务所的强制轮换要求期限以避免对审计市场的过度干预及对审计质量带来的不利影响

公司整体治理环境的建设需要一个过程，在整体治理环境的建设期间，监管者可以考虑适当延长现行针对国有企业及金融机构实施的强制轮换期限。例如参考欧盟的要求，每 10 年进行会计师事务所招标，轮换期限最长为 20 年。较长的轮换期限能够缓解强制轮换对审计质量造成的不利影响。

当中国公司的治理环境及治理结构基本成熟的时候，中国监管者应该考虑取消对会计师事务所的强制轮换要求，而侧重于轮换签字审计师个人及其他对独立性的治理要求，并由公司的治理层对更换审计师进行决策。这样可以消除强制轮换带来的多项弊端，进一步提升中国会计服务的竞争力。

# 第六章 政府购买会计师事务所专业服务

## 一、国际经验



### （一）各国政府购买会计师事务所专业服务的现状分析

当今世界，社会公众对政府责任的关注度日益增加，目前在许多国家，政府机关和其他公共部门（以下简称“政府部门”）都需要向公众披露财务报表和财政支出情况，并由独立的机构对其进行审计。为满足日益增长的审计需求，许多国家除了建立一个独立的审计机构执行政府部门的审计外，也开始向会计师事务所购买审计服务。同时，除审计服务外，政府也会向会计师事务所购买非审计服务，比如优化内部控制、提升信息系统等咨询服务。鉴于政府业务的特殊性，政府向会计师事务所购买专业服务的优势和潜在的挑战已日渐成为一个热门话题。

因此，项目组研究了目前各国与政府从会计师事务所购买专业服务相关的政策、法规以及具体实例，以便为我国相关政策的制定提供借鉴。项目组的研究将主要集中在美国和英国。其中，美国政府遵循的是“分权制衡原则”，而英国则是议会制度的代表。此外，在其中一些问题上，我们也会参考新加坡、澳大利亚、新西兰和香港的情况，这些是欧美地区以外的发达国家/地区的代表。

1. 政府购买专业服务的范围

在美国、英国、新加坡、澳大利亚、新西兰和香港，法律都允许会计师事务所从事政府部门的审计或审计相关服务。具体来说，在美国，联邦政府和州政府都可以向会计师事务所购买这些服务。而在英国，地方政府可以向会计师事务所购买这些服务，但中央政府目前仍然由英国国家审计署（National Audit Office，NAO）审计。NAO是一个独立于政府的机构，它对政府部门进行审计并直接向议会报告，从而保护纳税人的利益。新加坡对于政府购买审计和审计相关服务的范围在法律上没有详细规定。在澳大利亚，尽管政府机关以及归属于财政支出范畴的公共部门均要求由审计署长（Auditor - General）领导的政府审计部门进行审计，并最终由审计署长签署审计意见，但审计署长可以考虑将部分或全部具体的审计工作外包给会计师事务所执行。新西兰与澳大利亚在这一方面的做法一致。在香港，政府的合并财务报表由香港特别行政区政府库务局（Treasury Department）编制，香港审计署（Audit Commission）审计。但是，很多由政府资助但独立核算的政府下设机构和公司，比如证券与期货事务监察委员会、机场管理局、医院管理局、香港科技园公司、香港贸发局等，可自行选任审计师对其财务报表进行审计。



政府购买的审计和审计相关服务主要包括财务报表审计、内部控制和合规性审计、审阅和其他鉴证服务（比如对具体财政项目进行绩效审计等等）。而非审计业务，例如管理咨询、绩效改进咨询等，由于没有法定需求，各国的法律没有针对政府采购这部分内容作明确的规定。政府采购非审计服务更多是基于各部门具体的需求。同时，由于审计或审计相关服务与政府责任的相关性更为密切，目前有关政府采购会计师事务所服务相关的法律法规和政策的讨论大多是围绕着审计服务展开的，因此，我们在以下对政府采购具体问题的讨论上，也将主要针对审计服务展开。

2. 会计师事务所对公共部门的审计与政府审计的关系

在我们研究的国家中，会计师事务所和政府审计机关，例如上面提到的英国的NAO，都会为政府部门提供审计或审计相关服务。那么，我们从以下几个方面来对比研究会计师事务所对政府部门的审计和政府审计的关系和区别。

• 独立性——在我们研究的这些国家中，会计师事务所和政府审计机关都遵循同样的独立性要求。通常来说，各国都会设立一个独立的政府审计机关，来执行政府审计工作，比如上文提到的英国的NAO、美国的Government Accountability Office（GAO）、新加坡的Auditor - General's Office（AGO），以及澳大利亚的Australia National Audit Office（ANAO）。这些机构都直接向议会或国会报告。具体来看，NAO是一个独立于政府的机构，代表议会来监督政府财政开支，通过对中央政府各部门执行审计并直接向议会报告，来保护纳税人的利益。议会下设的政府账目委员会（Public Accounts Commission）对NAO进行监督，聘用外部审计师来审核NAO的工作。与英国的NAO相似，美国的GAO常常被称为国会的“看门人”。GAO为国会工作，独立审计政府账目，调查联邦政府财政资金的使用情况。GAO还负责调查涉嫌非法和不正当使用财政拨款的情况，研究并汇报政府具体项目和政策实施效果，以及执行政策分析，并向国会提供可行性建议，以帮助政府提升业绩表现、确保政府履行对公众的责任。新加坡的AGO也是一个独立于政府机关的国家审计机构。它的任务是审计政府的财务信息以及公共资源的使用情况，并向总统和议会汇报。AGO的审计范围包括财务报表审计、合规性和内部控制审计以及其他一些政府部门和基金的特殊审计。澳大利亚的ANAO是独立的专业机构，它在审计署长（Auditor - General）领导下为议会和政府部门提供审计服务。



（1）适用的准则与法规。针对政府部门的审计，在我们研究的国家中，绝大多数都制定有一套专门的准则和法规，供会计师事务所和政府审计机关遵守。我们将在下面的部分更为详细地讨论这些准则和法规。

（2）角色与职责。在我们研究的国家中，会计师事务所和政府审计机关为政府提供审计服务时，若提供的服务一致，二者在角色和承担的责任上没有实质区别。他们的报告使用者也是相同的。

（3）监督机制。由于会计师事务所在政府事务和实践方面的知识和经验可能没有政府审计机关丰富，会计师事务所在提供政府部门的审计服务时会接受国家审计机关（如NAO、GAO、AGO和ANAO）或他们授权的机构的监督，以保证审计质量。我们将在下面部分详细讨论这些监督活动。

3. 审计服务的采购程序

总地来说，政府采购审计服务的采购程序没有特别的法律规定，通常遵循政府对商品和服务的一般采购程序，例如美国的联邦政府采购条例（Federal Acquisition Regulation, FAR）和英国的公共合同法规（Public Contracts Regulations）。然而，在美国，由于社会越来越关注州和地方政府向会计师事务所购买的审计服务的质量问题，GAO在1987年制定了一个政府审计服务采购框架，供各个政府部门参考和使用，从而确保政府部门能够购买到有效的审计服务。这个框架提出了采购程序中的四个关键因素：竞争机制、招标询价、技术评估和书面协议。GAO 建议政府部门在法律允许的范围内，尽量符合这四个关键性因素。具体建议如下：

第一，在选聘审计师时，确保至少考虑两个会计师事务所以保证竞争机制的存在；

第二，准备全面的招标询价文件，列明具体审计要求，公布给有意竞标的会计师事务所；

第三，在选择会计师事务所时制定明确且具体的技术指标以便对事务所进行评估；

第四，使用书面协议确定双方权利和责任；

第五，建议签署服务期限为多年的协议，5 年为最佳；

第六，配备经验丰富且具备政府会计和审计专业知识的官员来帮助计划和实施采购流程；

第七，考虑使用审计委员会帮助计划和监督采购流程。

下面，我们研究采购程序中的几个关键环节。

（1）审计师的任命。有关政府部门审计师的任命，美国和英国都建立有一个独立于政府机关的组织来负责监督审计师的任命。具体而言，在美国，各政府部门的监察长（Inspector General，IG）负责监督该部门审计师的任命。IG 是每个政府部门设立的独立调查官员，通过审计、督察、评估和调查等方式来监督和追踪该部门的财政资金使用情况。IG 每半年向国会下属的相关委员会或附属委员会报告。此外，在 1990 年的 CFO 法案出台之后，GAO 发布了政府采购的采购指南，指南指出各部门都应指派一个技术代表监督整个采购过程中的各项日常活动，而这个代表的最佳人选就是 IG 或者 IG 的代表。同时，1978 年出台的监察长法案（IG Act）的 4（b）部分要求监察长制定相关规则，用来判断使用会计师事务所而非政府审计师的恰当性。英国的情况与美国类似。英国 1998 年通过了审计委员会法案（Audit Commission Act 1998），根据该法案，审计委员会作为一个独立的直接向议会报告的机构，负责集中任命地方政府部门的审计师，并制定相关的审计准则。最新的变化是，自 2015 年 3 月 31 日起，审计委员会法案将被 2014 年通过的地方审计和责任法案（Local Audit and Accountability Act 2014）所取代，根据新的法案，地方政府可以自行任命当地的审计师执行审计工作。但是，每个地方政府需要组建一个审计专家组，其职责包括为地方政府审计师的选择和任命提供意见以及督导地方政府与其审计师之间的独立性。新加坡的情况与英国相似。新加坡的政府指导手册要求政府机构在指派审计师时征求 AGO 的意见。在澳大利亚和新西兰，如果部分政府审计工作外包给会计师事务所来执行，则执行这些审计工作的审计师由审计署长来指定。在澳大利亚和新西兰的政府审计项目中，审计署长的角色是该审计项目组的总负责人，而外包的会计师事务所则作为核心项目组成员执行具体的审计程序。会计师事务所需要将所有在审计工作中注意到的问题定期向审计署长进行汇报，审计署长为最终签署审计报告的签字人。在澳大利亚，这种政府审计外包的协议通常是 5 年的服务期限，审计工作底稿最终归属于审计署长。

（2）竞争机制。美国认为完全的公开竞争是政府采购的基础因素。因此，美国鼓励符合要求的会计师事务所参与竞争，通过这种竞标的方式获取高质量且价格合理的审计服务。当然这项要求不是绝对的，在紧急情况下，比如某项审计具有特殊资质要求，而某个事务所恰好具有这样的资质，那么政府部门也可以不通过竞争机制而直接聘用这个事务所。同样在英国，"公开竞争"也是政府采购的一项关键原则。



（3）对审计师任命情况的公告。美国和英国都强调政府机构审计师任命情况的公告。在美国，GAO 要求政府部门在正式开始招标之前在商业日报（Commence Business Daily）中公告招标方案。英国同样要求有关当局必须在自任命审计师之日起 28 天内公布该任命情况，公告需包括审计师的名称以及审计专家组对审计师选择和任命的意见。

（4）政府审计招标文件应涵盖的内容。针对招标文件应涵盖的内容，各国并无特别的规定，通常来说，招标文件包括项目背景、招标机构介绍、费用情况、时间表、投标安排等。此外，英国财务报告委员会（Financial Reporting Council，FRC）建议审计招标文件（不局限于政府审计招标）中包含充分有效的信息，使审计师更好地了解潜在客户的业务。

（5）针对审计服务的招标文件要求会计师事务所提供的信息。各个国家在进行政府部门审计招标时对参与投标的会计师事务所提供的信息各自有一些具体的规定，但总体上可以归纳为两个方面的信息，即投标的会计师事务所的一般信息和与招标项目相关的具体信息。

①会计师事务所的一般信息。

• 会计师事务所的总体情况——这主要包括会计师事务所的一些基础信息，如事务所名称、主要联系人信息、事务所注册地址及组织类型等、事务所的注册情况（英国等国家要求会计师事务所在指定的会计职业组织注册以获得执行审计工作的资格）、事务所是否无不良或违法行为（涉嫌欺诈等）、公司网络和影响力，以及事务所的规模和人员情况。

• 会计师事务所的财务状况——通常包括资本额、营业收入、利润等。有些国家要求事务所提供近期财务报表等作为其财务状况的佐证。

• 事务所内部控制政策和制度。

• 事务所已接受的外部检查的审核结果。

②与招标项目相关的具体信息。

• 专业技术与执业能力——该项信息主要是指事务所在提供招标项目类似服务的经验，也包括事务所与招标服务相关的服务资历、执业资格证书等。

• 项目方案——通常，招标部门会要求参与投标的事务所提供一份与招标服务相关的具体服务方案（审计策略、方法等），详细描述准备如何完成所要求的各项工作，概述事务所为了完成所要求的各项工作而建议实施的程序和使用的资源，包括如何遵守时间表、如何适当管理风险，以及如何遵照规定的执业质量准则。服务方案也可包含任何增值活动以及确保完成高质量服务的措施等。

• 项目团队——该项包括项目团队人员配置情况、核心项目组成员的教育背景、专业资格、以往工作经验和服务质量等。

• 时间表及项目报价——该项包括事务所预计的审计工作时间表和项目的费用报价。

• 独立性——有些国家要求事务所提供有关利益冲突的声明或独立性确认函（如英国、韩国）。其他有些国家要求事务所提供职业责任保险的合规情况（如澳大利亚，该保险需满足澳大利亚监管机构和注册会计师协会的最低要求）。

（6）会计师事务所开展政府部门审计的特定要求/评选标准。从我们研究的国家来看，有关会计师事务所开展政府审计的特定要求/评选标准可以归纳为如下几点：

• 独立性——不管是政府审计机关还是会计师事务所和注册会计师，执行政府审计工作时都必须具备独立性。

• 专业知识和技能——会计师事务所开展政府部门的审计必须拥有足够的与政府事务相关的知识和技能。

• 良好的品行——为政府部门提供审计服务的会计师事务所或注册会计师需具有良好的品行，涉及停职、处罚、行为过失等情况的事务所或注册会计师不得执行政府部门的审计。

• 资格要求——审计人员需拥有国家承认的审计行业执业资格。

• 继续职业教育——（仅限美国）执行政府机构审计的审计师每2年需要完成不少于24小时的政府审计、政府运营环境等相关知识的继续教育课程。此外，我们注意到在美国的注册会计师考试中也涵盖了政府会计和审计的内容。

除上述要求外，政府在具体审计项目上还会考虑会计师事务所投标书中涵盖的与项目相关的一些方面，包括：

• 对被审单位运营环境、主要运营风险的理解；

• 如何识别关键审计风险及审计风险与运营风险的关系，以及如何向政府审计部门报告这些风险；

• 审计项目组的政府部门审计经验及对被审计单位行业特性的经验；

• 审计项目组与政府审计部门的沟通计划；

• 预计审计时间及审计时间在不同级别成员之间的分配情况；

• 确保履行保密义务的措施；

• 语言能力（有些政府机构由于其存在一些特殊语言的官方文件而可能有特殊语言要求）。



（7）对会计师事务所提供的政府部门审计服务质量的监督。在美国和英国，主要由与政府审计相关的组织和机构负责监督会计师事务所提供的政府部门审计服务的质量。具体来说，美国要求每个政府部门的IG采取适当的措施，对会计师事务所提供的审计服务实施监督，确保执行的审计工作均遵守了相关的准则与法规。此外，GAO与其他一些与政府审计相关的机构，例如行政管理和预算局（Office of Management and Budget，OMB）也会对会计师事务所开展的政府部门审计工作实施一定的监督。例如，在21世纪初，美国各州和地方政府的审计质量受到越来越多的关注，OMB，作为总统办公室中最大的部门，其主要任务是编制和执行联邦政府的财政预算，OMB认为政府部门的审计质量需要在数据统计的基础上进行衡量。因此，OMB和几个联邦政府部门的IG决定合作推行一项审计质量检查项目，该项目被称为“全国单一审计抽样检查项目”（National Single Audit Sampling Project）。这个项目通过抽样的方式选取各州和地方政府审计项目的样本，进行质量检查，识别这些审计中的不足之处。具体检查工作由总统廉洁与效益委员会（President's Council on Integrity and Efficiency, PCIE）执行，PCIE 是一个由 OMB 副局长领导的跨部门委员会，在 OMB 的指导下，与美国教育局的 IG 协调工作。针对项目检查结果，GAO 进行了分析，同时对 PCIE 提出的审计质量改进建议进行评价并向国会的相关附属委员会报告。

与美国有些许不同，英国在地方政府的审计安排方面正处在一个过渡时期。在 2014 年地方审计和责任法案出台之前，审计委员会负责监督政府审计的质量。具体来说，审计委员会选择了几家会计师事务所作为他们主要的会计师事务所，包括“四大”会计师事务所、BDO、Grant Thornton 和 Mazars，每季度对这些事务所执行政府部门审计的情况进行检查。审计委员会设定了一系列合规性和质量控制指标，比如是否保持独立性、是否按时完成审计、是否按照政府审计准则执行审计工作等，每季度的检查就围绕事务所对这些指标的完成情况展开。针对每一家事务所，审计委员会发布季度和年度检查报告。其中，季度报告以表格的形式简述该季度事务所每一指标的完成情况（比如共执行多少项政府审计，其中多少项独立性存在问题），年度报告则会比较具体地总结全年的检查情况，除介绍各项指标全年完成情况外，还会讲述发现的主要问题及改进建议等。2014 年出台的地方审计和责任法案将于 2015 年 3 月 31 日起生效，此后，地方政府的审计安排将会有一个新的框架，审计委员会有可能被取消。在过渡时期，地方政府协会（Local Government Association, LGA）将会创建一个独立的过渡性机构，用来监管过渡时期内的地方审计项目。同时，审计和责任法案还赋予英国财务报告委员会（Financial Reporting Council, FRC）作为审计师的总监管者的新职责。此外，NAO 也将会编制新的政府审计实务准则，而一些审计专业团体也会参与到对审计师的监管工作中来。

2014 年的地方审计和责任法案废除了审计委员会对地方政府审计的统一调配，推行地方政府自行负责各自的审计工作，其动因主要有以下几点：

①近年来英国政府采取了许多措施，旨在增加地方政府透明度，实现地方公众对政府部门的监督，体现地方政府的责任。地方审计和责任法案正是体现了这一趋势。

②地方审计和责任法案出台后，审计委员会的职能将由地方政府自行完成，审计委员会的规模就可以得到大大的缩减，从而降低政府成本，精简政府机构。该法案也可以促使地方政府审计获得更为广泛、合理且更加体现地域性特点的方案。

③自审计委员会成立以来，其职责范围不断扩大，远远超过最初的预期。审计委员会作为所有地方政府审计工作的监管者、行政长官和提供者，其建立的系统缺乏有效的成本激励机制，同时，它更加关注于向中央政府而不是地方政府公众报告。

④由地方政府部门像企业那样自行管理和聘用审计师，有利于提高地方政府对其审计成本的控制力，从而提高透明度。地方政府也将不再需要负担审计委员会发生的与地方政府审计活动不直接相关的日常开支，这将促使他们有更大的动机降低成本。

⑤审计和地方责任法案将保留纳税人监督地方政府账目的权利，并对他们认为审计师需要报告的事项提出意见。地方公众可以持续利用这一监督机制来确保地方政府机关履行其职责。

(8) 政府部门审计的收费制度。目前在英国，地方政府的审计服务费用首先由审计委员会统一支付，之后再由审计委员会将相关费用分配至接受审计服务的地方政府部门。新的地方审计和责任法案下，审计委员会即将被取代，审计费用将由接受审计服务的地方政府机构直接支付给他们的审计师。美国也采用相似做法，由接受审计服务的政府部门承担审计费用。在澳大利亚，如果部分政府机关或是政府预算内的公共部门的审计工作外包给会计师事务所执行，其审计费用统一由政府承担。

(9) 会计师事务所对政府部门的审计与政府部门预算控制的关系。在我们研究的国家中，因为政府部门的审计及审计相关的服务是由立法强制要求的，所以其对应的成本包含在政府的财政预算中。



4. 会计师事务所开展政府部门审计的相关准则依据

在美国和英国，会计师事务所大量地参与了政府部门的审计，因而这两个国家都建立有一套专门的政府审计和会计准则。而在澳大利亚和新西兰，与政府会计审计相关的准则与一般企业会计审计准则关联性更强，准则本身也具有一定的弹性。表 7 概括了美国、英国、澳大利亚和新西兰的政府会计审计准则：

表 7　各国政府会计审计准则

| | 审计准则/法规 | 会计准则/基准 |
|---|---|---|
| 美国 | *一般公认政府审计准则*(*Generally Accepted Government Auditing Standards, GAGAS*)<br>GAGAS 是由 GAO 颁布的。GAGAS 引用了美国注册会计师协会(American Institute of Certified Public Accountants, AICPA)颁布的部分审计准则(Statement on Auditing Standards, SAS)。政府审计机关和会计师事务所对政府部门的审计和其他鉴证服务都遵循 GAGAS | *联邦政府会计指南*(*FASAB Handbook*)<br>联邦政府会计准则咨询委员会(Accounting Standards Advisory Board, FASAB)颁布了联邦政府会计指南,为联邦政府财务会计提供了会计准则、应用解释和报告框架<br>*政府会计准则*(*GASB codifications*)<br>政府会计准则委员会(Governmental Accounting Standards Board, GASB)颁布了政府会计准则,为美国州和地方政府会计和财务报告制定了标准。该准则不是联邦法律或法规,因而不具备强制执行的法律效力。但是有一些州的州立法则要求强制执行 |
| 英国 | *审计实务准则*<br>英国目前使用的审计实务准则是由审计委员会依照 1998 年审计委员会法案发布的。该准则是会计师事务所执行政府部门审计实务的依据。2015 年 3 月 31 日地方审计和责任法案生效后,NAO 将制定一套新的审计实务准则 | *政府财务报告手册*<br>政府财务报告手册是由英国财政部发布的政府部门编制财务报表的会计应用指南 |
| 澳大利亚 | 国际审计准则(ISAs) | 澳大利亚只有一套会计准则,基本与国际财务报告准则(IFRS)趋同,同时适用于企业和公共部门。但是,澳洲会计准则委员会(Australia Accounting Standards Board, AASB)也认识到该套准则并非 100% 适用于公共部门。因此,AASB 对其中一部分准则进行修改,添加了适用于公共部门的内容。对于这些修改,AASB 借鉴了由国际公共部门会计准则理事会(International Public Sector Accounting Standards Board, IPSASB)制定的国际公共部门会计准则(International Public Sector Accounting Standards, IPSASs) |
| 新西兰 | 国际审计准则(ISAs) | 新西兰将公共部门划分为四类,划分的标准为各部门的年度总支出,每类部门适用的会计准则有所不同。<br>一类部门(年度总支出高于新币 3 000 万):全面执行 IPSASs<br>二类部门(年度总支出介于新币 200 万至 3 000 万之间):总体上执行 IPSASs,但可减少部分披露要求<br>三类部门(年度总支出低于新币 200 万):按权责发生制<br>四类部门(法律批准的情况下):按现金收付制 |

### (二)政府从注册会计师事务所购买专业服务的原因、优势与挑战

基于以上研究，我们了解到促使政府向会计师事务所购买专业服务的一个主要动因是各种法律法规强制要求的政府审计数量增加，这些审计要求旨在证实政府是否正确且合理地使用财政资金。例如，美国的1984年单一审计法案（Single Audit Act of 1984）规定，所有州和地方政府部门在一个财政年度内得到的联邦政府资金超过一定金额的，在当年都要进行审计。但与此同时，政府审计机关自身缺乏足够的资源来完成日益增加的审计业务。因此，政府就需要到公共的会计师市场中获取可满足这部分新增审计需求的资源。

政府购买专业服务的另一个重要原因是社会公众对提高政府收支透明度、改进政府部门公共监督的需求不断加强。前文提到的英国审计委员会法案被地方审计和责任法案取代的案例就是一个例子。正如前文所提到的，在审计委员会法案下，审计委员会统一安排地方政府机构的审计事宜。尽管会计师事务所也被允许参与执行地方政府部门的审计，但实践中大部分地方机构的审计还是由审计委员会下属的政府审计师完成的。在2012年7月，社区和地方政府部门（Department for Communities and Local Government，DCLG）向议会提交“地方审计草案”，提出废除审计委员会，将地方政府审计政策的重心转移到帮助地方政府建立理事会或其他机构，由地方政府自己对自己的开支负责。DCLG在草案中也提出他们更愿意由会计师事务所承担地方政府的审计工作。DCLG认为新的体制对地方政府更加有益，它将允许地方机构在适当的独立性保护措施下在公开竞争的市场中选择他们自己的审计师。2014年的地方审计和责任法案因而出台。



综上，我们认为政府向会计师事务所购买专业服务的优势包括：

1. 减少国家审计机关的审计负担

适当减轻国家审计机关肩负的具体审计工作的重担有利于帮助审计机关专注于对政府审计工作的总体把握，比如建立和推进政府审计会计准则规范的有效执行、研究分析政府审计中识别出的政府部门内部控制缺陷、政府审计整体质量监督，等等。这样的安排也有利于提升政府部门的工作效率和效果，从而最终提高政府的公信力。举例来说，美国的联邦政府审计机关GAO在全国约有3000名工作人员，除执行政府机构的审计工作外，该机关还负责发布和更新政府审计准则、执行政策分析并向国会提供建议、调查违法或不当行为以及为提

升政府管理水平提供建议，等等。GAO 能够履行这些不同的职责，正是由于政府购买审计服务的存在为其提供了契机，确保其有充足的资源来完成这些职责。

2. 增加政府的透明度，确保地方公众对政府部门实施监督的权利，从而维护公共利益

如前文所提，英国地方审计和责任法案出台的主要动因就是由于地方公众要求增强政府透明度，而且地方公众认为将原英国审计委员会的工作转交给会计师事务所能够赋予当地民众从公开市场上自行选聘审计师的权力，这样政府的透明度就得到了保证。同时，这种方式也能减少审计委员会为协调各地方政府审计工作而发生的费用，降低政府审计成本。

3. 会计师事务所可以将其在为企业提供专业服务时获得的经验用于为政府部门提供的服务上，该优势在提供管理咨询等非审计服务时更为显著。

当然，政府购买专业服务也可能遇到以下挑战：

1. 由于市场竞争机制的存在，不同政府部门在公开的市场上采购类似的审计服务（比如类似的行业和规模等）所支付的审计费用可能有所不同，这就可能对政府统一的预算支出管理增加困难。但从长期来看，政府审计项目外包给外部审计师将为纳税人节约相当可观的资金。

2. 信息保密。政府的业务常常涉及高度机密的信息，会计师事务所为政府部门提供专业服务将有机会接触到这些机密信息，因此对这些机密信息需要进行额外的保护。

3. 政府部门和企业的审计目标是不同的。具体来说，企业的审计目标在于审核企业财务信息是否存在重大错报，以保护投资人的利益。而政府部门的审计旨在检查政府资金的使用情况以及资金的使用是否符合相关法律法规，从而维护纳税人的利益。同样地，企业审计的重点往往是与企业盈利相关的活动，而政府部门的审计更关心被审机构的现金流情况。此外，政府部门审计的范围更为广泛。除了财务报表和内部控制审计，合规性审计也是政府部门审计的内容之一。由此可见，会计师事务所在处理政府部门的审计时可能缺乏足够的背景和专业知识。因此，总的来说，会计师事务所开展政府机构审计，相比企业审计，需要更高水平的监管。

## 二、中国实践

与美国和英国相比，在中国，会计师事务所目前所涉足政府部门的专业服务的范围较为有限。政府机关的审计目前主要由国家审计机关执行，大多使用其内部审计师，但在必要时也会运用外部的社会力量。国家审计机关目前的审计范围主要包括中央政府部门，例如商务部（在国家审计署发布的2012年审计报告中提及57个中央政府机关）和某些大型金融机构和国有企业（SOE），例如中国银行（2013年国家审计署对13个国有企业发布了审计报告）。这些审计主要是针对政府预算执行情况的合规性审计和国有企业领导人员经济责任审计等，频率为每年一次（企业例外），审计结果由国家审计机关公布。值得注意的是，上述国家审计机关对国有企业的审计是特殊目的审计，并非针对其年度财务报表的法定审计，国有企业财务报表的法定审计已由其各自任命的外部审计师完成。



近年来，一方面，社会公众对政府透明度的要求越来越高，公众希望了解政府部门对财政资金的使用情况、政府部门的财务状况及审计情况等。为应对这些需求，中国政府越来越重视政府部门财务信息的标准化、透明化，在致力于提高政府部门财务信息披露质量的同时也在不断扩大政府部门审计的覆盖面，审计全覆盖理念日益深入。另一方面，为提高政府效率，优化政府财政结构，中央和地方政府也先后出台了一系列政府职能改革的举措。例如，自2014年起中央逐步允许地方政府自主公开发行债券，这一重大举措旨在拓宽地方政府融资渠道，使得政府债务阳光化，从而防范化解政府财政金融风险。国务院、财政部也相应发布了地方政府性债务管理相关的规范性文件，强调了地方政府发债相关的财务信息公开披露要求。此类举措和要求也衍生出可观的相关审计咨询服务的需求。

要应对日益增长的政府部门会计审计服务需求并实现上述目标，需要投入大量专业人士的力量，但国家审计机关相关专业资源在充分性、独立性方面都存在一定的局限性，因此，中国政府近年来一直在探索各项政府职能改革措施，希望更大地发挥市场机制在资源配置中的作用，特别是在政府部门会计审计中引入社会力量，提高政府部门审计工作的独立性，明确政府部门审计师对审计结果的民事责任。因此，目前各级政府在很多方面都有购买会计师事务所专业服务的切实需求，比如地方政府发债所需的财务报表审计服务、行政事业单位财务报表的审计服务、行政事业单位内部控制制度的建立和咨询服务、社保基金的内部控制审计服务、政府部门会计审计准则制度的建立和咨询服务、国有企业内部控制和管理会计咨询服务，等等。

与此同时，中国各级政府也表现出对政府购买专业服务的支持态度。中国政府近年来致力于创新公共服务提供方式，深化社会领域改革，提高政府工作水平和效率。国务院在 2013 年印发了《国务院办公厅关于政府向社会力量购买服务的指导意见》（以下简称《指导意见》），明确指出“国务院对进一步转变政府职能、改善公共服务作出重大部署，明确要求在公共服务领域更多利用社会力量，加大政府购买服务力度”，“政府向社会力量购买服务，就是通过发挥市场机制作用，把政府直接向社会公众提供的一部分公共服务事项，按照一定的方式和程序，交由具备条件的社会力量承担，并由政府根据数量和质量向其支付费用”。《指导意见》还详细说明并强调了政府向社会力量购买服务的重要性，同时提出了政府购买的目标原则、运营管理等各方面的具体指导意见。



该《指导意见》出台后，财政部陆续印发了《财政部、民政部关于支持和规范社会组织承接政府购买服务的通知》及《关于印发〈政府购买服务管理办法（暂行）〉的通知》。上述两个文件进一步强调了政府购买服务的重要性，并明确了购买内容及指导目录，其中，“会计审计服务”被特别列为适宜由社会力量承担的技术性服务事项之一。此外，2014 年 10 月，国务院印发的《关于加强审计工作的意见》（以下简称《意见》），明确指出凡是涉及管理、分配、使用公共资金、国有资产、国有资源的部门、单位和个人，都要自觉接受审计。《意见》还指出国家审计机关应推动审计方式创新，根据审计项目实施需要，探索向社会购买审计服务。这些举措都表明了中央政府勇于创新、推进政府职能改革以及对接受社会监督、增加透明度方面的决心，也为会计师事务所参与政府部门业务提供了机遇。

中国注册会计师协会（CICPA）在 2014 年公布了更新的中国注册会计师业务指导目录，目录列举了注册会计师可以提供的与政府部门有关的各类审计或非审计服务，例如政府资金合规性的专项审计、税务咨询服务、管理咨询服务、IT 系统咨询服务等。更新后的指导目录呈现出中国注册会计师的专业服务向非审计鉴证服务和政府事务等相关业务领域延伸的发展趋势。

当然，机遇与挑战往往是并存的，基于中国的现状，政府向会计师事务所购买专业服务面临的挑战，除上文提及的，还包括：

（1）目前在中国，会计师事务所参与政府部门的审计或与审计相关的工作的情况较为有限，政府部门的审计主要由国家审计机关负责执行。对比会计师事务所审计和国家审计机关审计，双方在独立性要求、职业道德要求等方面具有相似之处。但由于企业审计和政府部门审计的关注点不同（企业审计更关注财务报表的真实性公允性，政府部门审计除关注财务报表的真实性公允性外，还关注财政资金使用等合规性的执行情况）；会计师事务所审计主要针对财务信息发表意见，而国家审计机关审计主要对政府部门的合规性等发表意见（如财政拨款使用的合规性），因此会计师事务所审计与国家审计机关审计在审计目标和策略、适用的审计准则、接受的监管等方面都存在差异。此外，国家审计机关审计还包含对单位主要负责人的经济责任审计，对预算执行情况和特殊项目的财政收支情况等的专项审计。针对这些差异要求建立起一套适用于会计师事务所进行或参与政府部门审计工作的准则，来明确会计师事务所参与政府部门审计的范围、方式和行为规范等。



（2）中国目前在政府部门审计方面的准则规范还需要进一步明晰和完善。目前与政府审计相关的法律法规及准则主要包括《中华人民共和国审计法》、《中华人民共和国国家审计准则》等等。此外，针对审计署聘用外部人员参与政府审计工作的还有《审计署聘请外部人员参与审计工作管理办法》。与私营部门审计遵循的审计准则相比，这些法规准则更多的是一些基础规则，而不是审计师执行具体审计程序时应遵守的行为准则。因此，如果计划让会计师事务所大规模地参与到政府部门的审计工作中来，就必须制定及完善针对会计师事务所对政府部门进行审计的专业准则。政府部门审计准则可以参考企业审计的一般公认审计准则，但也需要针对政府审计目标的特殊性增加相应的要求，例如对政府机构相关信息合规性发表审计意见的标准。目前，中注协已经开始组织专员着手该准则制定工作。

（3）中国政府部门适用的会计准则体系尚未建立，会计师事务所对政府部门适用的会计准则的了解也是有限的。与中国企业会计准则比较，政府会计改革相对滞后，仍实行预算会计制度体系。因此，应加快推进政府会计改革，根据中国共产党的十八届三中全会的要求，积极推进政府会计准则体系的建立和以权责发生制为基础的政府综合财务报告制度。财政部也正在积极推进这一工作。

（4）需要推动和加快对政府部门会计审计人才的培养，尤其是要提升他们对政府会计、审计准则相关知识的掌握水平。一方面，政府财务报表的编制者，应当熟练掌握更新的政府会计准则和综合财务报告制度，同时相关领导阶层能对政府审计准则进行总体上的把握。另一方面，若计划让会计师事务所大规模地参与到政府部门的审计工作中来，还需要加强对会计师事务所和注册会计师与政府部门会计审计准则相关知识的培训。

（5）会计师事务所也许会因为缺少适当授权，在执行某些政府审计程序时遇到困难。政府审计的报告使用者是政府监督机构和公众，政府部门的审计师可能由国家审计机关或被审计单位自己任命。审计师代表的是独立的专业团体，可能因缺乏与国家审计机关相同的权力而不受被审计单位的重视，所以需要国家审计机关授予独立审计师相关权力以保证审计师在执行审计时能够获取足够的信息。

（6）虽然短期内在中国，针对政府机构的审计，会计师事务所的平均收费标准与国家审计机关内部审计师的预算支出相比可能略高，但从长远看，政府购买审计服务能够大大节省公共部门的总审计成本。因此，短期内如果外部审计服务费用由接受审计服务的机关承担，那么目前政府预算支出管理就需要进行调整，将这部分费用纳入财政预算的范围内。

（7）在中国，政府从会计师事务所购买专业服务尚处在初步探索阶段，还需要进一步建立和完善一套透明且公平的政府购买专业服务招标体系，而选聘符合要求的会计师事务所的评估标准将是该体系的一项重要内容。



## 三、有关建议

基于上述研究和分析，我们有关政府购买专业服务的建议如下：

（1）会计师事务所向政府部门提供专业服务可以增加政府财务状况的透明度，增强政府公信力，确保公众对公共机构实施监督的权利，对加快推进廉洁政府、透明政府能够起到积极的作用。我们预期在中国，会计师事务所的专业服务在政府部门的事务中拥有非常广阔的发展空间，比如行政事业单位财务报表审计、内部控制制度建立与实施咨询等。因此，中国应当在实施必要监督的基础上，大力支持和鼓励政府从会计师事务所购买专业服务，将专业人才的服务有效地应用于政府事务中，提高政府效率。

（2）政府部门应考虑建设一套标准的政府购买专业服务的体系，包括由哪些部门负责采购、采购方式（如公开招标还是直接指派）、公开招标文件、招标文件应涵盖的内容、要求事务所提供的信息、选聘事务所的评估标准以及对聘用的事务所工作质量的监督等。上文中讨论的其他国家在这些方面的实施情况可作为参考。

（3）政府在计划向会计师事务所采购专业服务的同时也要考虑其成本。这些成本需要被妥善地纳入政府预算控制体系。政府可自行决定成本应由财政直接支付还是由接受服务的部门自行承担。建立将政府采购专业服务纳入政府预算控制体系的机制需要考虑和分析政府部门审计的范围和频率要求、该类服务费用的市场价格，并明确购买的专业服务费用由谁承担，以及这类费用与政府绩效考核的关系。

（4）应按照中国共产党的十八届三中全会要求，尽快建立政府会计准则体系和以权责发生制为基础的政府综合财务报告制度。同时，应进一步改革和完善政府部门审计准则，使其标准化、具体化，明确会计师事务所作为政府部门审计师的责任，是保证政府购买专业服务顺利进行的决定性前提和关键因素。作为中国注册会计师审计准则的一部分，这些准则和应用指南需要具体且清晰，可以最大限度地参考企业审计的一般公认准则，并加入政府部门审计的特殊领域（如合规性）的特殊审计要求。这些准则和应用指南也为政府审计各方提供了一个行为标准的框架，并赋予会计师事务所执行政府审计工作所需要的适当授权，保证事务所在执行审计时能够获取足够的信息，执行必要的审计程序。

（5）应全面推进对政府部门会计审计人才的培养。首先，应当加强对政府部门财务报表编制者，即政府财务人员的专业培训，使其具备充分的政府会计准则知识及编制以权责发生制为基础的政府综合财务报表的专业胜任能力，并对政府审计准则有一定的了解。同时，为政府部门提供专业服务的会计师事务所和注册会计师应当熟练掌握政府部门会计准则、审计准则与实务，具备对政府部门事务尤其是特殊业务（如社保基金）的充分了解并具有相关经验和资质。对此，中国可以考虑在注册会计师考试和后续教育要求中增加政府部门会计准则、审计准则相关的内容，同时，各会计师事务所内部也应增加相关的培训内容，注重对政府部门专业服务人才的培养。

（6）与其他审计一样，财政部作为监管机构，应总体上对会计师事务所开展的政府部门审计业务实施监管。其他相关机构，主要是国家审计机关，也可以对其委托的审计业务参与监管。财政部对政府部门审计业务的监管可以在一些方面跟对私营部门审计业务的监管有效地结合起来，比如通过对事务所的检查来监管该事务所对私营部门的审计业务和对政府部门的相关业务。但是，由于政府部门的审计涉及的是社会公众的整体利益，因此对政府部门审计的监管需要更加广泛和严密。除对会计师事务所已完成的项目进行检查外，还应监督政府部门选聘审计师的过程，使对政府部门审计的监管贯穿审计的全过程。下一步，财政部、审计署应加强对推进公共部门注册会计师审计制度建设的沟通协调，促进政府审计与注册会计师审计相互补充、相互支持、相得益彰。

# 第七章 金融机构审计



金融机构是金融市场中的媒介。他们将资金从投资者的手中转移到有资金需求的公司或人员手中。金融机构的特殊性主要在于绝大多数的金融机构都是公众利益实体，利益相关者众多并且对社会公众利益具有影响。金融机构主要有三类：一是存款性的金融机构，如银行、住房公积金、信用合作社、信用社、信托公司和抵押贷款公司等；二是契约式存储机构，如保险公司、养老基金等；三是投资性金融机构，如投资银行、证券承销商和经纪公司等。

一个快速发展的经济体需要有一个活跃的金融市场作支撑。活跃的金融市场对于经济发展的作用主要表现在以下几个方面：

- 吸收存款：金融市场的一个重要的作用就是将积蓄或者盈余资金从家庭、个人、企业、公共部门单位、中央政府、地方政府等方面集中起来。
- 投资：金融市场的另一个重要功能就是将集中起来的资金投入到那些有资金需求的企业和个人手中。
- 国家经济增长：金融市场能够将资金从有资金盈余的产业导向存在资金需求的产业，从而利用资金流向刺激生产力的进一步发展并带动整个国家经济的增长。
- 鼓励创业：金融市场通过提供必要的资金协助那些创业公司的发展。
- 产业发展：金融市场通过其各个组成部分的功能，刺激国家的产业和经济在各个方面加速发展，从而有助于提高国家整体生活水平和社会福利。

相反的，金融危机对国家经济具有破坏性的影响。金融危机可以导致整个经济体的衰退，并且在大多数情况下一个国家需要花费很长的时间才能从衰退中复苏。重大金融危机对一个国家造成的经济损失无法用金钱来衡量。

因此，大多数国家对金融机构采取严格监管措施。每个国家的监管结构不同，但通常都涉及审慎监管、消费者保护和市场稳定。其监管目的是构建一个稳健与活跃并重的金融市场、预防金融危机的再次发生。在中国，随着人民币国际化及利率市场化的进程，金融机构面临着重大变革，这也为金融审计带来挑战。本章重点讨论法定审计在金融机构监管体系中发挥的作用以及如何进一步提高审计师[①]在这个监管体系中的功能。

## 一、国际经验

### （一）金融审计在政府监管中的作用

各国政府都试图通过直接监管金融部门来消除或减缓潜在的金融危机。监管的主要目标之一是提高透明度：通过要求金融机构定期提供并公开其按照相关会计准则编制的财务报告使公众了解金融机构的财务状况；监管的另一个目标是通过准备金、资本要求以及其他杠杆比率的限制确保金融机构有足够的资产以履行其契约义务。审计师在政府对金融机构的监管中发挥如表 8 所示的重要作用：



表 8　　审计师在政府对金融机构监管中的作用

| 监管目标 | 审计师的作用 |
|---|---|
| 透明度 | 对金融机构的财务报表执行高质量审计 |
| 资本充足率 | 对准备金、资本金及其他杠杆比率执行合规性审计工作[②] |

### （二）各国对金融审计的特殊规定和要求

鉴于金融机构的特殊性及金融审计的作用，各国对金融机构的审计都制定了特殊的规则和要求。以下我们介绍了世界上主要金融中心所在国家对金融审

---

① 在本章如无特别说明，审计师均指提供审计服务的会计师事务所。

② 通常金融机构的合规审计没有强制要求其法定审计师执行，金融机构可以聘请另一家有资格的会计师事务所提供该审计服务。然而，在实际操作中，法定审计师通常比其他事务所在执行合规审计方面更为高效，因此合规审计通常仍由法定审计师来执行。

计的特殊规范性措施：

1. 美国

在美国，联邦存款保险公司（Federal Deposit Insurance Corporation，FDIC）法规第363条规定了存款机构的年度审计和报告的特殊要求。它要求在会计年度初始合并资产总额超过5亿美元（含5亿美元）的存款机构必须公开发布年报，年报中须包含经审计的年度财务报告和独立审计师报告，并提交一份管理层对于财务报告内部控制架构及流程的评估报告以及一份审计师对该管理层内部控制评估报告的认证报告。它还对存款机构设立审计委员会及其职能和责任制定了详细要求。

为应对始于2008年的次贷危机，美国联邦政府于2010年颁布了《多德·弗兰克华尔街改革和消费者保护法案》（以下简称《多德·弗兰克法案》）。该法案被称为是对银行业“史上最严格”的监管，其目的是为了防止下一次金融危机和恢复消费者对金融业的信心。《多德·弗兰克法案》针对金融业制定了多种审计要求，归纳如下：



（1）美国审计总署（Government Accountability Office，GAO）需要对美国联邦储备系统（Federal Reserve System，Fed，简称美联储）进行多种不同的审计：

①对美联储2007年12月1日起至该法案颁布之日期间设立的所有紧急贷款和其他金融资助进行一次性审计；

②对美联储进行监管审计，以检查：

第一，目前对于联邦储备银行董事的任命体系能否保证其选举的董事能够代表“公众利益，没有种族、宗教信仰、肤色、性别或国籍的歧视，同时考虑到农业、商业、工业、服务业、劳动者和消费者的利益”；

第二，是否存在实际上的或潜在的利益冲突；

第三，每个机构的运营情况；

第四，针对美联储银行董事选聘程序或其他治理问题提出改进措施，使其更能够代表公众利益并且强化其提供的财务信息。

（2）在《多德·弗兰克法案》立法下成立了一个独立的金融稳定监督委员会（Financial Stability Oversight Council，FSOC），FSOC有权力要求资产超过500亿美元的任何银行或非银行金融机构提交以下相关报告：

①财务状况报告；

②风险监控系统报告；

③与受监管的子公司之间的交易报告；

④任何可能对金融市场或国家整体金融稳定性造成潜在的破坏性影响的活动报告。

（3）《多德·弗兰克法案》授予美国审计署长对金融稳定监督委员会及在其授权下活动的个人或实体进行审计的权力，同时审计署长有权力要求金融稳定监督委员会提供其掌握的任何信息。

（4）《多德·弗兰克法案》授予美国公众公司会计监督委员会（Public Company Accounting Oversight Board，PCAOB）对在美国证券交易委员会（Security Exchange Commission，SEC）注册的经纪人及承销商的审计进行监管的权力。在《多德·弗兰克法案》修正案的规定下，PCAOB 对在 SEC 注册的经纪人及承销商拥有与其对美国上市公司一样的监管权力，包括对其审计的准则制定、检查、调查和违纪处分①。

2. 英国

在英国，金融市场行为监管局（Financial Conduct Authority，FCA）要求对金融机构提供审计服务的专业人士必须拥有必要的金融机构审计技能，并且需要配合相关监管机构的调查回答问题、参加会议，以及提供相关信息给包括 FCA 在内的相关监管机构。详细要求摘录如下：

（1）SUP 3.4 审计师资格。

“公司拟委任的审计师应具备与该公司业务的性质、规模和复杂性及其所属的监管要求和标准相匹配的审计技能、资源和经验。公司应该考虑到其拟定的审计师是否就被审计单位的专业领域的相关规定和要求拥有充足的专门知识（其中可能涉及英国特有的专门知识）并且拥有或能够取得适当的专家技能，例如在对保险公司或社团审计时应该拥有与精算有关的专家技能。该公司应该从拟委任的审计师处取得确认函确认其拥有相关技能。

为了评估审计师对金融企业的审计能力，相关监管机构可以向审计师索取与其金融审计经验和技能有关的信息。对于初次执行金融审计的审计师，监管机构通常会以书面信函形式征询信息。审计师需要就信函全部问题给出合理解

---

① 更多有关《多德·弗兰克法案》信息请参见：http：//en. wikipedia. org/wiki/Dodd% E2% 80% 93Frank_ Wall_ Street_ Reform_ and_ Consumer_ Protection_ Act#Title_ VI_ . E2. 80. 93_ Improvements_ to _ Regulation

第二部分

答（如果该审计师未能就信函作出合理解答，则其不应该被聘任为该公司的审计师）。监管部门也可以在审计师聘任后要求其提供进一步的信息。”

（2）SUP 3.8 审计师的权利和职责。

“相关监管机构可能要求审计师出席会议并为其提供与被审计公司有关的信息。根据 SUP 3.8.2 R 条款规定，为配合相关监管机构依法履行其职责，审计师应出席这类会议并提供相关资料及信息。”

（3）SUP 3.10 审计师的职责：通知和报告客户资产。

“审计师必须向 FCA 提交一份有关被审计公司持有客户资产的报告，包含以下信息：

①首先，对 SUP 3.10.5 R[①] 条款要求的事项进行说明；

其次，具体说明 SUP 3.10.9 R 条款及 SUP 3.10.9A R[②]条款指定的事项；或者

②如果该公司声称没有持有客户资金或代保管的资产，审计师应声明在其审计过程中是否注意到任何使其相信在报告所涉期间该公司持有客户资金或代保管的资产的事项。”



3. 新加坡

在新加坡，新加坡金融管理局（Monetary Authority of Singapore，MAS）规定，所有金融机构必须聘请审计师对财务报表进行年度审计。如果金融机构没有按规定聘请审计师或者 MAS 认为其聘请的审计师不合适，MAS 可以为该金融机构指定审计师。除了财务报表审计以外，金融机构也应向 MAS 提交其压力测试的结果及审计师关于该机构内部控制流程的报告。

4. 澳大利亚

在澳大利亚，如果澳大利亚审慎监管局（Australia Prudential Regulation Authority，APRA）认为某个金融机构的审计师不合格，APRA 有权力对其解聘。对于金融审计师的基本要求是拥有最低 5 年的相关金融审计专业经验。在 APRA 执行对金融机构的审核期间，如果其认为有必要，也可以要求检查其审计师的审计工作底稿。APRA 要求金融机构提供多种报告，一类是常规报告，包括年度财务报表审计报告、对于金融机构的风险管理系统的报告和对于内部

---

① 指 FCA 手册中关于要求提供持有客户资产报告的条款。

② 指 FCA 手册中关于审计师不能形成对金融机构是否拥有客户资产的意见并出具相关资产报告的情况。

控制及金融机构向 APRA 提供数据的准确性的报告；另外一类是非常规报告，这些报告是根据 APRA 对个别项目特殊要求制定的报告。

### （三）金融监管的困难及为金融审计带来的挑战

我们的研究显示，金融监管中的难点之一在于金融服务行业中新产品层出不穷，发展极快，但是与新兴金融产品有关的法律和政策相对滞后。例如，有广泛观点认为在美国，对于信用违约互换产品的管制不严是导致 2008 年次贷危机发生的一个最重要的原因。金融行业的这种特点也对金融审计带来挑战：金融审计师需要充足的技术分析及运用能力，针对层出不穷的金融产品判断其会计处理是否合理并且管理层披露是否恰当。这要求审计师拥有充足的相关审计技术知识及经验。尤其是在新兴金融产品相关法律和政策滞后的情况下，如何准确判断金融产品的风险并进行合理披露，确保市场上潜在投资人能够通过财务报告对金融机构的风险进行合理判断，这无疑是一个严峻的挑战。



欺诈也是一个导致金融监管失败的主要原因。这样的例子很多，比如 20 世纪早期波士顿查尔斯·庞氏的骗局、1994 年俄罗斯 MMM 投资基金破产骗局、诈骗导致的 1997 年阿尔巴尼亚彩票起义事件、2008 年麦道夫投资证券的破产骗局等。在这些案例中，金融机构通过误导性投资策略吸引投资者进行投资，或者盗用投资基金进行欺诈。抵押贷款融资欺诈也被认为是导致 2008 年美国次贷危机的一个主要原因。2008 年 9 月 23 日，美国政府披露，联邦调查局调查按揭融资公司可能存在的欺诈行为，调查对象包括房利美①、房地美②、雷曼兄弟和美国国际集团保险公司等。另外有观点认为，许多金融公司在最近的危机中失败是因为他们的管理层未能履行其代理责任。欺诈带给审计师的挑战是毋庸置疑的。常规审计方法往往能够发现由于管理层疏忽导致的财务报表错误，但是较难发现由于管理层欺诈而引发的误导性财务计量。这要求金融审计师拥有特殊审计技巧及经验。

---

① 国家住房抵押贷款中心，与下文的房地美（Freddie Mac）一样，主要业务是在美国房屋抵押贷款二级市场中收购贷款，并通过向投资者发行机构债券或证券化的抵押债券，以较低成本集资，赚取利差。在 2008 年美国开始的次贷危机中遭受重创面临倒闭，后经美国联邦政府接管免于倒闭。

② 联邦住房抵押贷款公司，与上文房利美（Fannie Mae）相同的机构。见注解①。

### （四）金融审计的经验及教训

2008年开始的次贷危机，使各国的金融监管部门更加意识到金融机构提供“准确、翔实和透明”的财务报告的重要性。2009年以来，美国PCAOB发出多次警报，强调在金融危机时期的审计要求；英国FRC针对各大银行董事发表了有关偿付能力、流动性风险管理和持续经营会计核算基础的指导意见。无一例外地，上述监管机构对金融机构审计的关注重点集中在以下领域：

1. 电子计算机审计技能

在现代社会中，金融机构大多拥有庞大的计算机体系及网络，并通过这些计算机网络来进行大量的金融交易。随着电子计算机技术的提高及金融产品的演变，这些计算机系统越来越复杂。审计师要想对金融机构进行有效审计就离不开对这些电子计算机系统的审计，这些都要求审计师拥有先进的电子计算机审计技能以应对金融审计的特殊要求。



2. 公允价值评估

公允价值计量的金融资产、金融负债和衍生金融产品。由于市场上层出不穷的结构复杂的金融产品，公允价值计量也越来越复杂，特别是对各种衍生品和嵌入性衍生金融工具的估价往往需要特殊专长。大部分情况下审计师需要利用内部或外部专家进行估值，所以可能还涉及审计师利用专家的工作。

3. 减值评估

所有的金融机构都面临着信用风险，与其相关的资产减值评估存在高度的管理层估计和判断因素。在金融危机时，整个经济处于衰退之中，大部分的债务人深受价格下跌和通货膨胀的影响，因而减值风险更高。

4. 信息披露

对风险信息、关键的估计和判断的合理披露能够为投资者提供必要的信息。目前财务报告存在对风险信息披露不足的问题。另外一个关于披露的问题是披露信息的复杂性，在财务报告中披露的信息过于复杂导致普通投资者无法理解并对风险水平作出正确判断，因此无法作出正确的决策。

5. 欺诈风险

在经济低迷时期，公司业绩和经营成果面临更大的压力，管理层舞弊的风险比以往任何时候都要高。

6. 合并财务报告及对特殊目的实体的会计处理

金融机构通常利用特殊目的实体来进行高风险投资，由于风险很高，这些投资的价值波动通常很大。如果这些特殊目的实体没有被纳入金融机构的合并范围内，那么投资人就无法通过金融机构的财务报告来“全面”了解金融机构的信息。

此外，大型金融机构规模庞大，交易复杂，为这类金融机构提供审计服务的事务所需要拥有充足的人才储备及审计经验，以确保其审计服务的有效性。研究显示，在世界主要国家/地区，大型的金融机构一般倾向于选择大型会计师事务所为其提供专业服务。

## 二、中国实践



中国金融服务业在过去的 15 年间经历了重大的改革和发展。在这 15 年间，四大国有银行先后转制为股份有限公司并且在全球各主要的证券交易所上市；上海和深圳建立了股票交易市场；人民币汇率从对美元的固定汇率转变为半浮动汇率等。在当下，中国也面临着人民币国际化及利率市场化的转变。这些发展伴随着更多更复杂的金融交易和产品进入中国市场，为中国金融机构审计带来重大机遇和挑战。

和其他国家一样，中国政府对金融服务业实行高度管制，也特别重视对金融机构审计的要求。多年来中国财政部、银监会、中国人民银行针对金融机构审计发布了多项规章制度。2010 年 8 月，中国银监会发布了《银行业金融机构外部审计监管指引》；2010 年 12 月，财政部发布了《金融企业选聘会计师事务所招标管理办法（试行）》。上述文件规定了对金融机构审计师的资格要求，并且要求超过一定规模的金融机构必须通过强制招标程序聘请审计师。

2014 年 9 月，中国银监会发布了《商业银行内部控制指引》（以下简称《指引》），对银行的内部控制提出了新的指导意见。新的指引相比之前的规定在以下方面进行了完善：一是内部控制评价：修订后的《指引》补充完善了内部控制评价的工作要求。要求商业银行建立内部控制评价制度，明确内部控制评价的实施主体、频率、内容、程序、方法和标准，强化内部控制评价结果运用，推动内部控制评价工作制度化、规范化，以利于促进商业银行不断改进其内部控制设计与运行。二是监管约束：修订后的《指引》增加了有关违反规定的处罚措施。要求银监会及其派出机构对内部控制存在缺陷的商业银行，责成其限期整改，对逾期未整改的商业银行，根据有关规定采取监管处罚措施。

鉴于金融审计的复杂性和重要性，金融机构的审计委员会在选择审计师并向股东会推荐的时候都是非常谨慎的。他们会注重审计师的相关经验及背景是否符合财政部、银监会等监管机构的要求，审计师对金融业风险的掌控能力以及审计师的整体规模和综合实力。另外，由于大型金融机构一般都涉及多地上市或者存在海外上市的关联方，受到“多重监管”，这就需要审计师不仅要了解中国金融业的监管要求，也要了解海外的监管要求，并拥有相关审计经验。例如，在中国，国有大型银行的审计一般聘请“四大”会计师事务所执行。据了解，“四大”会计师事务所对“四大”国有商业银行的审计团队人数一般都超过 200 人，其中经理级别以上的人员一般为 30 ~ 50 名。这些人员拥有多年银行审计经验及在海外发行金融产品的相关财务及审计经验，其中项目主管合伙人是具有丰富审计经验的资深合伙人，其银行审计经验往往超过 30 年；项目经理的金融机构相关审计经验也都超过 5 年，一般为 8 ~ 10 年。另外，这些银行审计团队中也包括拥有特殊审计技能的专家，例如计算机系统方面的专家、精算方面的专家以及估值方面的专家等。



中国政府倡导的亚洲基础设施投资银行的成立预示着中国跻身世界金融中心的步伐正在加快，人民币国际化利率市场化以及新兴电子金融和电子银行将使金融服务业变得更加复杂。中国金融的发展为金融机构审计师带来新的挑战，注册会计师需要掌握新的技能以应对市场中越来越复杂的交易及产品带来的额外风险。

## 三、有关建议

针对金融审计的特殊性，我们就中国金融机构审计提出以下几个方面的建议：

### （一）夯实教育

金融机构的财务报表必须能够“透明且充分”地反映金融机构的财务状况。这样社会公众才能够通过其财务报表对金融机构的财务状况有正确的认识，市场上的广大投资者也才能够利用这些财务报表信息，作出正确的投资决策。

为了能够使金融机构的财务报表“透明且充分”地反映其财务状况，金融机构的管理层需要具有编制金融机构财务报表所需的相关知识及技能；金融机构的审计师也必须拥有审计金融机构的相关知识及经验。这些都要求通过教育及培训，使金融机构的管理层及其审计师对金融机构的高风险领域掌握足够的相关知识。另外，对市场上的潜在投资人进行这些方面的教育也是十分必要的，这样可以保证这些投资人能够正确阅读并理解财务报表，进而根据经审计的财务信息及其他信息作出明智的投资决定。结合中国实际情况，我们将金融机构的高风险领域总结为如下几点：

1. 金融资产的信用分析及减值准备

金融机构拥有大量的贷款、应收款项及其他类型的金融资产，这些都为金融机构带来交易对手风险和信用风险。对金融资产的信用分析和减值准备需要使用大量的管理层判断和估计。金融机构审计师需要拥有针对管理层估计进行审计的特殊技能，如确定估计中使用的关键因素和假设、考虑关键因素和假设的敏感性、历史数据的偏差、主观错报的风险和管理层偏见等。这方面的审计还通常需要使用回顾（即利用历史数据推理事件发生的规律和方向）和前瞻（即利用现有资料预测未来事件）等审计技巧。

2. 公允价值评估及利用专家的工作

根据会计准则规定，大量金融资产和负债需要在资产负债表中以“公允价值”计量。其中很多种类的投资，如拍卖利率债券、商业票据、房屋抵押或其他资产抵押债券、另类投资（如对冲基金、私募股权投资等）、担保债务凭证和其他投资都涉及复杂的公允价值评估。金融机构通常使用一个复杂的估值模型进行公允价值的评估，审计师需要具备与评估有关的专业技能，通常需要聘用评估专家对这些公允价值评估进行审查。审计师需要的专业技能包括评估对特定类型的资产或负债的估值模型是否合理、估值中关键性假设的使用是否合理——尤其是当这些假设并非来自市场上能够观测到的数据，以及这些关键假设的敏感性等。

3. 合并报表和对特殊目的实体的会计处理

金融机构通常使用特殊目的实体来开展某些高风险项目。这些特殊目的实体可以以不同的形式存在。如果这类特殊目的实体没有被包含在该金融机构的合并范围内，将导致对投资者提供误导性信息。为了防止出现这种问题，审计师需要特殊技能来对这种特殊目的实体相关的复杂的法律协议进行审核并衡量该业务安排的商业实质。

4. 内部控制和欺诈风险

由于金融机构交易规模大、数量多且交易性质复杂，它需要有一个完善有效的内部控制系统。金融机构通常利用复杂的 ERP 系统来完成处理交易的需要。相应的，审计师需要拥有熟练的 IT 技能以对复杂的计算机系统执行审计，并识别漏洞。内部控制中的任何不足之处都可能为欺诈提供机会，审计师需要考虑欺诈活动对金融机构审计的影响。

5. 披露

为了使报告使用者能够全面掌握金融机构的风险并作出合理的投资决策，在金融机构的财务报告中对风险状况和管理估计的无偏差披露是十分重要的。这需要对金融机构的控制环境、风险评估、控制活动、用于作出估计和判断的系统和方法、关键假设的敏感性等拥有全面详细的了解。好的披露绝对不是按照一个标准的模板复制出来的东西，它应该从管理者的角度提供所有必要的信息，同时信息的披露应该简洁，避免使用过于复杂的语言。审计师应发挥“守门员”的角色来确保这样的披露得以实现。



上述 5 个领域的审计技能在现代金融机构的审计工作中是非常重要的，尤其是越来越多的复杂的金融产品将不断涌现。提高这些技能的方法包括通过安排各种培训，如注册会计师专业协会提供的培训、研讨会；通过相关审计工作经验积累以及通过阅读书籍进行自学等。例如，美国公众公司会计监管委员会在 2008 年次贷危机后发布各种警报以要求审计师在金融机构审计的高风险领域给予特别关注，并提供了这些高风险领域审计的指导说明。

除以上领域以外，在现代金融审计服务中，金融审计师还必须拥有的一项至关重要的技能就是与时俱进的电子计算机技术及相关审计技能，从而能够对金融机构使用的复杂的电子交易系统及网络进行有效审核。

### （二）人才储备

如前文所述，大多数金融机构都具有规模庞大、系统复杂的特点。会计师事务所要想对这类大型金融机构提供有效的审计服务就必须注重自身的人才储备、培养及吸收有金融审计经验的审计师以及拥有特殊审计技能的人才，例如精算专家、评估专家、电子计算机系统专家等。这样才能够提高会计师事务所在金融审计领域的竞争力，赢得金融审计客户。同时随着金融审计客户数量的增加，审计师应进一步培养金融审计人才，不断壮大金融审计队伍，形成良性循环。

中国财政部一直以来注重培养会计专业人才，并推出若干会计专业人才培养计划。其中，会计领军人才培养及特殊支持计划旨在发掘并培养中国会计领域的高端人才。中国会计师事务所可以结合财政部推出的会计领军人才培养计划，有针对性地培养金融审计方面的专业人才，充实人才储备，壮大团队规模，提升在金融审计方面的竞争力。

## （三）监管检查

监管检查可以保证法定审计服务的质量。在中国，财政部、银监会、保监会等监管机构都对金融机构的审计师执行定期或不定期的质量检查。鉴于金融机构对整个国家经济的重要性，监管机构可以考虑进一步提高对金融机构审计师的检查频率和扩大覆盖范围，以营造一个稳健有效的金融管理控制体系。各监管机构可以互相配合并且进行整体协调，建立一个以财政部门检查为主的质量检查体系，避免对同一个审计师在同一时间进行多次重复检查，这样可以节省监管机构的成本，将资源运用到提高检查频率及扩大覆盖面上。例如，财政部作为审计师的直接监管部门，应该主导对审计师进行的质量检查；其他监管部门如银监会等，应该主要针对金融企业进行质量检查，如果在其检查过程中发现的问题可能涉及金融企业的审计，这些监管部门可以与财政部配合进行对审计师的检查，这样就避免了重复监管。另外，为了提高检查频率和扩大覆盖范围，相关监管机构也可以考虑使用政府采购审计师服务，从会计师事务所购买这类服务有助于提高政府监管的独立性和客观性。本书第六章讨论了政府采购会计服务的相关问题。

监管机构的检查机制应公开透明，向公众提供其采用的抽查方法、检查范围及检查结果等信息，这将进一步提升公众信心并建立市场信任。以美国为例，美国公众公司会计监管委员会对各金融机构审计师进行各种检查，检查方法、范围及结果都刊载于其官方网站。澳大利亚监管机构也将这些信息全部公开于其官方网站。基于对会计师行业的保护，公开的检查结果往往不会提及审计师名称，而是将普遍存在的问题以不记名方式公之于众，以便其他审计师在审计中遇到同样的问题时，给予重视，避免同样的问题再次发生。

监管检查应该集中考察审计师的经验、能力和审计工作的质量。监管机构可以根据检查目的，要求事务所提交报告，说明其事务所及相关合伙人对金融机构审计的相关资质和经验以进行检查。例如，英国金融市场行为监管局对于初次执行金融审计的审计师，通常会以书面信函形式征询其关于金融审计经验和技能有关的信息，审计师必须以书面形式进行回复。如果金融市场行为监管局认为其金融审计经验和技能不足，可以要求更换审计师。

### （四）惩戒措施

良好的质量控制环境离不开合理的惩戒措施，这些措施通常包括通报批评、经济处罚以及通过限制事务所的业务范围来进行惩戒。例如限期禁止有问题的事务所及其合伙人对金融机构提供审计服务，那么这些事务所及其合伙人就需要在限期内证明他们进行了相关的学习培训并提高了他们的金融审计技能。此外，在金融机构审计检查中发现的问题也可能反映了被审计金融机构也许存在合规性问题，这些问题应该通过合理的渠道向金融机构的监管者进行反映，以便在必要情况下对相关金融机构采取惩戒措施，确保市场的稳定性。

# 第八章　会计师事务所职业责任保险

会计师事务所提供的所有服务，无论是审计还是非审计服务，都面临着在服务完成后被利益相关者起诉的风险。提供审计服务的专业人士（以下统称为“审计师”）的疏忽或者过失不仅对被审计公司会产生很严重的后果，对其他利益相关者也是如此。例如被审计公司的每一个股东、债权人以及潜在的投资者都可能由于审计师的疏忽或者过失而蒙受损失。职业责任保险是一种针对会计师事务所可能因执业活动使委托人或其他利害关系人遭受经济损失而提供的保险。



## 一、国际经验

### （一）是否强制保险

世界上大多数国家均通过立法或者由会计职业组织的行业自律条款强制要求注册会计师或会计师事务所购买职业责任保险。表 9 总结了世界上主要有代表性的国家/地区对于会计师职业责任保险要求的相关规定。

表 9　　各国关于会计师职业责任保险的相关要求

| 国家/地区 | 强制保险相关要求 |
| --- | --- |
| 英国 | 主要会计职业组织均强制规定了责任保险最低投保额，比如英格兰及威尔士特许会计师协会（ICAEW），英国特许公认会计师公会（ACCA） |
| 德国 | 公共会计法案中规定了强制保险的最低投保额度 |
| 法国 | 法律规定了强制保险的最低投保额度 |

续表

| 国家/地区 | 强制保险相关要求 |
|---|---|
| 澳大利亚 | 会计师协会规定了强制保险的最低投保额度，例如澳新特许会计师协会（CAANZ） |
| 新加坡 | 新加坡会计师法规定了强制保险要求的最低投保额度 |
| 香港 | 香港会计师公会（HKICPA）规定了强制保险的最低投保额度 |
| 美国 | 美国注册会计师协会（AICPA）鼓励所有会计师事务所购买责任险，大多数会计师事务所均购买了一定数额的责任险 |

## （二）保险范围

对于那些有强制购买职业责任保险要求的国家/地区，这些要求或者是对注册会计师个人的，或者是对会计师事务所的。在英国和澳大利亚，强制保险的要求是针对具有执业资格的注册会计师个人的，不论这些执业会计师在任何法律形式的事务所中执业都需要购买职业责任保险。在其他一些国家/地区，比如德国、新加坡和香港，强制保险是针对事务所的，而且只有涉及有限责任形式的事务所需要购买职业责任保险，例如会计师事务所有限责任公司或者有限责任合伙制事务所。由于无限责任形式的事务所其组织形式保证了提供审计服务的专业人士对其过失或者疏忽承担无限的法律责任，这些会计师事务所为了控制其面临的风险，都会自发地采取一定的保护措施，例如自发性地购买保险或者提取风险储备基金。这样大多数国家的强制保险要求不包含无限责任形式的事务所，而是给予这些事务所一定的自由选择空间。表 10 总结了各主要国家/地区的保险范围要求：

**表 10　　各国/地区保险范围要求**

| 国家/地区 | 保险范围 |
|---|---|
| 英国 | ACCA 和 ICAEW 都要求其拥有执业资格证书的会员进行投保 |
| 德国 | 具有执业资格的注册会计师、会计师有限公司和有限责任合伙制事务所需要购买强制保险 |
| 澳大利亚 | 全部拥有执业资格证书的会员需要购买保险 |

续表

| 国家/地区 | 保险范围 |
| --- | --- |
| 新加坡 | 全部在新加坡会计师法下注册登记的会计师事务所有限责任公司和有限责任合伙公司需要购买保险（对承担无限责任的普通合伙制会计师事务所没有强制购买保险的要求） |
| 香港 | 每一个会计师事务所有限责任公司都需要购买保险（对承担无限责任的普通合伙制会计师事务所没有强制购买保险的要求） |

## （三）保险额度

最低保险额度通常要求是以注册会计师个人或者事务所的收入为基础计算得出的。在一些国家，通过区分审计客户中是否有上市公司对会计师事务所规定了不同的投保要求（见表 11）：



**表 11　　各国/地区保险额度要求**

| 国家/地区 | 保险额度 |
| --- | --- |
| 英国 | • ACCA 规定的注册会计师责任保险的最低额度为该注册会计师上一年度全部收入总额 2.5 倍或者单笔最大服务收费的 25 倍中较高者，且最低保险额度不得低于 5 万英镑①；<br>• ICAEW 针对收入超过 60 万英镑的事务所规定的最低投保额为 150 万英镑。对于收入总额没有超过 60 万英镑的事务所，其投保额应为收入的 2.5 倍，且不少于 10 万英镑。 |
| 德国 | 对非上市公司的服务最低投保额为 100 万欧元，对上市公司的服务最低投保额为 400 万欧元。 |
| 法国 | 最低投保额为每次事故赔偿限额 250 万欧元 |

① 在英国，会计师职业责任保险的要求是针对各会计职业组织会员个人提出的，但是在实践中，由于执业会计师必须在一个经注册许可的会计师事务所中执业，这种职业责任保险往往都是对事务所承保。对于那些由会计职业组织会员与非会员共同成立的事务所来说，整个事务所都需要购买这种职业保险。例如，在一个由会员与非会员组成的合伙制事务所中，合伙制的连带责任导致那些会员合伙人需要对非会员合伙人的过失承担责任，这样，保险就需要覆盖整个事务所，而不仅仅是那些会员合伙人，所以对最低投保额的要求也是针对事务所来要求的。

续表

| 国家/地区 | 保险额度 |
|---|---|
| 澳大利亚 | 根据CAANZ成员手册要求，审计服务的最低投保额度（按照每个事务所的年审计收费额计算①）为：<br>• 审计收费在澳币10万元以下的项目投保额度不得低于澳币200万元；<br>• 审计收费在澳币10万元到30万元之间的项目投保额度不得低于澳币500万元；<br>• 审计收费在澳币30万元到50万元之间的项目投保额度不得低于澳币1000万元；<br>• 审计收费在澳币50万元到100万元之间的项目投保额度不得低于澳币2000万元；<br>• 审计收费在澳币100万元到250万元之间的项目投保额度不得低于澳币5000万元；<br>• 审计收费在澳币250万元以上的项目投保额度不得低于澳币7500万元 |
| 新加坡 | 最低保险额度为以下各项中较高者：<br>• 100万新币；<br>• 按照会计师事务所中全部签字会计师每人50万元新币计算的总额；或者<br>• 如果适用，会计师事务所上个完整财务报告年度收入的2.5倍，最高额不超过5000万元新币 |
| 香港 | 最低投保额为以下最高者：<br>• 根据香港会计师公会的最低保险额度要求的金额（目前是500万港币）；<br>• 上一年度收入总额的2.5倍，最高不超过1500万港币；<br>• 用该事务所在投保年度开始日的合伙人人数乘以300万港币得出的金额 |

### （四）离任后保护

离任后保护是指当一个注册会计师或会计师事务所停止执业后，注册会计师或会计师事务所还需要在多长时间范围内继续购买保险。由于会计师事务所有可能在一个合伙人离任后仍然因该合伙人在任时负责的项目被起诉，或会计师事务所在停止执业后仍因以前年度的执业活动被起诉，因此这种离任后的保护是有必要的。表12总结了主要国家/地区离任后保护的具体要求：

① 与英国一样，澳大利亚的会计师职业责任保险要求是针对各会计职业组织会员个人提出的，但是最低投保额是按照事务所规模计算的。原因与英国相同，详见上页附注。

表 12　　各国/地区离任后保护要求

| 国家/地区 | 保险范围 |
|---|---|
| 英国 | ICAEW：执业会计师个人 2 年；如果会计师事务所关闭，则需要额外 4 年保护期；ACCA：6 年 |
| 澳大利亚 | 7 年 |
| 香港 | 7 年 |

### （五）特别保险措施

为确保注册会计师/会计师事务所能够通过支付合理的费用购买到相应的职业责任保险，各国政府及会计职业组织都致力于采取一定的措施。

在英国，就以 ICAEW 为例，ICAEW 为其会员采取了如下措施确保其会员能够在市场中购买到相应的职业责任保险：ICAEW 职业责任保险委员会明确规定了最低限度的保险条款要求，这主要是用来避免保险条款中包含含糊不清的条款以及确保事务所在签署保单之前的服务也被包含在保险公司的承保范围内。保险公司如果想加入 ICAEW 会员保险计划并为其会员提供保险服务，就必须同意按照 ICAEW 职业责任保险委员会规定的最低限度的保险条款提供保险服务。此外，ICAEW 还要求加入其会员保险计划的保险公司在保险条款中加入对“意外情形”进行的承诺。即在投保人和承保人对保险条款产生争议的时候，按照上述承诺，如果保险公司提供的保险条款相比 ICAEW 职业责任保险委员会规定的最低限度的保险条款对投保人更不利，则适用 ICAEW 职业责任保险委员会规定的最低限度的保险条款。ICAEW 网站公布了加入其成员保险计划的保险公司名单。在这些保险公司购买职业责任保险的 ICAEW 会员可以确保他们的保险条款都满足了 ICAEW 职业责任保险委员会的最低要求。

除此之外，如果事务所被证明无法从加入 ICAEW 成员保险计划的保险公司那里购买到相应的责任保险，ICAEW 将对这些事务所进行识别并提供“指定风险池”服务。

无法购买责任保险分为两种情形：一是直接被加入 ICAEW 保险保障计划的保险公司拒绝提供保险服务；二是会计师事务所为购买保险需要支付的保费额度过大，导致其无法承担，或者如果该事务所支付相应保费，则其将会陷入财务困境。在这种情形下，事务所可以提出要求，加入 ICAEW 的“指定风险池”，直到其能够从市场上购买到相应保险为止。“指定风险池”为那些无法从市场上获得保险的事务所提供了一个短期保障服务，所有加入 ICAEW 成员保险计划的保险公司均为风险池中的公司共同承保。

根据 ICAEW 网站上公布的信息，目前有 65 家在英国注册的保险机构及 49 家在爱尔兰注册的保险机构加入了 ICAEW 的成员保险计划①。

在美国，AICPA 与大型保险公司合作开展了“美国注册会计师责任保险计划”项目，并提供三种不同程度的保险计划以供会计师事务所选择（见表 13）：

**表 13　　美国注册会计师责任保险计划**

| 保险项目 | 主要特征 |
|---|---|
| CPA 价值计划 | 针对那些不超过 3 个合伙人且年收入少于 40 万美元的事务所，CPA 价值计划涵盖了会计、税务和咨询业务，包括：<br>• 税收筹划及报税<br>• 个人理财计划<br>• 代理记账<br>• 整理财务数据<br>• 审阅<br>• 审计<br>• 管理咨询服务<br>• 信息技术服务<br>• 基本业务规划<br>• 法律顾问 |
| 超值计划 | 针对具有 4 个或 4 个以上合伙人并且年收入超过 40 万美元的会计师事务所。该项保险计划覆盖的专业服务范围包括：<br>• 税收筹划及报税<br>• 审计和其他鉴证业务<br>• 综合会计服务<br>• 上市公司服务<br>• 计算机软硬件服务<br>• 经营顾问<br>• 个人理财<br>• 诉讼支持及法律顾问<br>• 管理咨询服务及更多 |

① 更多关于 ICAEW 强制保险要求及安排可以在以下网址中查找：http：//www. icaew. com/en/members/regulations - standards - and - guidance/practice - management/professional - indemnity - insurance - regulations - guidance - current#ICAEW151

续表

| 保险项目 | 主要特征 |
|---|---|
| 大公司计划 | 大公司计划是为大型会计师事务所以及总收入超过 1000 万美元的事务所专门订制的保险项目计划（“四大” 会计师事务所除外）① |

在澳大利亚，各州政府都制定了法律，规定了执业会计师提供专业服务的最高法律责任限额。也就是说，职业会计师如果在工作中出现疏忽或者过失，需要对第三方进行赔偿，那么最高赔付额不会超过法律规定的限额。其中，提供审计服务的责任限额为澳币 7500 万元，其他服务的责任限额通常为其服务收费的 20 到 30 倍。这种规定使保险公司能够对提供会计师职业责任保险的潜在风险进行衡量并将其控制在一定可保范围内②。

### （五）注册会计师职业责任保险的重要作用

在一定程度上，注册会计师职业责任保险可以让会计师事务所避免由于过失或者疏忽等原因引发大额民事赔偿而倒闭，从而保护会计师事务所的可持续发展，进而维护资本市场的稳定。任何一个大型会计师事务所的倒闭将给资本市场带来巨大的冲击。根据《审计师责任制度的经济影响研究》③一书中的分析——“这种情形（指现有大型会计师事务所倒闭）显然后果严重并且任何市场调整只会带来更多的问题。首先，由于对审计师以及审计行业价值的质疑，投资者的信心会产生巨大的动摇。投资者对公司经审计报告的信心会严重受损，其结果可能导致资本成本的大规模上升。同时，由于风险过高，具有丰富经验的审计职员以及合伙人可能会退出审计这个行业，导致审计服务市场供给缩水。由于倒闭的事务所之前的审计客户需要寻找新的审计师，同时审计服务市场供给缩水将导致市场上供需不平衡，很多公司，尤其是那些需要特殊审计技能的公司将无法及时提交法定审计报告。审计服务的费用由于供需不平衡而提高，而且由此导致的审计费提高不会是暂时的。”

① 更多关于美国注册会计师责任保险计划的信息可以从以下网址中查询：http：//www. cpai. com/business - insurance/professional - liability/index

② 参见以下新南威尔士州法律对最高责任限额的要求：http：//www. legislation. nsw. gov. au/maintop/view/inforce/act + 81 + 1994 + cd + 0 + N

③ 由伦敦经济杂志及德国 Goethe 大学的 Ralf Ewert 博士于 2006 年 9 月发表。

第二部分

注册会计师职业责任保险的另一个好处是可以保护由于审计师疏忽或者过失所受损的第三方的利益。特别是针对那些没有足够备用金来赔偿损失的中小型事务所来说，这个优点尤为突出。

### （六）注册会计师职业责任保险的复杂性

在市场操作中，注册会计师职业责任保险面临着一些复杂的市场因素，下面对这些问题进行详细讨论：

对于保险业来说，一项风险能够被承保的因素之一是这个风险必须能够被分散，并且这个风险在可能性及影响程度上均能够被量化，而在历史上，由于种种原因，注册会计师职业责任保险面临以下一些挑战：

（1）市场上有限数量的大型会计师事务所限制了保险公司分散风险的能力。例如，在欧洲，由于四大会计师事务所主导了市场上主要审计服务业务，同时会计师事务所都是由其网络统一为全部成员所进行投保，这就导致为审计服务提供的保险只能在四个参保对象中进行分散，这个数字显然太小了。

（2）对于风险的规模及未来的补偿无法预测。根据国际知名保险公司 AON 披露的 1975 至 2003 年的信息，在欧洲四大/五大会计师事务所的年度责任赔偿损失成本①由 1500 万美元上升至 2.24 亿美元。在个别年度，事务所的赔偿成本远远高于其他年度。

在 19 世纪 80 年代，会计师职业责任保险在欧洲及美国获利并不多，有些甚至亏损。表 14 显示了自 1997 至 2002 年各个国家责任保险盈利水平：

**表 14　　责任保险盈利水平**

| 国家 | 平均损失比重（发生的诉讼费用/保费） |
|---|---|
| 美国 | 99.7% |
| 法国 | 113.2% |
| 德国 | 65.1% |
| 意大利 | 102% |
| 英国 | 99% |

数据来源：Swiss Re Sigma, The economics of liability losses - insuring a moving target, No. 6/2004

① 此处指欧洲四大/五大会计师事务所全部加总的年度责任损失赔偿额。

第二部分

以上问题导致的结果是，保险公司为保持盈利，不再为会计师事务所提供责任保险或者大幅度提高会计师职业责任保险的保费金额并缩减责任保险涵盖范围。由于注册会计师行业的激烈竞争，会计师事务所很难将提高的保险费用通过提高审计费用而完全转嫁到审计服务收费中。尽管注册会计师行业对职业责任保险的需求很高，但是相对较高的保费以及缩减的保险范围令会计师事务所对购买职业责任保险仍持有一定观望心态。

另外，研究显示会计师事务所保险诉讼案件需要较长时间才能够得以解决，通常需要 5 到 10 年的时间，对于一些大型诉讼案件花费的时间会更多。这对于商业保险公司和会计师事务所来说，由于双方都需要雇佣律师及其他专业人员解决诉讼问题，双方均需要花费大量成本。这就让这种保险对于保险公司和会计师事务所双方来说都削弱了吸引力。

由于上述原因，为保证会计师事务所能够从市场上购买到职业责任保险，各国/地区政府或者会计职业组织都采取了一定措施。我们在本书前面的部分对这些特别保险措施进行了详细讨论。同样的，由于上述原因，一般来讲在市场上购买的职业责任保险往往不能为大型会计师事务所提供其所需要的全部保障，尤其是对四大这样的大型事务所来说，由于这些事务所面临的责任风险很高，很难从市场上找到愿意提供相应保险的公司满足其全部责任保险需要。比如，在上文中提到的美国注册会计师保险计划中涉及的三类保障计划都没有包含四大会计师事务所。这样，这些大型的会计师事务所通常会采取一些其他的保障措施作为自身风险控制体系的一部分。例如，大型会计师事务所，诸如“四大”，一般会成立专业自保公司为其网络事务所提供更全面的保险。专业自保是为防范来源于网络事务所的风险所专门设立的保险。每个网络事务所都要定期缴纳一定额度的“保证金”构成自保份额并据此享有被保险权利。保证金的数额大小以及保险水平取决于事务所在整个网络事务所内的相对规模以及网络内部质量检查结果。规模大或质量差的网络事务所需要交纳的保证金数额相对较高。通常这种专业自保公司能够从市场上购买到比较有限的再保险。除此之外，专业自保主要是将各个网络事务所的风险在网络中“平均化”，是一种自我保护举措。

在西方，劳合社是有限的能够为大型会计师事务所提供保险服务的保险机构之一，它能够为高额风险提供辛迪加式（即由若干在法律形式上保持独立，在商业上互相合作的保险公司或保险机构共同提供一项或几项服务的形式）保险保障。劳合社机构设置分为“劳合社公司”和“劳合社市场”两部分。其中，劳合社市场由57个管理顾问和93个辛迪加组成，为客户提供保险安排；劳合社公司对劳合社市场进行监督及提供支持，以确保其有效运作。劳合社的保单都是由劳合社保险顾问与客户面对面按照客户的需求定制的，其承保的风险通常由参与劳合社的辛迪加成员共同承担，由此来分散风险。这样就使劳合社能够承保相对高额的风险。我们注意到，四大的专业自保公司的再保险也大多是由劳合社提供的。

除了个别情形外，中型会计师事务所国际网络一般没有专业自保的安排，它们的保险主要来源于市场。这主要是由于中型会计师事务所的结构较为松散，没有像四大会计师事务所那样进行集中管理、统一协调。中型会计师事务所国际网络通常是由几个成员所组成的，成员所分享特定的管理服务并按照各成员所的收入百分比或者各成员所使用的管理服务量缴纳一定的成员费。通常这些成员所的主要经营活动是各自分开的，不受统一管理。



## 二、中国实践

相对欧美来说，注册会计师职业责任保险在中国处于起步阶段。在1994年颁布的《中国注册会计师法》中规定了会计师事务所应当建立职业风险基金或购买保险。然而，责任保险制度真正开始实施是在2000年左右，当时深圳的一家会计师事务所与平安保险公司签约购买了相应的责任保险。

为了保证会计师事务所能够在市场上购买到适合的职业责任保险产品，在2011年年末，上海市注册会计师协会在上海市为会计师事务所开展了集体公开招标。在这次招标活动中，上海市注册会计师协会鼓励保险公司提出招标建议并且形成了一个5人招标协商专业小组进行协商。专业小组成员包括上海市注册会计师协会的代表、会计师事务所的代表及保险行业专家。该招标活动的目的旨在代表上海会计师事务所协商降低保费及扩大保险承保范围，以提高会计师事务所投保积极性。

招标协商的结果是会计师事务所和保险公司之间实现了双赢。会计师事务所不仅扩大了保单中涵盖的责任保险范围并且降低了保险成本。对于事务所来说，在一定程度上就提供了可靠保障。对于保险公司来说，中标的保险公司业务会得到显著发展。中国太平洋保险公司上海分公司在这次招标活动中成功入选承保人后，其责任保险的保险客户由原来的 3 家增加到 54 家，同时这也有助于保险公司在提供该类保险中更好地分散风险，降低成本。

2014 年年末，财政部会同保监会也发布了关于会计师事务所职业责任保险相关办法的征求意见稿，对会计师事务所购买职业责任保险作出了一系列规范性的要求，预计将于 2015 年正式发布，从而填补中国注册会计师行业在职业责任保险领域的制度空白。

## 三、有关建议

会计师事务所应当建立稳健的内部风险控制系统从而应对由于其自身过失或者疏忽所带来的风险损失。会计师事务所为取得合理风险控制，应该衡量其自身通过备用金等形式承担的风险和通过商业保险转嫁给第三方的风险，并在两者中取得一个合理的平衡。



对于会计师职业责任保险的要求应当结合事务所的组织形式加以分析。从 2010 年开始，财政部陆续出台了各种文件鼓励会计师事务所将组织形式转变为特殊普通合伙制。中国四大会计师事务所在 2012 年以前均陆续完成了向特殊普通合伙制的转制。然而，市场上仍然存在着众多中小型会计师事务所，其组织形式为有限责任制。由于有限责任制会计师事务所的赔偿限额以公司的净资产为限，对投资者保护也就相应受到限制。在这种情形下，职业风险基金与注册会计师责任保险相结合的要求将有助于保护投资者的利益并维持资本市场的稳定。

对于特殊普通合伙制的会计师事务所，一个或数个合伙人在执业活动中因故意或重大过失造成合伙企业债务的，应当承担无限责任或无限连带责任，其他合伙人以其在合伙企业中的财产份额为限承担责任。合伙人在执业活动中非因故意或者重大过失造成的合伙企业债务及合伙企业其他债务，由全体合伙人承担无限连带责任。在这种责任形势下，事务所应执行高标准风险控制程序，并建立必要的准备金以应对潜在的大额诉讼。职业责任保险和事务所的内部风险控制，以及风险保护备用金都是会计师事务所风险管理系统的一部分，共同组成了会计师事务所的风险控制体系。这类会计师事务所应当根据风险管理系统的要求自主决定相应的投保程度及范围。如果会计师事务所自身制定了完善的保护制度，就无需强制性要求其购买固定额度的职业责任保险而是给予其一定程度的灵活性。此外强制性职业责任保险要求也应该结合对会计师事务所执行的质量检查结果。对于质量好、信誉高、内部控制完善的事务所可以允许其根据自身需要，灵活安排投保额度；相反的，对于质量差、信誉低的事务所，强制购买一定额度的保险是对审计市场的有效保护。

为了促进会计师事务所职业责任保险的推广以及更好保护注册会计师行业，市场上需要存在能够为注册会计师提供有效保障的保险产品，这种产品应当专业性强、覆盖面广、保费灵活，能满足不同规模的事务所的需求。保险公司应有一定的人才储备，能对注册会计师执业活动进行判断及认定，从而提供专业的理赔服务。对于中国的保险公司来说，由于缺乏对相应保险产品定价的信息及经验，提供这种保险产品就存在一定的挑战。解决这个问题的方法之一是在政府主导下增强会计职业组织的参与，由会计职业组织直接提供相应的保险产品或者由会计职业组织出面与保险公司协商，提供相应的保险产品。上海市注册会计师协会开展的集中投保提供了较好的经验，其结果实现了会计师事务所与保险公司的双赢。集体招标的安排可以在分散风险的同时降低保费。中国其他地区可以借鉴上海市的做法来解决注册会计师职业责任保险的问题。



另外，由于越来越多的会计师事务所向海外市场提供专业服务，这样他们也面临着海外市场的责任风险。一些国际保险组织联合起来组成专业保险市场，为高额风险提供“辛迪加”式的保障服务，例如劳合社。中国监管机构可以考虑从这些国际保险组织获取国际上保险业及再保险的操作经验，从而为会计师事务所提供全球化的保险服务提供借鉴[①]。

① 更多关于劳合社的信息可以从以下网站中找到：http：//www. lloyds. com/lloyds/offices/asia/china – in – chinese

# 第九章　会计师事务所联合审计

## 一、国际经验



### （一）联合审计简介

联合审计起源于1930年的丹麦，当时的会计师事务所普遍缺乏对大型且复杂的跨国企业进行审计的能力，因此政府要求强制执行联合审计，以确保有足够的审计资源对此类公司进行审计。当时法律规定，自1930年起，丹麦所有上市公司须任命两位审计师对其年度财务报表执行联合审计。然而，该规定在实施了75年后，于2005年因其导致“不必要的高审计费用”而被废除。自那时起，联合审计在丹麦由强制执行改为自愿执行。

目前，除丹麦外，联合审计主要存在于少数几个欧盟国家。其中，法国自1966年以来一直实施强制性的联合审计制度，是目前联合审计最大的市场，而瑞典和奥地利则是允许但不强制要求联合审计。法国商法规定：“所有要求公开披露合并财务报表的法律实体均须委任至少两个法定审计师。”这种实体主要包括上市公司和其他公共利益实体。实施强制性联合审计制度的主要目的是在一段时期内扶持中小型的会计师事务所，增强其在国际市场上的影响力，以减少审计市场的集中度，而在自愿实施联合审计的瑞典和奥地利，实践中一家公司聘用两个审计师的情况极为少见。

除欧盟国家外，加拿大的银行也曾于1923至1991年间被强制要求聘用两个审计师进行审计，以便更好地对贷款组合进行独立审查，并为当地小型会计师事务所提供机会与大型国际会计师事务所联合工作以获得经验。然而，该联合审计未能有效阻止1985年加拿大商业银行的危机。因此，该制度于1991年被废除。此后，在加拿大，银行可自愿执行联合审计，但目前实践中没有一家银行聘用两家审计师。此外，澳大利亚于25年前曾有个别大型银行使用过联合审计（非强制执行）。澳大利亚最近一次联合审计发生在15年前，当时有两家大型企业合并，合并后的首个财务期间，合并双方都希望继续聘用各自以前年度的审计师，最终双方决定由各自的审计师对合并后的财务报表进行联合审计。该联合审计只持续了一年。目前，美国、英国、澳大利亚或亚洲市场均没有联合审计的实例。

### （二）联合审计与单一审计的比较

表15列举了联合审计的关键特征及其与单一审计的区别。



**表15　　联合审计与单一审计的区别**

| | 联合审计 | 单一审计 |
|---|---|---|
| （1）有多少事务所参与审计 | 至少两家来自不同网络的会计师事务所作为联合审计师参与审计① | 通常只聘用一家事务所，有些情况下，对于集团合并财务报表，可能聘用来自相同或不同网络的多个事务所分别作为集团审计师和组成部分审计师参与审计 |
| （2）事务所之间审计工作如何分配 | 法国法律要求审计工作按照定量（如工作小时数）和定性（如专业知识及资质）的标准在审计师之间均衡分配，以确保实现高效的双重控制机制②。丹麦和其他自愿实行联合审计的国家则无法律法规明确要求审计工作或审计收费如何在审计师之间分配。 | 集团财务报表审计中，如果由多个事务所参与，根据国际审计准则600号（ISA 600）特殊考虑事项——集团财务报表审计（包括组成部分审计师的工作）的规定，集团审计师遵循职业准则和相关法律法规，对集团整体审计工作进行指导、监督，并对出具的审计报告是否恰当负责。具体而言， |

① London Economics公司2012年的一项研究表明，大多数使用联合审计的法国公司聘请两家会计师事务所执行年度审计，极少数的公司聘用两个以上的会计师事务所。

② London Economics公司2012年的一项研究就法国联合审计制度下审计师之间审计费用如何分配进行了统计，以调查研究联合审计中实际审计工作量的分配情况。研究结果表明，在联合审计中，平均一家事务所的审计收费是另一家事务所审计收费的2.7倍。

续表

| | 联合审计 | 单一审计 |
|---|---|---|
| （2）事务所之间审计工作如何分配 | 实践中，审计工作被拆分为具体项目在联合审计师之间进行分配，但并非总是平均分配。例如，职工薪酬和税项由一个审计师审计，收入和应收账款等由另一个审计师审计。这种分配将在审计业务约定书中明确规定，因此审计客户也清楚地知晓各个审计师具体负责哪些审计工作 | 集团审计师须履行下列职责：<br>（1）集团项目组应制定集团整体审计战略和审计计划；<br>（2）集团审计师需要评估组成部分审计师的独立性及其执行组成部分审计工作的胜任能力；<br>（3）集团审计师还应决定组成部分审计师所需执行工作的重要性水平以及审计程序的性质、时间和范围 |
| （3）如何形成审计意见及签署审计报告 | 虽然审计工作被分拆为各个具体项目分配给各个审计师分别完成，但联合审计要求审计师之间必须进行有效的协同与合作。在审计过程中，各方审计师都将出席与客户的重要会议，分享各自的审计计划，以确保在审计重要性水平、审计风险识别、审计战略制定等方面各方均达成一致意见。在审计完成阶段，各审计师对审计底稿进行交叉复核，并对其他审计师形成的审计结论负责。由于每个审计师均需对最终的整体审计意见完全负责，该交叉复核必须在签署审计报告之前完成。<br>联合审计中，所有审计师联合签署审计报告，因而共同承担所有责任。如参与联合审计的各审计师最终形成不同的审计意见，需在审计报告中进行明确的披露。<br>因此，联合审计中各审计师分别完成审计工作，但承担联合责任 | 对于集团财务报表审计，如果涉及多个事务所，集团审计师单独签署审计意见，对集团合并财务报表是否存在重大错报发表意见。<br>根据国际审计准则600号（ISA 600）特殊考虑事项——集团财务报表审计（包括组成部分审计师的工作）的规定，集团财务报表审计报告不得提及组成部分审计师，相关法律法规有特殊规定的除外。如果根据相关法律法规需在审计报告中提及组成部分审计师，审计报告也应说明这并不会减少集团审计项目合伙人或集团审计项目合伙人所属事务所对集团审计意见的责任 |
| （4）遵循什么审计准则 | 联合审计与单一审计应遵循的审计准则一致 | |

第二部分

续表

| | 联合审计 | 单一审计 |
|---|---|---|
| (5) 联合审计在实践中应用的范围如何 | 在法国，联合审计对于所有公开披露合并财务报表的实体（主要为公共利益实体）是强制性的，在丹麦、瑞典和奥地利，由于联合审计是自愿性的，实践中只有极少的公司使用联合审计① | 不适用 |

### （三）联合审计产生的原因及优缺点

如前文所述，在法国实施强制性联合审计制度的主要目的是将非“四大”会计师事务所引入大型公司的审计市场，从而降低审计市场集中度。此外，关于联合审计的讨论还集中在审计成本与审计质量两个话题上。针对市场集中度、审计成本和审计质量这三个话题，联合审计的支持者，主要是中小型会计师事务所，认为联合审计的优点主要包括：

- 促进“四大”会计师事务所（“四大”）与非“四大”会计师事务所（非“四大”）之间的知识共享，从而提高非“四大”会计师事务所在大型公司的审计市场竞争性；
- 联合审计制度下，若某一个事务所被轮换或出现重大过失，另外的事务所可继续提供服务，以保持连续性；
- 提高审计的独立性和审计质量。

相应地，联合审计反对者则认为联合审计：

- 增加审计成本；
- 可能带来潜在风险，如“搭便车”问题、审计分工不均问题或分工不明晰导致的重大审计程序遗漏的问题，因而不一定能提高审计质量，反而可能降低审计质量；



① London Economics 公司 2012 年的一项研究表明 2012 年瑞典 100 家上市公司中仅 4 家使用联合审计；奥地利 39 家上市公司中仅 1 家使用联合审计。研究还表明，在丹麦，自 2005 年强制性联合审计要求被废除后，联合审计的使用大幅减少（超过 92%）。数据显示截至 2012 年 3 月，哥本哈根证交所交易的丹麦上市公司共 171 家，其中 152 家 2005 年以前已经挂牌交易。这 152 家公司中，有 77 家 2005 年度审计聘用两家事务所联合审计，但 2012 年只有 6 家仍使用联合审计。

- 可能增加市场集中度、减少审计师的可选择性；
- 阻止审计委员会获得最佳的审计方案。

对于联合审计的可行性，一直以来存在诸多意见分歧，因此，各国专家学者对其优缺点进行了多项调查研究与理论分析。其中，法国和丹麦的研究较为突出，这两个国家由于曾经或现在仍然对联合审计有强制性要求，因而能够取得相关统计数据对联合审计相关的三项重要指标（审计成本、审计质量和市场集中度）进行实证分析，从而判断其优缺点。此外，我们也参考了对瑞典等自愿实施联合审计的国家进行的调查研究，用以参照。

以下我们针对联合审计相关的三项重要指标：审计成本、审计质量和市场集中度，逐一进行分析。

1. 审计成本

理论上讲，由于存在协调的问题，联合审计很可能比单一审计需要耗费更多时间和精力，而一些数据分析也恰恰显示了类似的结果。

（1）法国和其他国家审计收费的比较。2012 年的一项研究比较了法国、意大利和英国市场的审计费用，却发现法国的审计费用明显较高，具体来说，法国与意大利相比约高 26%，法国与英国相比约高 26%。

（2）丹麦强制性联合审计要求废除前后的审计费用比较。2010 年的一项研究表明，丹麦废除强制性联合审计的要求后，多数公司从联合审计转变为单一审计，审计费用平均减少 25%。

（3）瑞典使用联合审计和单一审计的公司审计费用比较。2011 年的一项研究发现，在瑞典，选择使用两家审计师进行联合审计的公司所支付的审计费用，与其使用单一审计的可比公司相比，若可比公司审计师为“四大”，联合审计费用平均高出 13.2%，若可比公司审计师为非“四大”，联合审计费用平均高出 76.9%。

*对审计成本研究结果的分析*

以上数据研究结果显示，在大多数情况下，联合审计会增加审计成本。同时，我们应当注意到，国家之间的比较有其固有的局限性。即使选取的可比公司具有非常相似的行业性质、收入规模、子公司数量等，审计费用也可能受到其他各种因素影响，而这些因素在不同国家之间可能存在差异，比如审计准则及其他相关法律法规、审计市场竞争情况等等。因此，国家之间的比较数据可能只能作为参考。

另一方面，理论分析也可以得出类似推定，与单一审计相比，联合审计会导致额外的审计和协调工作。如在“联合审计简介”中所提到的，联合审计中，各方审计师均需出席与客户的关键会议，并分享审计计划以确保有效的协同与合作。此外，审计完成阶段，各审计师需对审计底稿进行交叉复核，对项目整体，包括其他审计师形成的审计结论负责。因此，与单一审计相比，联合审计会导致更多的协调工作和底稿复核。参与的审计师之间在审计方法和内部质量控制系统等方面差异越大，联合审计需要的额外工作可能就会越多。

2. 审计质量

总地来说，各项调查研究均未能从数据统计的角度说明联合审计可促进审计质量的提高，对审计质量的讨论主要集中在以下几个方面：

（1）交叉复核和独立性。一些研究指出联合审计要求审计师之间进行交叉检查，从而保证审计质量。联合审计也会削弱公司管理层可对每个审计师施加的压力，以保证审计师的独立性。然而，London Economics 的一项调查发现，大型会计师事务所自身就拥有专业的技术部门处理复杂的会计审计事项和进行审计质量复核。同时，一些参加该调查的受访者认为，当联合审计师在审计策略等方面差异较大甚至无法相提并论时，联合审计反而会降低审计质量。



（2）搭便车问题。联合审计制度的潜在缺点之一就是可能导致搭便车问题，即参与联合审计的一家事务所直接利用其他事务所执行的审计工作和形成的审计结论。当参与联合审计的两家事务所在审计策略和声誉风险方面差异很大时，搭便车问题就容易出现。举例来说，如果一个大型事务所和一个小型事务所共同参与一项联合审计，两者相比小型事务所的声誉风险较低，同时，大型事务所通常经验丰富并建立有一套完整且广泛的审计方法和策略，这种情况下，小型事务所就很可能选择“搭便车”，直接依赖大型事务所执行的审计工作。搭便车问题的产生正是由于联合审计需要各事务所在审计过程中紧密合作，那么对每个事务所各自分别完成的工作就很难加以区分。

（3）审计质量与分工情况的联系。许多调查研究都注意到，如果审计工作在事务所之间的分配不均衡，联合审计可带来的事务所之间交叉复核能够提高审计质量的优势会被弱化。这是因为，当一名审计师只是承担一些非重要的审计工作而在重大方面更多是辅佐另一名审计师完成审计工作时，其复核对方审计工作的能力和有效性是非常有限的。然而，前文提到的法国联合审计制度下审计费用在审计师之间分配情况的统计表明，联合审计师之间完全均衡的分工在实际操作中几乎是不存在的。此外，审计工作分工不明晰也会损害审计质量。如前文所述，审计工作通常按照会计科目在审计师之间进行分配（比如审计师A审计职工薪酬科目，审计师B审计税金科目）。但是，很多时候有些审计程序是跨科目的，所以由于这些程序的分工不能做到很明确的界定，就可能出现一些必要的审计程序被遗漏掉的情况。

（4）联合审计对审计质量影响的实证分析。针对审计质量，有专家学者选取了一些法国和德国的可比公司，比较其审计质量，也有一些调查研究对丹麦公司从联合审计转变为单一审计前后的审计质量进行了分析。研究结果未发现联合审计可以提高审计质量。

*对审计质量研究结果的分析*

关于联合审计对审计质量的影响，各项调查研究的观点未能达成一致，同时没有任何一个观点有实证性的统计数据支持。我们注意到，认为联合审计提高审计质量的观点，比如联合审计能够加强审计独立性和交叉复核是基于理论假设，并不绝对。交叉复核并不一定能够提高审计质量。很多其他因素，如事务所的专家资源、内部质量控制系统、执行项目过程中的培训等，会在整个审计过程中影响审计质量。仅依靠审计工作底稿的交叉复核来确保审计质量是远远不够的。例如，如果一个事务所执行某些审计程序时由于专业知识和经验有限而没有发现某个重大问题，因而未在审计底稿中做任何描述；另一家事务所，不管经验多么丰富，仅通过复核审计底稿也很难发现问题。因此，联合审计中的交叉复核有其固有的局限性，而且审计工作在审计师之间的分配越是不均衡，交叉复核的有效性越弱。此外，我们还需要考虑到联合审计的其他一些问题可能会影响甚至损害审计质量，比如搭便车问题以及审计工作不均衡、不明晰的问题。这些问题的产生是由于联合审计中审计师责任划分不明晰，审计师之间的沟通若出现偏差就可能会损害整体的审计质量。

3. 市场集中度

如前文所述，法国引入强制性联合审计制度是为了让广大中小型事务所参与到规模较大、结构复杂的公司的审计中来，从而促进审计市场逐步走向多元化。然而，针对法国审计市场本身以及法国与其他国家审计市场比较的一些统计数据却发现，联合审计制度在改善市场集中度方面并没有达到预想的效果。

（1）法国审计市场集中度演变。London Economics 2012年的一项研究发现，与其他欧洲国家相比，法国尽管存在强制性联合审计制度，审计市场仍高度集中，近年呈现更加集中的趋势。该研究着重调查了纽约泛欧交易所集团（*CAC All - Tradable*）指数的公司，这包含在所有巴黎泛欧证券交易所上市的公司。研究发现，2010 年纽约泛欧交易所集团（*CAC All - Tradable*）指数公司中由“四大”审计的比例为：

- 若按审计公司数量简单计算，该比例为50%，比2003 年增加了13.5%；
- 在按审计公司数量计算的基础上，若按被审计公司的营业额对审计公司数量进行加权，该比例为71%，比2003 年增加14%；
- 若按审计收费金额计算，该比例为83.5%。

研究还发现，自 2003 至 2010 年间，玛泽会计师事务所（Mazars）是中小型事务所中唯一一家实际增加市场份额的事务所。自 2003 至 2010 年，按审计公司数量简单计算，Mazars 市场份额上升 5%；按审计公司营业额加权的公司数量计算，Mazars 市场份额上升 2.5%。玛泽市场份额的增长还需作多因素具体分析。



（2）法国与其他国家审计市场集中度的比较。学者 Piot 在 2007 年的一项研究中指出，1997 年法国的市场集中度与英国类似。

*关于市场集中度研究结果的分析*

以上统计资料清楚地显示：联合审计没有实现降低审计市场集中度的预期目的。即使强制性联合审计制度能够使得某些中小型事务所被聘用，但缺乏具有竞争力的专业技能及资源的事务所终将在市场选择中被自动淘汰。过度的保护还会损害中小型事务所的竞争力。

### （四）关于联合审计的公众意见

2010 年 10 月，欧盟委员会（EC）就审计这个话题发起公开咨询，发布绿皮书“审计政策——危机的教训”。这一举动的起因是众多被出具无保留意见审计报告的银行在 2007 到 2009 年均出现了巨额亏损。欧盟委员会旨在通过该咨询寻求不同群体对一些审计政策问题的看法，从而改革审计市场的监管政策。这份公开咨询中的第 28 个问题即是探讨引入强制性联合审计制度的可行性。

欧盟委员会收到包括审计师、监管机构、投资者、专家学者、公司、政府机关、职业组织和个人等不同群体约 700 个回复，其中“四大”会计师事务所分别代表其整个网络各自提交了一个回复。欧盟委员会于 2011 年 2 月发布了回复的摘要。

根据 Böcking 等学者针对回复进行的分析，初步统计，剔除掉200多家德国小型审计事务所的相同回复，大约61%的回复反对引入联合审计制度。如果继续剔除掉所有来自审计师的回复，联合审计支持率下降到12%，而反对率增加到76%。分群体比较，除了审计师群体，其他群体绝大多数都反对强制性联合审计见表16。

表16　　对于联合审计制度的回复统计

| | 审计委员会 | 财务报表编制者（公司） | 政府机关 | 审计报告使用者 | 专家学者 | 审计师 |
|---|---|---|---|---|---|---|
| 反对率 | 100% | 86% | 73% | 65% | 56% | 38% |

联合审计制度的反对者指出，如果联合审计中审计师之间出现意见分歧，尤其是当一家“四大”事务所和一家小型事务所搭配时，或者其中一家审计师出现重大过失时，联合审计就会导致无法明确地判断参与的事务所各自的责任。



### （五）联合审计分析结果总结

根据上述分析，联合审计的主要影响可总结为如下几点：

1. 设想的联合审计的优点（降低市场集中度、提高审计质量）在实践中并未得到体现：

（1）实证和理论依据都无法证明联合审计提高了审计质量；

（2）法国强制性联合审计未能阻止法国市场集中度增加。

2. 多项研究表明联合审计的缺点确实存在：

（1）绝大多数数据统计结果证明联合审计导致审计成本增加，这也正是丹麦废除强制性联合审计要求的主要原因；

（2）联合审计可能带来一些潜在风险，损害审计质量，比如搭便车问题和联合审计师之间分工不均或分工不明晰导致的重大审计程序遗漏的问题。

3. 市场对联合审计的态度多是否定的，这体现在：

（1）除法国外，极少数的公司选择使用联合审计，并呈现越来越少的趋势；

（2）欧盟委员会针对联合审计的公开咨询（剔除掉德国小型审计事务所提交的相同答复）显示绝大多数回复反对强制性联合审计制度。

## 二、中国实践

引入联合审计制度对中国有益吗？下面我们讨论中国审计市场的现状以及如果在中国实行联合审计可能遇到的挑战。

### （一）中国审计市场的现状

与“四大”主导欧洲上市公司审计市场的情况不同，中国审计市场并非完全由少数会计师事务所特别是“四大”主导。根据中国注册会计师协会（CICPA）披露的2013年审计情况统计数据，中国国内资本市场2537家上市公司，按审计客户数量简单计算，中国境内前十大的会计师事务所所占的市场份额合计约为68%。其余32%的公司的审计师涵盖约30个会计师事务所，其中任何一个事务所单家的审计客户数量均未超过2%。此外，在中国，很多大型的会计师事务所也为在香港和美国等海外资本市场上市的中国公司提供服务。因此，相比欧洲市场，中国审计市场的分布相对更加分散和均衡。



### （二）中国实行联合审计将会遇到的挑战

基于以上分析，我们认为中国实行联合审计，可能会遇到以下挑战：

（1）鉴于中国会计师事务所之间现实存在的重大差异以及欧洲市场的经验教训，联合审计很可能会导致联合审计师之间大量的协调及重复工作，从而导致审计费用的大幅度增加。

（2）如上文所述，联合审计师之间审计工作分配不均会导致交叉复核失效，因而不能提高审计质量。然而，从中国会计师事务所在资源、专业技能等方面现实存在的重大差距来看，均衡地分配审计工作是很难实现的，尤其是当大型事务所与中小型事务所作为联合审计师参与一项审计时，均衡分配工作的难度很大。

（3）如果联合审计师最终得出不同的审计结论，或者其中一名审计师不能完全信赖另一名审计师执行的审计程序而导致其无法对整体财务报表发表意见，就会影响审计报告的及时出具。即使各审计师就具体差异在审计报告中进行充分披露，审计报告也将会给报告使用者带来困惑。

## 三、有关建议

基于以上分析，我们关于联合审计的建议是：

（1）基于中国审计市场现状，引入联合审计是一个不经济的选择。无论是欧洲市场的实践经验，还是基于中国现状的理论分析都表明联合审计将导致大量额外的审计师之间的协调甚至重复工作，这些额外的工作除增加审计费用外，也会增加被审计公司管理层参与和配合这些工作的负担。因此，在中国引入联合审计制度很可能增加资本市场的经济负担，并且可能很长一段时间内不会产生经济效益。

（2）鉴于中国会计师事务所在规模、资源、专业技能和审计方法等方面确实存在的明显差距，以及联合审计在会计师事务所责任划分方面的固有局限性，现阶段在中国引入联合审计可能弊大于利。一方面，事务所之间的各项差距会导致审计工作的均衡分配难以实现，也无法避免联合审计中事务所在审计策略和方法上产生各项冲突与矛盾。另一方面，联合审计在事务所责任划分方面的固有局限性将带来审计分工不明晰从而导致重大审计程序遗漏的问题和“搭便车”的问题。这些冲突和问题都可能损害审计质量。

（3）联合审计在提高独立性和审计质量有关方面的潜在优势可以通过其他替代途径来获得，如提高独立性及合规性的要求，并加强审计行业监管。有关加强审计行业和注册会计师监管的建议在前面的议题中已进行了详细论述，比如调整事务所检查方案、改进纪律处罚方式等等，这些改进措施均能够进一步保证和提高审计质量。

（4）尽管联合审计模式在中国现阶段可能并不适用，但在集团审计模式下推动具有一定经验的会计师事务所作为参审所更多参加金融审计是可行的选择。中国除“四大”之外的会计师事务所可先在中小金融机构审计中积累经验，并逐步以参审所的形式加入到大型金融机构的审计业务之中。假以时日，必将发挥更为重要的作用。

# 第十章　跨境会计监管与合作

## 一、国际经验



### （一）各国国际监管合作情况介绍

随着资本市场全球化进程的推进，海外上市越来越受到那些有募集资金需求的快速成长的公司的青睐。根据世界交易所联盟（World Federation of Exchange, WFE）公布的数据，截至 2014 年 9 月，WFE 的 57 家成员中，41 家交易所挂牌交易的海外公司达 2425 家（该数据不包括在中国香港上市的中国内地公司）。其中绝大多数集中在纽约证券交易所、纳斯达克、泛欧证券交易所、卢森堡证券交易所、澳大利亚证券交易所、香港证券交易所和新加坡证券交易所，这些交易所代表的是世界上最大、最活跃的资本市场。由于各个资本市场在会计审计准则、公众监督系统、市场风险特征等方面存在差异，跨境监管冲突便由此而生。因此，需要建立有效的国际监管合作机制来解决这些监管冲突，以保护全球资本市场上投资者的利益。

一方面，各国的监管机构和一些国际性的组织正在努力促进会计和审计准则的标准化进程，这就为国际监管合作奠定了一定的技术性基础。德勤会计师事务所的一份报告显示，截至 2011 年，世界上近半数国家都要求其境内所有上市公司采用国际财务报告准则。同时，其他的一些国家，比如中国，一直致力于使本国的会计准则向国际财务报告准则趋同。另一方面，为了实现跨境监管和信息交换，许多国家也正在积极地加入到各种双边和多边合作的谈判中。本书附录列举了一些具有代表性的国家目前在跨境监管合作方面的实践方案，我们可以将其归纳为两种模式："欧盟模式"和"美国模式"。其中，"欧盟模式"立足于相互信任和相互支持，而"美国模式"则旨在实施联合审查和信息交换。

1. 欧盟模式

包括英国在内的欧盟各国对欧洲资本市场上市公司的监管采取"相互信任、相互支持"的方式。欧盟委员会（European Commission，EC）通过了"等效性决议"，确认10个国家的审计监管体系与欧盟审计监管体系等效，即以所在国的监管代替上市地监管机构的检查。该决议为促进欧盟成员国之间以及欧盟与其他国家之间的合作扫清了障碍。这一决议同样也给予了20个国家会计师事务所在欧盟从事年度财务报表审计业务的过渡期，在这个过渡期内欧盟将进一步对这些国家的审计监管体系进行评估。目前欧盟确认审计监管体系等效的10个国家/地区包括澳大利亚、加拿大、中国内地、克罗地亚、日本、新加坡、南非、韩国、瑞士和美国。尚处在过渡期的20个国家/地区包括阿布扎比、百慕大群岛、巴西、开曼群岛、迪拜国际金融中心、埃及、英属格恩西岛、中国香港、印度、印度尼西亚、英属马恩岛、以色列、英属泽西岛、马来西亚、毛里求斯、新西兰、俄罗斯、中国台湾、泰国和土耳其。

根据该决议，若上市公司所在国是上述10个等效国家之一，欧盟各成员国即可选择依赖上市公司所在国的监管体系。依赖的程度及合作的范围需由各成员国与这10个国家通过签署合作协议来进行具体的规定。

EC在欧洲审计师监管机构（European Group of Auditors Oversight Bodies，EGAOB）的帮助下，对上述国家/地区的审计监管体系进行了评估，评估范围主要包括对审计师及被审计公司的公开监管、质量复核以及检查和处罚制度。这些评估是基于EC指令2006/43中的第29条、30条和32条的标准进行的。具体来说，这些条例确定了一系列审计监管体系的标准，主要包括监管机构的独立性、检查频率、质量复核系统的资源及复核范围、监管机构的专业知识、责任和透明度、有效的检查和处罚制度等方面。

2. 美国模式

作为全球最强大的经济体和最大的资本市场之一，美国在促进跨境监管合作方面一直努力作出实践探索，以保护美国资本市场投资者的利益。随着2002年公众公司会计监督委员会（Public Company Accounting Oversight Board，PCA-

OB）的成立和《2002年萨班斯－奥克斯利法案》（Sarbanes－Oxley Act of 2002，简称《萨班斯法案》）的出台，美国一直致力于对所有为美国上市公司提供审计服务的会计师事务所进行监督和审查，这也包括在PCAOB注册的美国境外的会计师事务所。同时，PCAOB在对境外会计师事务所进行检查时也积极寻求与当地监管机构的协调，以加强合作与信息共享。PCAOB的检查可通过两种形式来实施：（1）PCAOB现场检查，即PCAOB通过和事务所所在国家的监管机构沟通协调，入境自行实施检查；（2）联合检查，即PCAOB与事务所所在国的监管机构建立合作检查框架，并在这个框架下联合实施检查。这种形式将允许PCAOB在一定限度内合理依赖当地监管机构执行的检查程序。表17汇总了一些PCAOB检查的相关规定和程序。

**表17　　PCAOB检查的相关规定和程序**

| 项目 | 相关规定 |
| --- | --- |
| 检查对象 | 所有在PCAOB注册的会计师事务所，包括美国境外会计师事务所。 |
| 检查频率 | • 为超过100个美国上市公司出具审计报告的事务所每年审查一次；<br>• 为不超过100个美国上市公司出具审计报告的事务所至少每三年检查一次；未单独出具审计报告，但在至少一家上市公司审计中扮演重要角色的事务所也是至少每三年检查一次 |
| 整体审查方案 | PCAOB对事务所审计质量的检查包含两个方面：<br>• 第一，PCAOB独立选取事务所的具体审计项目进行检查，事务所无权拒绝PCAOB的检查安排，也无权干涉PCAOB的选样；<br>• 第二，对事务所的内部质量控制政策和程序进行评估，内部质量控制体系会影响事务所的整体表现 |
| 具体审计项目的检查 | PCAOB对具体审计项目的选样基于对经审计的财务报表出现重大错报风险的评估。评估该风险时考虑的因素包括被审计公司及其行业特征、常见的审计问题、提供审计服务的事务所及其下属具体执行审计程序的分所、负责项目的合伙人以及以前年度的检查结果等等。<br>总地来说，各年被检查的具体审计项目的数量是不固定的，但检查的被审计公司的平均资本规模和审计的复杂程度是逐年上升的。<br>此类检查对审计师是否按照PCAOB的审计准则执行审计程序进行评估。同时，PCAOB还会抽选一些具体的审计领域进行检查，评估审计师是否发现并妥善地处理所审财务报表中偏离相关会计准则的情况。若检查发现审计存在过失，则会记录在检查报告中 |

续表

| 项目 | 相关规定 |
| --- | --- |
| 事务所内部质量控制体系的检查 | 对事务所内部质量控制体系的检查主要考虑以下几个方面：<br>• 高层的态度；<br>• 合伙人业绩评估、薪酬安排、职责分配、纪律处分政策；<br>• 非审计服务、商业合作、个人经济利益、佣金及或有收费方面就保持独立性的执行情况；<br>• 客户承接与续接程序；<br>• 对会计、审计和美国证监会相关问题的咨询程序；<br>• 事务所内部检查情况；<br>• 审计策略和程序的建立与沟通，以及相关培训；<br>• 审计项目人员配置的政策和程序；<br>• 事务所对其外国网络成员所完成的审计客户国外经营部分的审计工作的监管 |
| 具体检查程序 | 在检查过程中，检查组成员会与事务所的代表就检查注意到的问题一一进行讨论。通常情况下，检查组成员会首先与审计项目组成员讨论关于具体审计项目的问题，但也可能同时或者之后与事务所负责协调 PCAOB 检查的专员以及总所的专家进一步讨论这些问题，有些时候事务所的高级管理层，比如主管合伙人和总裁，也可能参与讨论。<br>现场检查后未解决的重大问题，PCAOB 将出具意见书，并要求事务所进行书面回复。检查组和其他检查人员会认真考虑发现的问题和事务所的回复，并考虑如何将其反映在检查报告中以及是否需要采取进一步措施 |
| 检查报告 | PCAOB 对每个被检查的事务所出具检查报告。该报告包括公开的和非公开的部分。公开的部分主要描述重大的审计缺陷（通常按具体审计项目逐一描述）。检查发现的事务所内部质量控制体系存在的问题，则属于非公开部分。如果自检查报告发布之日起的 12 个月内事务所未能对检查发现的问题进行整改并令 PCAOB 满意，则原来保留在非公开部分中的描述将被公开 |
| 联合检查 | 在一些国家，PCAOB 会与当地监管机构合作进行联合检查。联合检查在检查内容、检查选样方法和检查程序方面并无区别。联合检查的一个主要目的就是合理利用当地监管机构的工作，避免重复检查。例如，PCAOB 和澳大利亚证券与投资委员会（Australian Securities and Investments Commission，ASIC）在对美国上市的澳大利亚公司进行检查时，就在一定程度上进行合作。具体而言，针对事务所的内部质量控制体系，由于 ASIC 也对会计师事务所执行相似的检查，并且检查的内容通常已包含在 PCAOB 的检查范围内，因此，PCAOB 和 ASIC 会发表联合通知要求事务所准备检查需要审阅的材料，同时，PCAOB 和 ASIC 也会一起访谈事务所的相关人员，对事务所的内部质量控制体系的情况进行了解和讨论。对于具体审计项目的检查，由于 PCAOB 和 ASIC 的检查对象不同 |

续表

| 项目 | 相关规定 |
| --- | --- |
| 联合检查 | （PCAOB 检查在美国上市的澳大利亚公司而 ASIC 检查澳大利亚本土上市公司），除非两者恰好选中了同一个公司的审计项目，不然 PCAOB 和 ASIC 在这项检查上通常不进行联合检查。如果进行联合检查，PCAOB 和 ASIC 会尽量安排同一时间实施检查，并一起与事务所人员进行访谈。然而，访谈过后，他们将分别按照各自的标准检查审计底稿和支持性文件，并独立形成检查结论。上述两种检查，PCAOB 和 ASIC 均按照各自的检查标准，分别出具检查报告 |

目前，PCAOB 现场检查已涵盖 30 多个国家/地区，这些国家包括加拿大、新西兰、墨西哥、俄罗斯、印度、中国香港等等。此外，PCAOB 也与英国和其他欧盟国家、澳大利亚、迪拜、新加坡、日本等国签署了正式的双边合作协议，实施联合检查。各双边协议的关键条款大致相同，以下是我们总结的这些协定的主要条款：

合作目的——履行双方法定职责，确定未来双方相互依赖的程度。

合作范围——协调信息共享、联合检查审计工作底稿和会计师事务所质量控制系统、交换检查指引和监管经验以及实施联合检查等等。

法律依据——美国萨班斯－奥克斯利法案和协议对方国家的相关法律法规（如英国 2006 年公司法）。

保密性要求——对检查中涉及的非公开的信息、个人信息、商业秘密及其他敏感商业信息，需采取保护措施，严格保密。

协议期限和终止条款——PCAOB 与英国及其他欧盟国家签订的协议绝大多数为 2013 年 7 月 31 日到期。然而，EC 通过了两项决议（“充分性决议”和“等效性决议”2013 年 8 月 1 日生效），这两项决议使得 PCAOB 与欧盟的双边合作协议到期后继续有效。其他一些国家/地区，比如日本和台湾地区与 PCAOB 的协议未明确有效期。所有协议均允许协议任何一方单方撤销协议。

根据 PCAOB 的规定，少数几家为超过 100 家美国上市公司出具审计报告的事务所必须每年检查一次，为不超过 100 家美国上市公司出具审计报告的事务所则是至少每三年检查一次。截至目前，PCAOB 尚不能实施现场或联合检查的国家/地区包括欧洲国家（希腊、爱尔兰、比利时）、中国内地以及香港的事务所具体审计项目中涉及审计客户在中国内地经营业务的部分。

3. 其他资本市场的情况

除美国和欧盟外，世界上其他活跃的资本市场，如澳大利亚、新加坡和中国香港，要么得到欧盟的等效认同，要么和美国签订了双边协议，与 PCAOB 实施联合检查，或者二者兼而有之。此外，值得一提的是，这些资本市场对于本地上市公司的法定审计，并不像欧盟和美国那样对境外的注册会计师或事务所开放。不同国家对于境外注册会计师或事务所参与法定审计的具体规定在本书之前讨论的话题中已经进行了详细的介绍，表 18 是针对除欧盟和美国外其他活跃的资本市场相关规定的概括性总结。

**表 18　　其他活跃资本市场的相关规定**

| | |
|---|---|
| 澳大利亚 | 澳大利亚上市公司的法定审计师（负责审计项目的注册会计师个人）需要在 ASIC 注册，且必须为澳大利亚居民 |
| 新加坡 | 在新加坡，会计师事务所须在相关政府机构注册才能成为上市公司的审计师，且该事务所 2/3 以上的主管合伙人须具有新加坡当地认可的执业资格 |
| 中国香港 | 中国香港上市公司的审计师（会计师事务所）须与香港会计师公会注册，取得法定审计资格。此类事务所全部主管合伙人均须具有香港执业注册会计师资格，但香港会计师公会认可的少数几家（目前为 11 家）中国内地的会计师事务所除外 |

以上信息显示，在欧盟和美国以外的活跃资本市场，上市公司的法定审计师局限于当地注册并受当地监管机构监管的会计师或会计师事务所。那么，这些资本市场就不会像欧盟和美国那样，迫切地需要寻求一种合作机制，来实现对境外会计师及事务所的监管，从而保护本地资本市场上投资者的利益。此外，欧盟与美国资本市场对境外会计师及事务所的开放程度也有所不同，我们将在以下的部分对此作详细的分析。

## （二）国际性组织

除上文提到的双边协议和等效性决议，一些国际性组织也对促进国际监管合作作出了积极的努力。其中，最具代表性的两个组织是独立审计监管机构国际论坛（International Forum of Independent Audit Regulators，IFIAR）和国际证券事务监察委员会（International Organization of Securities Commissions，IOSCO）。

IFIAR 则致力于对事务所和审计师个人的督察、促进国际间监管事务的合作和协同，而 IOSCO 则主要负责发展、实施和促进一套国际公认的对资本市场的监管标准。到目前为止，这些国际性组织的角色和责任仅仅局限于标准的制定和信息交换，并不具有强制性的法律效力。但是，这些组织为国际监管合作提供了相互依赖与合作的基础和平台。以下是有关这两个组织具体工作范围的详细信息。

1. IFIAR

IFIAR 成立于 2006 年，截至目前已有来自 51 个国家/地区的机构加入该组织，其成员是来自世界各地的独立审计监管机构，比如美国的 PCAOB、英国的财务报告委员会（Financial Reporting Council，FRC）、澳大利亚的 ASIC 等等。自成立以来，IFIAR 每半年召开一次全体会议，每年召开一次审计监管研讨会，供各成员机构就审计监管问题进行信息交流和经验分享。



除为各国的独立审计监管机构提供交流平台以外，IFIAR 建立了一套有关建立独立审计监管机构的标准，许多国家按照该标准建立了自己的审计监管体系。这套标准共 11 条，涵盖设置独立审计监管机构的三个方面，即组织结构、运营管理和检查活动。总体来看，该标准强调了监管机构的独立性和责任，也对最低检查要求提出了一些建议。此外，该标准还提出各国监管机构间应建立适当的合作机制。

2. IOSCO

IOSCO 成立于 1983 年。作为一个国际性组织，IOSCO 将全世界的证券监管机构联系在一起，并负责制定有关资本市场监管的全球标准。目前，IOSCO 的成员已涵盖全球 95% 以上的证券市场，遍布 115 个国家/地区。

自成立以来，IOSCO 在国际监管合作方面的主要研究成果包括以下两方面：

第一，IOSCO 证券市场监管目标与准则（IOSCO Objectives and Principles of Securities Regulation）。该套准则于 1998 年被启用，目前已成为全球各个资本市场监管体系的基准，也被称作 IOSCO 的核心准则。

第二，IOSCO 多边谅解备忘录（IOSCO Multilateral Memorandum of Understanding Concerning Consultation and Cooperation and the Exchange of Information，IOSCO MMoU）。IOSCO 多边谅解备忘录是促进各国证券监管机构实现跨境监管合作和信息交流的纲领性文件，它就各国监管机构之间的信息交流提出了各项具体要求，旨在促进跨境监管中各国监管机构的相互协助。目前，全世界已有超过 100 个国家/地区签署了该备忘录，这些国家/地区包括美国、英国、中国内地、法国、德国、中国香港、澳大利亚、新加坡等等。

### （二）欧盟模式与美国模式解读与优缺点分析

1. 欧盟模式

（1）欧盟模式的发展历程及产生原因。欧盟模式的特点是相互信任，相互支持。欧盟于 2006 年开展了一项针对非欧盟国家法定审计欧盟策略的公开咨询，并在 2007 年公开了咨询收到的回复。回复总体上提议欧盟对非欧盟国家的审计监管体系进行评估，确认其是否与欧盟的监管体系等效。2008 年，欧盟同一些非欧盟国家在布鲁塞尔召开了一次国际审计研讨会，会议讨论了如何加强国际合作以及如何提升非欧盟国家的审计监管体系。同年，欧盟通过一项决议，给予 30 个国家会计师事务所在欧盟从事年度财务报表审计业务的过渡期，在这个过渡期内欧盟将对这些国家的审计监管体系进行评估，并最终通过了上文提及的“等效性决议”。在此之前，欧盟各成员国已经与美国、澳大利亚、日本和瑞士在交流审计底稿方面进行合作。



欧盟采用这种模式最主要是考虑了成本效益，并且希望借此增强欧洲资本市场对非欧盟国家的投资者和发行人的吸引力。为进一步分析欧盟和美国形成两种不同模式的原因，我们再次详细对比了一下欧洲资本市场和美国资本市场的现状。WFE 公布的统计数据显示，欧洲资本市场对全球的投资者和发行人在一定程度上也是比较开放的，尤其是泛欧交易所和卢森堡交易所。截至 2014 年 9 月，泛欧交易所上市的 1065 家公司中有 120 家是外国公司，而在卢森堡交易所上市的 223 家公司中有 198 家是外国公司。值得注意的是，WFE 统计的数据中并没有包含在卢森堡交易所上市交易的投资基金和债券，而这些是卢森堡交易所交易的重要组成部分。然而在对欧洲上市公司法定审计师资格要求的管理上，欧盟的规定与美国有所区别，根据法定审计指令（Statutory Audit Directive）的第 45 条和 46 条规定，非欧盟成员国的注册会计师和事务所只能对在欧洲上市的“外国”公司（在欧盟成员国以外成立的公司）出具审计报告。在欧盟境内注册的公司应由欧盟承认的注册会计师或事务所进行审计，这些注册会计师和事务所受欧盟监管机构的监管。因此，欧盟资本市场的审计师的组成并不像美国那样多样化，因而风险偏低。这就为欧盟就采取与美国相比更为“友好”的跨境监管方式提供了可能性。

（2）欧盟模式的优点。

①欧盟模式为建立一个均衡的会计监管国际合作机制提供了可行性框架，有利于完善各个国家的监管体系。

②欧盟模式考虑了各国在经济、法律和文化等方面现实存在的差异及管辖权冲突，并且认识到单方面的监管是无法解决这些冲突的。

③欧盟模式在很大程度上减少了跨境监督的行政负担，更加具有成本效益。

④欧盟模式提倡合作中的互惠原则和相互尊重，这将更容易被其他国家接纳。

（3）欧盟模式的不足之处。

①欧盟模式 2011 年才被第一次正式提出，因此其是否足以有效解决跨境监管问题尚待历史的验证。同时，欧盟模式完全依赖其他国家自有监管，因而在跨境监管的实施方面缺乏执行力度。



②单纯地依赖其他国家的监管体系有其固然风险，可能无法使投资者建立信心。因此可能需要一个国际公认的机构按照国际公认的标准对每个国家的监管体系进行定期评估。

2. 美国模式

（1）美国模式的发展历程及产生原因。

美国模式起源于 2002 年，当时安然丑闻爆发后，美国成立了 PCAOB 并出台了《萨班斯－奥克斯利法案》。在过去的十余年间，PCAOB 致力于对所有在 PCAOB 注册的会计师事务所的监管，其中也包括美国境外的会计师事务所。自 2004 年 PCAOB 出台具体检查方案以来，PCAOB 对某些国家/地区的事务所的检查未能顺利开展，其中最大的困难来自于欧盟和中国。截至 2008 年，与 PCAOB 签订审计监管合作双边协议的仅有新加坡和澳大利亚两个国家。于是，PCAOB 与多个国家的监管机构、审计行业业内人士以及机构投资者代表举行了多次圆桌会议，并于 2011 年与大部分欧盟国家、日本和一些其他国家在联合检查和交换信息方面达成了共识。

PCAOB 的成立目标是制定有效的标准，监督为美国上市公司提供审计服务的会计师事务所编制的审计报告，从而保护美国资本市场上投资者的利益，而这一目标也正是跨境监管美国模式产生的关键动因。PCAOB 的目标是建立在市场需求的基础上的，具体原因可归纳为以下两点：

①美国资本市场是世界上最活跃和最开放的市场之一。WFE 发布的数据显

示，截至2014年9月，共有5175家公司在纽约证券交易所和纳斯达克上市，其中有854家是在美国境外注册及运营的公司。这些外国公司财务信息的可靠性和透明度对美国资本市场投资者的利益有重大影响。

②美国法律允许境外的注册会计师或会计师事务所对任何美国上市公司提供审计服务并出具审计报告。当然，这些会计师事务所必须在PCAOB登记注册。截至目前，在PCAOB注册的大约2300家会计师事务所中有超过900家为美国境外的事务所。具体来看，这900家事务所中有100家以上来自中国（包括香港），60家以上来自英国，50家以上来自加拿大，40家以上来自澳大利亚，其余覆盖了80多个国家。鉴于此，投资者期望并要求美国的监管机构在一定程度上对这些事务所进行监管，评估这些公司是否遵守PCAOB和SEC的规定，执行的审计程序是否符合专业标准，从而确保这些公司审计的美国上市公司财务信息的可靠性。

（2）美国模式的优点。

经过上述分析，我们认为美国模式具有以下优点：

①美国模式在跨境监管的具体实施上具有执行力，能够有效地保护美国资本市场投资者的利益。

②美国模式侧重于跨境监管标准的统一。PCAOB对事务所实施的检查均按照PCAOB的统一标准执行。

③美国模式积极寻求解决跨境监管冲突的可行性方案，不断进行实践探索，推动了国际监管合作进程。

（3）美国模式的不足之处。

①美国模式忽视了各国在会计审计准则、法律结构、市场风险特征等方面存在的差异。由于这些差异的存在，PCAOB一味按照其自己制定的准则和规定在各国实施检查，就会与其他国家自有监管机构的管辖权产生冲突。PCAOB在实施跨境检查时遇到的困难实际上就源于这些差异。换言之，美国模式要求存在超越区域管辖权的立法才能保证美国具备实施跨境检查的能力。

②美国模式对监管标准的统一存在局限性。尽管PCAOB评估境外会计师事务时均遵守PCAOB的统一标准，但其与其他国家签订的双边协议也提到联合检查依据包含上市公司所在地的法律法规。这就给实际检查工作增添了复杂性和不确定性。比如，若实施联合检查时就某一事项PCAOB的检查标准与上市公司所在地的相关规定存在差异，那么对该事项的处理就涉及如何协调标准差异的

问题。

③PCAOB 的检查与其他国家自己的检查有一定的重复，因而存在浪费资源的情况。同时，重复检查也会影响会计师及会计师事务所从事跨境活动的积极性。

④PCAOB 单独承担跨境监管，成本极高。

综上所述，无论欧盟模式还是美国模式目前都不足以解决国际监管合作中的冲突和挑战，但是欧盟模式为我们提供了更多的机遇。我们需要寻求一个更为均衡且同时具有成本效益的方案，在保护投资者利益的同时也可以体现对各国国家主权的尊重，并有效避免重复监管造成的资源浪费。此外，各个国家/地区的共同努力和相互了解是十分必要的，国际监管合作中的冲突与矛盾仅靠任何单方的力量是无法解决的。



## 二、中国实践

### （一）中国在全球资本市场活动中的特殊性

中国在全球资本市场活动中的情况非常特殊。一方面，有相当数量的中国公司在海外上市，且上市方式极为复杂，既包括直接上市，也包括反向收购等间接上市方式。但与此同时，目前还没有任何一家外国公司在中国上市。在国际监管合作中，中国目前的角色呈现“被动”的特性，是纯粹的上市资源输出国。因此，中国目前面临的主要问题和挑战是应该如何应对包括美国和欧盟在内的海外资本市场监管机构的跨境监管要求。

### （二）中美合作的挑战

中国目前面临的一项挑战是中美在 PCAOB 跨境监管问题上的不同立场。PCAOB 尚未与中国签署跨境检查的双边协议，因而无法对中国的会计师事务所直接实施现场检查。PCAOB 会定期向所有现有和潜在的投资者公开 PCAOB 无法实施检查的会计师事务所清单及其所属国家/地区，同时 PCAOB 也在一些公开研究分析中表示了因实施现场检查遇到困难而导致的对中国会计师事务所审计质量的担忧。长此以往，在美国上市的中国公司的形象可能受到损害，可能削弱投资者信心。同时，中国会计师事务所在美国审计市场的竞争力也将受到负面影响。

### （三）欧盟模式对中美跨境监管合作的启示

通过前述的分析，我们了解到对于跨境监管，欧盟对中国采取了一种较为“友好”且可行的方式。尽管欧盟模式也存在局限性，但它为中国妥善解决美国跨境监管与中国管辖权的冲突问题提供了可能和指引。

首先，欧盟承认中国的审计监管体系与欧盟等效，短期内在一定程度上缓解了中国在处理与美国跨境监管冲突中承担的压力。其次，欧盟成员国之间的合作实践，以及欧盟提出的“相互信任、相互支持”的理念提供了一个可行的国际合作框架，中国可依据该框架进一步研究对中国有利且可行的合作方案。最后，欧盟的做法意味着中国有机会与欧盟在不久的将来进行合作，共同致力于改善当前的跨境监管国际合作安排。

## 三、有关建议



基于以上的研究分析，有关国际监管合作我们的建议总结如下：

（1）解决跨境监管冲突、实现有效合作的根本是在保护投资者利益的同时，尊重各国国家主权，尊重各国对经济信息安全的关注，加强相互理解与协助，构建系统性的国际合作机制，既重视整体的协调又重视个体的差异，既重视标准的形成又重视执行中的落实，从整体效果最优的角度来考虑合作机制中各要素的相互关系。

（2）具体来说，中国可以考虑与欧盟进行更多的交流与合作，在全球范围内推动相互信赖与相互协助这一合作理念，以解决目前的跨境监管冲突。在这一理念下，如果外国监管者发现中国的会计师事务所在为海外上市的中国公司提供审计服务时存在潜在的过失，外国监管者可将这些发现告知中国的独立审计监管机构，并要求其对该事务所实施检查或调查，并将检查或调查结果以及对该事务所的处罚决定与上市地的外国监管者进行沟通。适当的情况下，也可以考虑采用联合检查的形式实施检查。

（3）中美在跨境监管合作方面的冲突源于美国推行的跨境检查方案与地域管辖权的固有矛盾，若这些冲突不能尽快得到很好的解决，在美国上市的中国公司的形象将受到不必要的损害，中国会计服务开放的进程也会受到一定的阻碍。对此，中国可以考虑主动举办圆桌讨论或对话，促进双方在存在的冲突和困难上达成共识，呼吁通过共同努力来解决冲突。同时，中国应考虑加强对以间接上市的方式进入海外资本市场的中国企业的监管，向全世界展示中国解决跨境监管冲突的信心和决心，为进一步开展多层次的跨境监管合作奠定基础。

（4）中国在跨境监管合作的国际活动中需要发挥更加积极的作用。作为世界上最大的经济体之一，中国参与全球范围内的活动是必需的。中国应当考虑主动参与或举办定期的圆桌讨论，与其他国家共同讨论全球跨境合作中面临的冲突和挑战，探讨可行的解决办法。中国也可以考虑就跨境合作问题与其他国家协商和签订一些谅解备忘录或双边协议，附件中所列的各国目前签署的合作协议可作为参考。此外，中国也可以对包括独立审计监管机构国际论坛（International Forum of Independent Audit Regulators，IFIAR）和国际证券事务监察委员会（International Organization of Securities Commissions，IOSCO）在内的大型国际组织的平台加以更好的利用。目前中国已是 IOSCO 的成员之一，并已签署了《IOSCO 多边谅解备忘录》，但还未加入 IFIAR。如前文所述，IFIAR 将全球的独立审计监管机构聚集在一起，讨论分享各自在审计监管方法、检查方案等方面的经验和心得。如果中国能够参加到这些讨论中，中国可以学习到其他国家在审计监管方面的先进经验，也可以将中国的监管体系展示给其他国家，从而提高世界对中国监管体系的认可，同时增强中国在国际规则制定方面的话语权，增强中国在审计监管方面对其他国家的影响力。

（5）中国可以考虑加强对各国法律法规和实践的研究与分析、为中国法律法规的修订提供建议等等；学习国际上的先进经验，及时解决其他国家或国际机构提出的中国市场目前的缺陷和问题，消除这些国际机构对中国市场的误解，进一步树立中国作为负责任大国在国际上的形象，增强全球资本市场投资者对中国及中国上市公司的信心。

# 参考文献

**中文部分：**

1.《中外合作会计师事务所本土化转制方案》，财会〔2012〕8号，2012年5月2日。

2.《会计师事务所分所管理暂行办法》，财会〔2010〕2号，2010年1月15日。

3. 商务部台港澳司，《内地与香港（澳门〈关于建立更紧密经贸关系的安排〉关于内地在广东与香港（澳门）基本实现服务贸易自由化的协议）》，2014年12月18日。

4.《关于证券期货审计业务签字注册会计师定期轮换的规定》，证监会计字〔2003〕13号，2003年10月31日。

5.《金融企业选聘会计师事务所招标管理办法（试行）》，财金〔2010〕169号，2010年12月3日。

6.《关于会计师事务所承担中央企业财务决算审计有关问题的通知》，财会〔2011〕24号，2011年12月29日。

7.《银行业金融机构外部审计监管指引》，银监发〔2010〕73号，2010年8月11日。

8.《金融企业选聘会计师事务所招标管理办法（试行）》，财金〔2010〕169号，2010年12月3日。

9.《商业银行内部控制指引》，银监发〔2014〕40号，2014年9月12日。

10.《国务院办公厅关于政府向社会力量购买服务的指导意见》，国办发〔2013〕96号，2013年9月26日。

11. 《财政部、民政部关于支持和规范社会组织承接政府购买服务的通知》，财综〔2014〕87 号，2014 年 11 月 25 日。

12. 《关于印发〈政府购买服务管理办法（暂行）〉的通知》，财综〔2014〕96 号，2014 年 12 月 15 日。

13. 《国务院关于加强审计工作的意见》，国发〔2014〕48 号，2014 年 10 月 9 日。

14. 《注册会计师业务指导目录（2014）》，会协〔2014〕28 号，2014 年 5 月 19 日。

**英文部分：**

1. "Practice Monitoring Programme", Accounting and Corporate Regulatory Authority Singapore, 2014 – 8.

2. Reiner Quick, Atuart Turley and Marleen Willekens on behalf of European Auditing Research Network, "Auditing, Trust and Governance Regulation in Europe", Routledge Taylor & Francis Group, 2008.

3. Australia Corporations Act 2001.

4. "A Manual of Disciplinary Guidelines and Model Disciplinary Orders", California Board of Accountancy, 2013.

5. "Transforming Singapore into a Leading Global Accountancy Hub for Asia – Pacific", Committee to Develop the Accountancy Sector Singapore, 2010 – 4.

6. "Report on Independent Audit Oversight", Deloitte and Financial Reporting Council Hong Kong, 2013 – 9.

7. "Quality Control for an Audit of Financial Statements", Hong Kong Institute of Certified Public Accountants, 2013 – 5.

8. Certified Public Accountants Act Japan.

9. "Memorandum of Understanding on Enforcement Cooperation between the Public Company Accounting Oversight Board of the United States and The China Securities Regulatory Commission and the Ministry of Finance of China", 2013 – 5.

10. Single Audit Act Amendments of 1996, United States .

11. "Audit of Banks, Lessons from the Crisis", ICAEW, 2010 – 6.

12. "The economics of liability losses – insuring a moving target", Swiss Re Sigma, 2004.

13. London Economics in association with Professor Ralf Ewert, Goethe University, "Study on the Economic Impact of Auditors' Liability Regimes", 2006 -9.

14. "Enhancing the auditor's contribution to prudential regulation", Financial Services Authority & Financial Reporting Council UK, 2010 -6.

15. Financial Services and Markets Act 2000.

16. "Guidance on Risk Management, Internal Control and Related Financial and Business Reporting", Financial Reporting Counsel UK, 2014 -9.

17. "Objectives and Principles of Financial Supervision in Singapore", Monetary Authority of Singapore, 2004 -4.

18. "The Relationship between the External Auditor and the Supervisor: a Code of Practice", Bank of England, 2013 -4.

19. UK Financial Services Act 2012.

20. UK Local Audit and Accountability Act 2014 .

21. UK Audit Commission Act 1998.

22. "Audit market not serving shareholders", Competition Commission, 2013 -2.

23. "Statutory audit services for large companies market investigation: a report on the provision of statutory audit services to large companies in the UK", Competition Commission, 2013 -10.

24. "Audit policy: lessons from the crisis", European Commission Green Paper, 2010 -10.

25. "Analysis of the EU Consultation on the Green Paper 'Audit Policy: Lessons from the Crisis'", Goethe - University Frankfurt, 2011 -11.

26. "Temporary Suspension of Mandatory Audit Firm Rotation", Statement by the Monetary Authority of Singapore, 2014 -6.

27. "Significant upturn in Audit tenders across FTSE 350", Pricewaterhouse Coopers UK, 2014 -7.

28. HR1564 "the Audit Integrity and Job Protection Act", 2013 -7.

29. M. Cameran, A. Prencipe and M. Trombetta, "Auditor Tenure and Auditor Change: Does Mandatory Auditor Rotation Really Improve Audit Quality?", Working Paper Bocconi University and IE Business School, 2010.

30. Soo Young Kwon, Youngdeok Lim and Roger Simnett, "Mandatory Audit Firm

Rotation and Audit Quality: Evidence from the Korean Audit Market," 2010 - 11.

31. "CG Watch 2014", CLSA Limited, 2014 - 9.

32. Inspector General Act of 1978, 2014 - 9.

33. Single Audit Act of 1984, 1984 - 10.

34. Single Audit Act Amendments of 1996, 1996 - 7.

35. Audit Commission Act 1998, 1998 - 6.

36. Local Audit and Accountability Act 2014, 2014.

37. Government Auditing Standards 2011 Revision, U. S. Government Accountability Office, 2011 - 12.

38. Code of Audit Practice 2010, U. K. Audit Commission, 2010 - 3.

39. "Guide for Federal Procurement from IPAs", U. S. Government Accountability Office, 1987 - 4.

40. "Actions Needed to Address Persistent Audit Quality Problems", U. S. Government Accountability Office, 2007 - 10.

41. "Local Audit and Accountability Bill - A Plain English Guide", U. K. Department of Communities and Local Government, 2013 - 5.

42. "Study on Joint Audits", London Economics, 2012 - 7.

43. "Green Paper, Audit Policy: Lessons from the Crisis", European Commission, 2010 - 10.

44. "Summary of Responses, Green Paper, Audit Policy: Lessons from the Crisis", European Commission, 2011 - 2.

45. Hans - Joachim Böcking, Marius Gros, Christoph Wallek, Daniel Worret, "Analysis of the EU Consultation on the Green Paper 'Audit Policy: Lessons from the Crisis'", Goethe - University Frankfurt, 2011 - 11.

46. C. Piot, "Auditor concentration in a joint - auditing environment: the French market 1997 - 2003", Managerial Auditing Journal, vol. 22, 2007.

47. Nicole Ratzinger - Sake, Sophie Audousset - Coulier, Jaana Kettunen, Cédric Lesage, "What Do We Know about Joint Audit?", ICAS, 2012.

48. Directive 2006/43/EC of the European Parliament and of the Council of 17 May 2006, European Commission, 2008 - 3.

49. "Consultation on Implementation of Articles 45 - 47 of the Directive of Statu-

tory Audit (2006/43/EC)", Cooperation with Non – EU Jurisdictions on Auditor Oversight, European Commission, 2007 – 1.

50. "Commission Decision of 19 January 2011 on the equivalence of certain third country public oversight, quality assurance, investigation and penalty systems for auditors and audit entities and a transitional period for audit activities of certain third country auditors and audit entities in the European Union", European Commission, 2011 – 1.

51. "Commission Decision of 11 June 2013 on the adequacy of the competent authorities of the United States of America pursuant to Directive 2006/43/EC of the European Parliament and of the Council", European Commission, 2013 – 6.

52. "Multilateral Memorandum of Understanding Concerning Consultation and Cooperation and the Exchange of Information", International Organization of Securities Commissions, 2002 – 5.

网站：

1. http://membershandbook.charteredaccountants.com.au/im/result Detailed.jsp? hitlist = index.jsp&commentaries = Ai0ped6AIR4JFJABRP6rZd&mappedTocId = Ai0ped6AIR4JFJABRP6rZd.

2. http://www.icaew.com/en/members/regulations – standards – and – guidance/practice – management/professional – indemnity – insurance – regulations – guidance – current#ICAEW151.

3. http://www.cpai.com/business – insurance/professional – liability/index.

4. http://www.legislation.nsw.gov.au/maintop/view/inforce/act + 81 + 1994 + cd + 0 + N.

5. http://www.lloyds.com/lloyds/offices/asia/china – in – chinese.

6. http://pcaobus.org/Registration/Firms/Pages/RegisteredFirms.aspx.

7. http://en.wikipedia.org/wiki/Dodd%E2%80%93Frank_Wall_Street_Reform_and_Consumer_Protection_Act#Title_VI_.E2.80.93_Improvements_to_Regulation.

8. http://www.comlaw.gov.au/Details/C2014C00519/Download.

9. https://www.fdic.gov/regulations/laws/rules/5000 – 2400.html.

10. http://www.docin.com/p – 96209351.html.

11. http://wenku.baidu.com/link?url = iBTpZJaeviGyhjaqxgSzB4QL_Q5DFT

274p72acIEH - 0CM70_Dksc_E9Cy4h9X4bXdeQ8PrRDcHugnz_Lw1FFPUz - veQw-PtR090JNC4_DSqi.

12. https://www.fdic.gov/regulations/laws/rules/2000 - 8500.html.

13. http://www.ilga.gov/commission/jcar/admincode/068/06801420sections.html.

14. http://www.wpk.de/rechtsvorschriften/.

15. https://www.ifiar.org/.

16. http://pcaobus.org/Pages/default.aspx.

17. http://www.sec.gov/.

18. http://www.asic.gov.au/for - finance - professionals/company - auditors/.

19. http://www.asic.gov.au/asic/ASIC.NSF/byHeadline/For%20auditors.

20. http://www.caldb.gov.au/CALDB/CALDBWeb.nsf/byheadline/Welcome + %28Home + Page%29?opendocument.

21. http://www.cpab - ccrc.ca/en/Pages/default.aspx.

22. https://frc.org.uk/Home.aspx.

23. https://www.frc.org.uk/About - the - FRC/FRC - structure/Former - FRC - structure/Auditing - Practices - Board.aspx.

24. http://www.acra.gov.sg/.

25. http://www.acra.gov.sg/About_ACRA/Public + Accountants + Oversight + Committee.htm.

26. http://www.acra.gov.sg/About_ACRA/Our + Divisions + and + Departments.htm.

27. http://www.eaigweb.org/home.php.

28. http://www.nao.org.uk/.

29. http://www.audit - commission.gov.uk/.

30. http://www.gao.gov/.

31. http://www.anao.gov.au/.

32. http://www.ago.gov.sg.

33. http://www.world - exchanges.org/.

34. https://www.iosco.org/.

35. http://www.apak - aoc.de/index.php/en/.

36. http://www.cvm.gov.br/subportal_ ingles/index.html.

# 附录　国际监管合作的全球实践

| 国家 | 主要监管机构 | 国际合作实践 |
| --- | --- | --- |
| 美国 | 公众公司会计监督委员会（PCAOB） | PCAOB 与约 18 家外国监管机构进行合作，实施联合检查。通过这些合作安排，PCAOB 致力于减少境外会计师事务所可能面对的行政负担和潜在的法律冲突等问题。对于缺乏独立健全的监管机构的国家/地区，PCAOB 在开展检查之前会与该国/地区相关金融监管机构或政府部门进行协调。PCAOB 也会协助别国/地区监管机构对美国公司实施监管 |
| 加拿大 | 加拿大公共责任委员会（Canadian Public Accountability Board，CPAB） | CPAB 长久与 PCAOB 保持良好的合作关系，并且已与英国财务报告委员会（FRC）、澳大利亚证券和投资委员会（ASIC）、日本金融服务管理局/注册会计师和审计监管局（FSA/CPAAOB）、荷兰金融市场管理局（AFM）、法国审计人高级委员会（H3C）和德国审计监督委员会（AOC）签有合作协议 |
| 欧盟 | 法定审计指令（Statutory Audit Directive，SAD） | SAD 的第 33 至 36 条制定了成员国之间相互认可、主管部门指定、保密要求和监管合作等方面的规范。SAD 要求欧洲经济区（EEA）的各国审计监管机构在一定条件下进行合作。合作需基于互惠原则，并允许审计底稿在成员国的监管机构之间共享，因国家安全获得豁免的除外，当然这并不是成员国之间审计监管体系等效认同的必要条件之一 |
| 德国 | 审计监督委员会（Auditor Oversight Commission，AOC） | AOC 与其他国家（包括欧盟和非欧盟国家）监管部门进行的合作，根据具体案例的具体情况而定，如在他国监管机构提出对某特殊事项进行检查时提供一定帮助。AOC 与 PCAOB 签有合作协议 |

续表

| 国家 | 主要监管机构 | 国际合作实践 |
| --- | --- | --- |
| 英国 | 财务报告委员会（Financial Reporting Council，FRC） | FRC 与其他国家监管机构就审计人员的监管问题进行多项合作与信息交流。FRC 在其 2012 年和 2013 年的审计质量检查年报中承诺将持续与其他国家独立的审计监管机构保持合作关系，定期与他国监管机构进行交流。FRC 还是欧洲审计检查机构的成员之一 |
| 澳大利亚 | 澳大利亚证券和投资委员会（Australian Securities and Investments Commission，ASIC） | ASIC 与众多国际组织、外国监管机构和执法机关进行密切合作，讨论研究各项关乎共同利益的问题。合作范围也包括对澳大利亚的会计师事务所施联合检查 |
| 新加坡 | 会计与企业监管机构（Accounting and Corporate Regulatory Authority，ACRA） | ACRA 在 2011 年与马来西亚和泰国的审计监管机构组成了被称为东盟审计监管机构（ASEAN Audit Regulators Group，AARG）的非正式合作组织，以促进审计监管机构之间的协作，进而提高东盟地区的审计质量。AARG 与“四大”会计师事务所的区域领导举行定期对话，讨论审计质量相关的问题。ACRA 与 PCAOB 也有信息共享的安排。此外，欧盟委员会（EC）确认 ACRA 的监管体系与欧盟的监管体系等效 |
| 巴西 | 巴西证券交易委员会（Commissão de Valores Mobiliários or Securities Commission，CVM） | 巴西证券法明确要求 CVM 与巴西的其他监管部门建立有效的系统，实现各自监管活动的信息交换。证券法还授权 CVM 与外国监管机构和国际组织签订合作协议，为对巴西或海外证券市场发生的违规行为的调查活动提供帮助与合作。目前，CVM 已与多个其他国家的监管机构签署双边或多边谅解备忘录，以实现信息共享以及监管合作。CVM 还积极参与包括 IOSCO 和 IFIAR 在内的多个国际组织的活动 |

# 后 记

经过一年多的深入调研和艰辛努力，《中国会计服务市场开放与监管》研究报告（亚行技援项目 TA8912_Comp 3）终于如期完成并付梓。本项目研究工作得到财政部副部长余蔚平的关心指导；亚洲开发银行给予立项资助；澳大利亚、新西兰、英国、美国和我国香港特区的相关政府监管部门、行业协会和普华永道全球成员机构网络对本项目给予了大力支持并提供了许多第一手资料；财政部国际财金合作司、中国财政经济出版社和有关单位给予指导和帮助。在此，表示诚挚的感谢！

本书由财政部会计司高一斌司长审定，刘光忠副司长拟定研究框架并主持起草修改工作，普华永道中天合伙人吴蔚、高级经理丁松、于玮和经理董洁具体执笔，普华永道中天管委会成员及合伙人吴卫军、合伙人 Paul F. Winkelmann、Addison L. Everet 和财政部会计司王宏、韩冰、王晶、冯翠平、邱颖全程参与本书的研究起草和审稿工作。在编写过程中，普华永道中天管委会成员及合伙人李丹、合伙人沈洁、中南财经政法大学会计学院陈波和黄洁莉教授提供了相关资料和指导。此外，本书还受到了普华永道全球公共政策及监管事务合伙人 Jan McCahey 和 Kenneth R. Chatelain 的大力支持及协助。

限于时间和水平，本研究报告难免存在疏漏和不当之处，敬请业内同仁及各界读者批评指正。